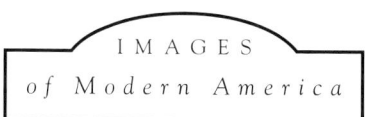

Fifty Years of Meadow Brook Theatre

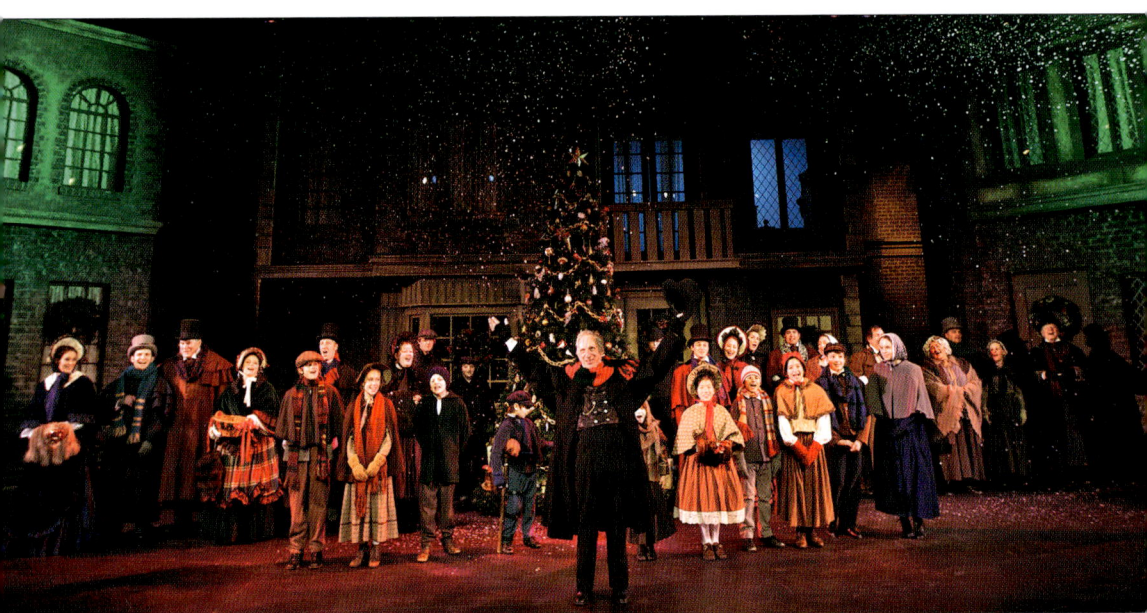

Meadow Brook Theatre has been happy to perform the popular Charles Dickens story *A Christmas Carol* for the past 33 years. It started in 1982 and has become an annual event for many local families. The Charles Nolte adaptation used today is preferred by audiences. The elaborate, two-story set has a center section that rotates from the outside street scene to the interior of Scrooge's home and business. It is the only set reused year after year. (Courtesy of Meadow Brook Theatre.)

On the Front Cover: Clockwise from top left:
Meadow Brook Theatre sign, Wilson Hall; Ruth Crawford and Julia Glander in the 2011 drama *Mary Stuart*; Kara Dombrowski and Teddy Toye in *Lysistrata Jones*; Will Lee-Williams, Tyrick Wiltez Jones, and Alexander Elisa in *From My Hometown* (see page 88); Adam Carpenter as Tiny Tim and Booth Colman as Ebenezer Scrooge in the 1993 production of *A Christmas Carol* (see page 33). (All courtesy of Meadow Brook Theatre.)

On the Back Cover: From left to right:
The 2011 renovation of the theatre's interior (see page 89); artistic director Travis W. Walter presents actor Katie Hardy with the Andes Award for her performance in *Harris Cashes Out!* (see page 68); members of the Meadow Brook Theatre Guild provide refreshments at the 2014 Andes Awards (see page 69). (All courtesy of Meadow Brook Theatre.)

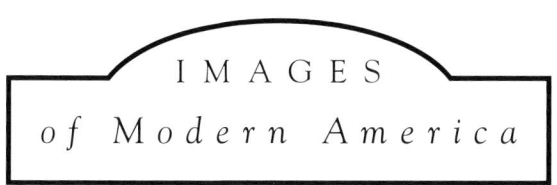

IMAGES
of Modern America

FIFTY YEARS OF MEADOW BROOK THEATRE

Thom F. and Maryann Foxlee

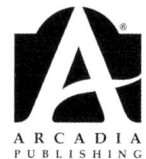

Copyright © 2015 by Thom F. and Maryann Foxlee
ISBN 978-1-4671-1420-2

Published by Arcadia Publishing
Charleston, South Carolina

Printed in the United States of America

Library of Congress Control Number: 2014959315

For all general information, please contact Arcadia Publishing:
Telephone 843-853-2070
Fax 843-853-0044
E-mail sales@arcadiapublishing.com
For customer service and orders:
Toll-Free 1-888-313-2665

Visit us on the Internet at www.arcadiapublishing.com

To the thousands of staff, actors, and guild and audience members who have been, and are part of, the Meadow Brook Theatre family.

Contents

Acknowledgments   6

Introduction   7

1. The Start of Something Special   9
2. Building a Legacy   23
3. Meadow Brook Theatre Guild   41
4. Behind the Scenes   53
5. Family and Community   65
6. Moving Forward   77

Acknowledgments

Maryann and I were students at Oakland University when Meadow Brook Theatre (MBT) began. We never knew the story behind its formation. Research for this book has provided some insight, and we are happy to share that with you. We have to thank many people for their help, starting with the Oakland University Library Archives and, particularly, Shirley Paquette, for guiding us through the process of learning about the early history of the theatre. We could not have told the story without the great photographs from the archives. Former OU chancellor and board member Donald O'Dowd provided his perspective and history of the events behind, leading up to, and launching MBT. Dr. Richard and Edie Haskell shared with us the history and beginning of the "Saturday Niters," a group that has been hosting a dinner party for the cast and crew of each show since the 1970s. Actor Marianne Muellerleile shared stories and cast photographs from her time on the MBT stage. Associate director Terry W. Carpenter and master electrician Reid G. Johnson are still telling us stories from their long and complex memories of MBT, some of which we were able to include. MBT board member Holly Powell helped comb through the archives and gather photographs. She also worked with Arcadia and MBT's marketing and communications coordinator Paige Vanzo to ensure all the photographs were organized and submitted on time. Vanzo and Amanda Rae Evans made sure all our photographs were properly scanned and met Arcadia's requirements. Vanzo also found some hard-to-locate photographs that were required in order to tell our story. MBT's artistic director, Travis W. Walter, provided both photograph recommendations and insights regarding the recent history of MBT and chapter six. Without the continued input and support of managing director Cheryl Marshall, this book could not have been written.

Unless otherwise noted, all images appear courtesy of the Oakland University Library (OUL) and Meadow Brook Theatre (MBT).

Introduction

Meadow Brook Theatre, founded in June 1966 by the Michigan State University (MSU) Board of Trustees, has a long history of producing quality theatre. It officially began on January 3, 1967, with the first performance of *The Caucasian Chalk Circle* by Bertolt Brecht. Things really got going when Chancellor Durward B. Varner decided that, for Oakland University (OU) to become recognized as a center for fine arts, it needed to have a professional theatre company on campus. Provost Donald O'Dowd was given the responsibility to convince John Fernald, an internationally acclaimed director and head of the Royal Academy of Dramatic Art in London, to establish a resident professional theatre company at Oakland University. A theatre was not in the original plans for Wilson Hall. Wilbur W. "Bud" Kent, an associate professor of music, drew up plans to modify a planned lecture hall to accommodate the needs of a theatre.

The Academy of Dramatic Arts (ADA), led by Fernald, was established in the fall of 1967. The ADA was not part of the university and did not offer academic credit. The intent was to have experienced actors teach aspiring actors how to become professionals. Instructors were the actors and technical staff from the Fernald Company, who were veterans of the Royal Academy of Dramatic Art. ADA was organized as the Studio Company with a separate season. Initially, it performed on the MBT stage in-between Fernald Company productions. In 1970, it moved to Varner Hall, and it lasted until 1977.

Fernald mostly selected plays that were well known and had seen success in Europe or New York. He spared no expense for his productions; by the spring of 1970, the theatre was in debt. A budget disagreement led to a management change. Fortunately, Terence "Terry" Kilburn, a teacher at the ADA, had already acted and directed at MBT. He was named acting artistic director in July 1970 and was later named artistic director. The theatre flourished under his leadership. One of his special talents was the ability to create a season of plays and musicals that appealed to MBT audiences. He was also proficient at keeping costs in line, partially by careful planning and not picking plays with extremely large casts, and also by doing things himself. For example, he designed the costumes for many shows. An important commitment was to continue to deliver the high-quality productions MBT audiences grew to expect during the Fernald years. His recruitment of Charles Nolte was a key part of the success during his tenure. Nolte, a professor emeritus at the University of Minnesota, enjoyed teaching as well as acting, writing, and directing. For 30 years, he directed some of MBT's most distinguished productions, among them *The Andersonville Trial*, *Inherit the Wind*, and *Death of a Salesman*. He directed the premieres of his own plays *A Summer Remembered* and *The Last Days of Mr. Lincoln* at MBT.

For the first several decades of its existence, Meadow Brook Theatre produced high-quality, professional shows that featured classic playwrights such as Shakespeare and Molieré, along with more popular musicals appealing to both educated playgoers looking for an intellectual experience and those simply looking for good entertainment. During this period, the subscriber rate was very high, to the point where it was difficult to get tickets if one was not a subscriber, and the best seats were held by people who had season tickets for many years. Managing directors over the years included David Robert Kanter, Frank Bollinger, and Gregg Bloomfield, who oversaw theatre operations from 1993 to 2003.

MBT's competition has changed over the years. The Fisher Theatre and Music Hall are focused on Broadway hits brought in by national touring companies. In recent years, increased competition from smaller local theatres, combined with local economic issues, has also taken a toll on MBT ticket sales. The number of different events vying for people's entertainment dollars has increased to include traveling ice shows, cable television, online streaming, and a revitalized movie industry.

Initially, the relationship between Oakland University and the theatre was very strong, with overall governance provided by the MSU Board of Trustees and, later, the OU Board of Trustees when Oakland separated from Michigan State. This union was dissolved in 2003, and the Theatre Ensemble, a nonprofit professional theatre governed by its own board, was formed to continue the Meadow Brook Theatre legacy by producing professional theatre in the same location, doing business as Meadow Brook Theatre.

The Theatre Ensemble was created by a few key people who worked at MBT and did not want to see it disbanded. Fortunately, Cheryl L. Marshall had the experience and associated working knowledge of how to run the 584-seat facility. Her passion for MBT and incredible energy are important elements of the theatre's success. A contract with OU was a key ingredient, along with support during the first several years. Retaining the core technical team was also critical. Terry Carpenter (resident stage manager and associate director), Sarah Lin Warren (production manager/assistant stage manager), Reid G. Johnson (master electrician), Mike Duncan (audio engineer), and Kitty Gentile (box-office manager) provided the knowledge and skill sets needed to recreate MBT. Bill Campbell volunteered to do the weekly payroll until his death in 2013. He was board president when he passed away.

The Theatre Ensemble struggled in its first few years; it has begun to show progress over the past five seasons. Initially, a season consisted of five plays plus *A Christmas Carol*, and now consists of six plays plus *A Christmas Carol*, with a goal of adding one more play in the future. Thanks to artistic director Travis W. Walter's vision, talent, and hard work, show quality and consistency has improved, and the number of subscribers has climbed. This progress is primarily due to a strategy focused on producing high-quality plays using Equity actors and offering a season appealing to theatre enthusiasts. This strategy has evolved to focus on Michigan premieres and a mix of comedies, musicals, and dramas. Now, 10 years later, the public view is that MBT once again produces Broadway-quality plays and puts together a season that offers something for everyone.

As MBT begins its 50th anniversary season, there are reasons to be optimistic about its future. It has developed a clear strategic plan and establishes supporting business plan objectives each year. MBT's relationship with Oakland University and the Department of Music, Theatre and Dance has flourished and will continue to develop.

MBT's mission statement is as follows: "To create a season of innovative, Broadway-quality theatre productions that make audiences smile, laugh and cry, enriching the cultural experience of the community in southeast Michigan." Its marketing tagline is: "Michigan's Answer to Broadway."

One
THE START OF SOMETHING SPECIAL

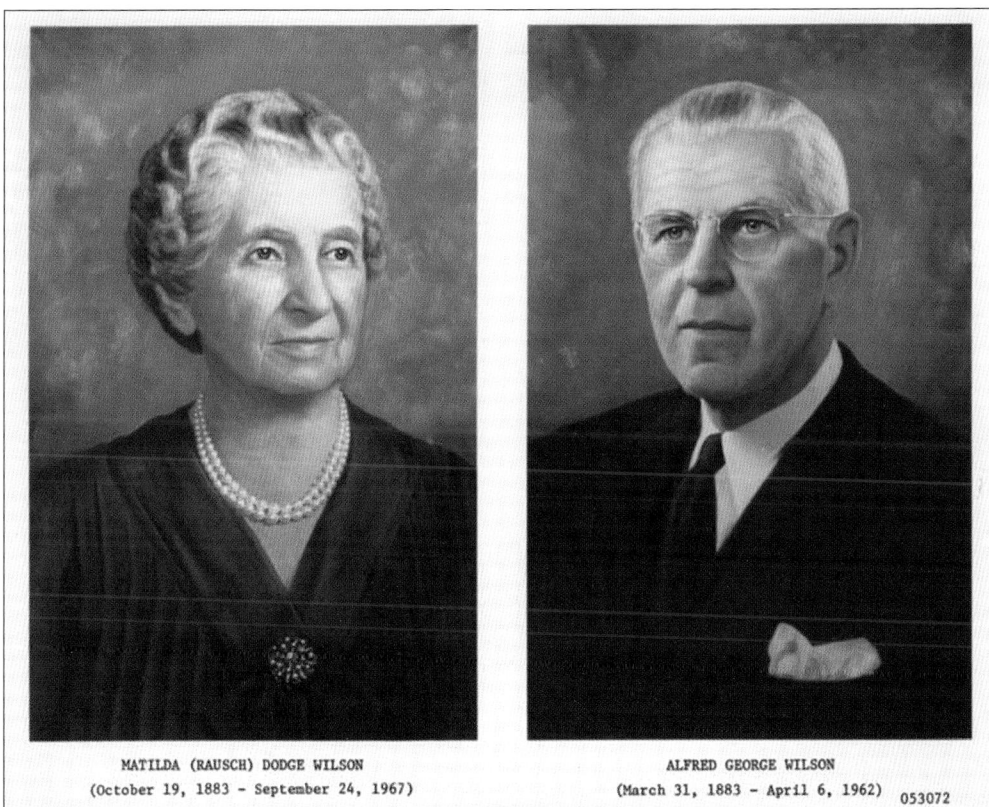

MATILDA (RAUSCH) DODGE WILSON
(October 19, 1883 – September 24, 1967)

ALFRED GEORGE WILSON
(March 31, 1883 – April 6, 1962)   053072

It all started in 1957, when Alfred G. and Matilda Wilson donated their 1,600-acre estate, Meadow Brook Farms, and $2 million to establish Michigan State University at Oakland (MSUO) in northern Oakland County. The school was to focus on academics and would not have sports or fraternities and sororities. (OUL.)

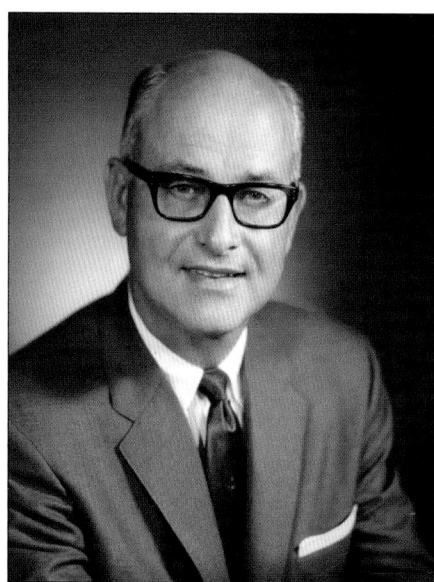

Durward "Woody" B. Varner was the first chancellor of Oakland University (OU), in Rochester, Michigan. He guided the school from its inception in 1957 through its formal separation from Michigan State University in 1970. One of his key strategies was to bring professional music and theatre to OU to firmly establish it as a center for the fine arts. (OUL.)

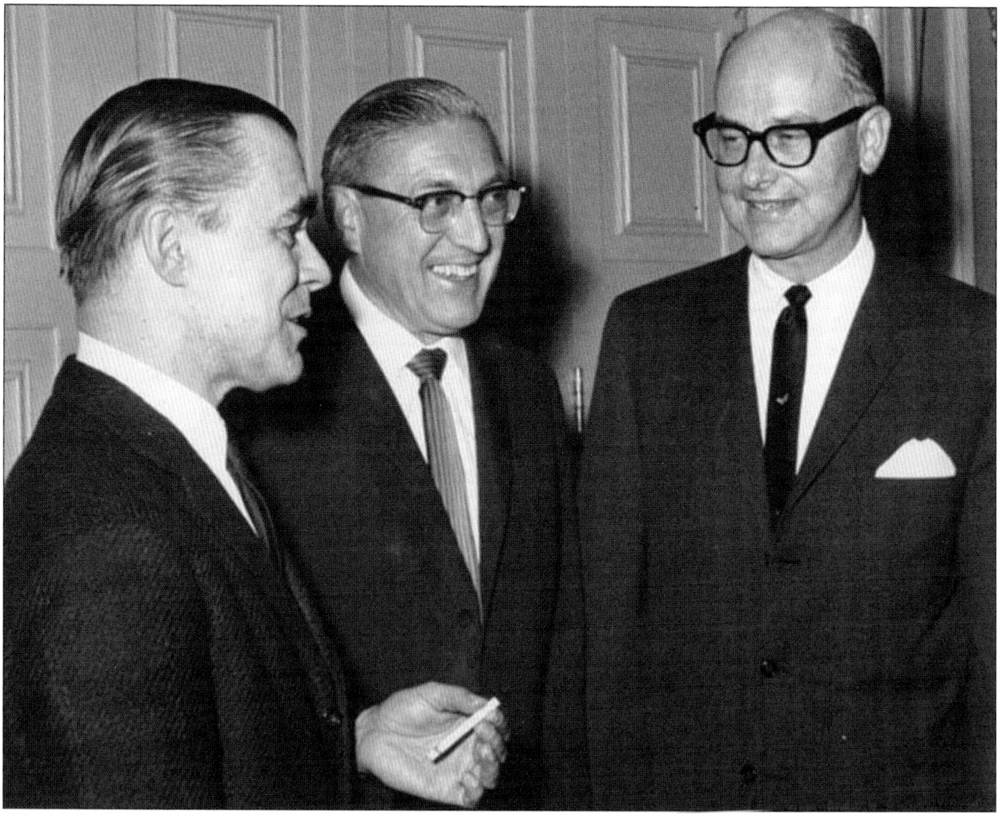

The model for Meadow Brook Theatre (MBT) was formulated during the establishment of Meadow Brook Music Festival (MBMF) in 1964. An accomplished orchestra and a group to garner support of local businesses were needed. The key players were, from left to right, Sixten Ehrling (Detroit Symphony Orchestra), Semon Knudsen (General Motors vice president), and Woody Varner. (OUL.)

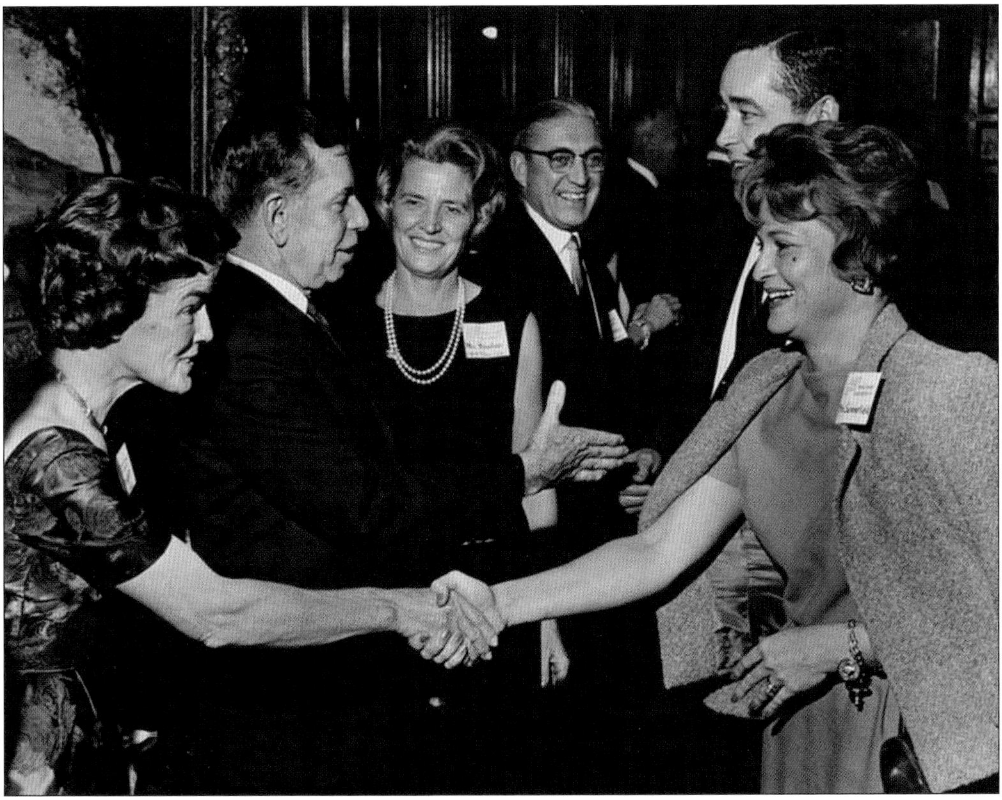

The Meadow Brook Music Festival Executive Committee, chaired by Mr. and Mrs. Semon Knudsen (center), was formed to provide both financial and marketing support. Subcommittees, set up geographically, were responsible for engaging friends and businesses from their respective areas. A similar committee was set up for Meadow Brook Theatre. (OUL.)

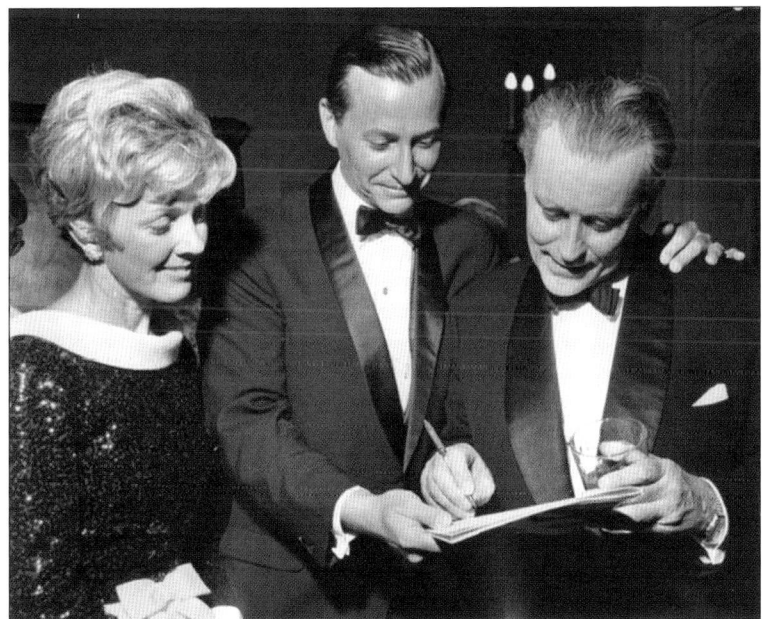

The Meadow Brook Theatre Committee was formed to generate interest and support for the facility. Ruth Adams and Charles F. Adams, the first chairmen, are shown here getting the autograph of John Fernald (right). Ruth Adams later served as a charter trustee for the newly independent Oakland University in 1970. (OUL.)

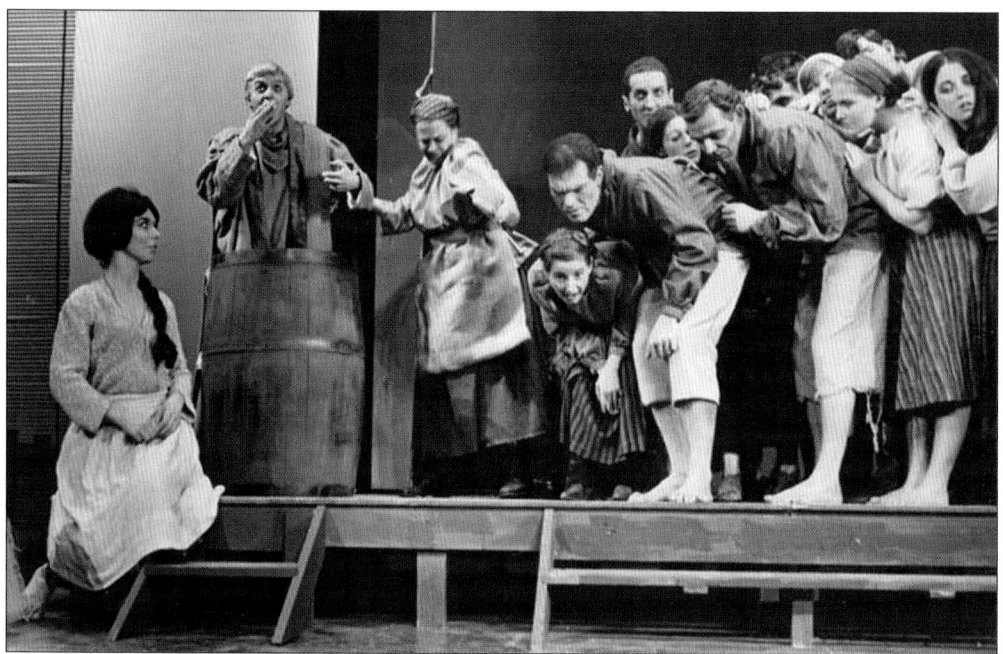

The Meadow Brook Theatre Executive Committee was responsible for fundraising and assisting with promotional and marketing programs, as well as special events. The "Patron's Night Premiere Performance" of *The Caucasian Chalk Circle* on January 3, 1967, included a black-tie afterglow at Meadow Brook Hall, hosted by Matilda Wilson. (OUL.)

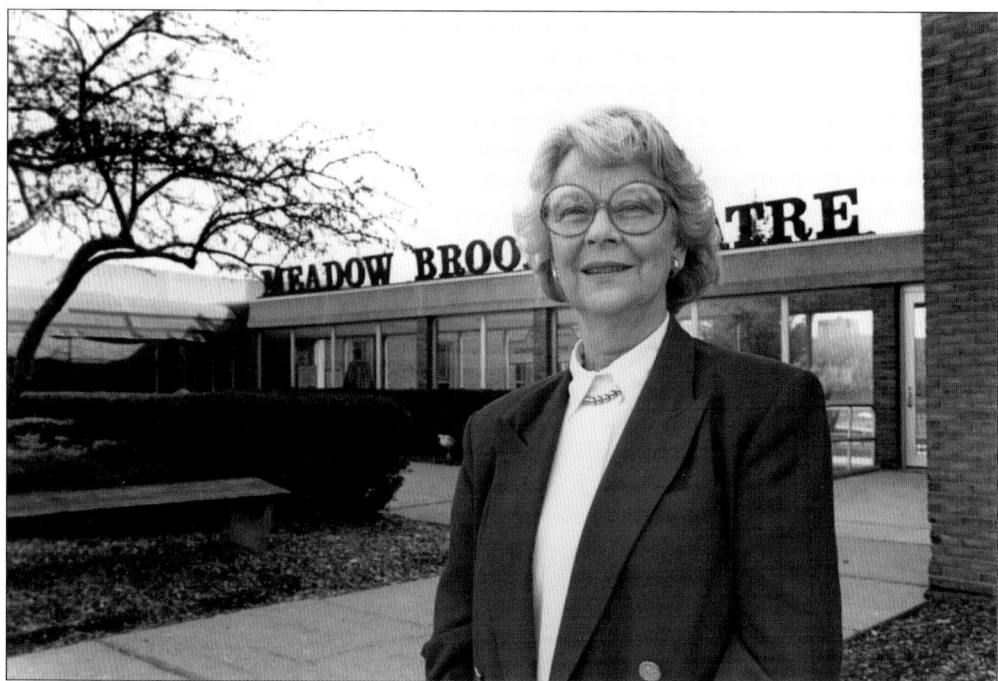

Jane Mosher, director of community relations for OU, was responsible for forming the women's committee. Comprised of volunteers, its mission was to generate ticket sales for MBT. Her contributions and leadership were critical to the success of MBT. (OUL.)

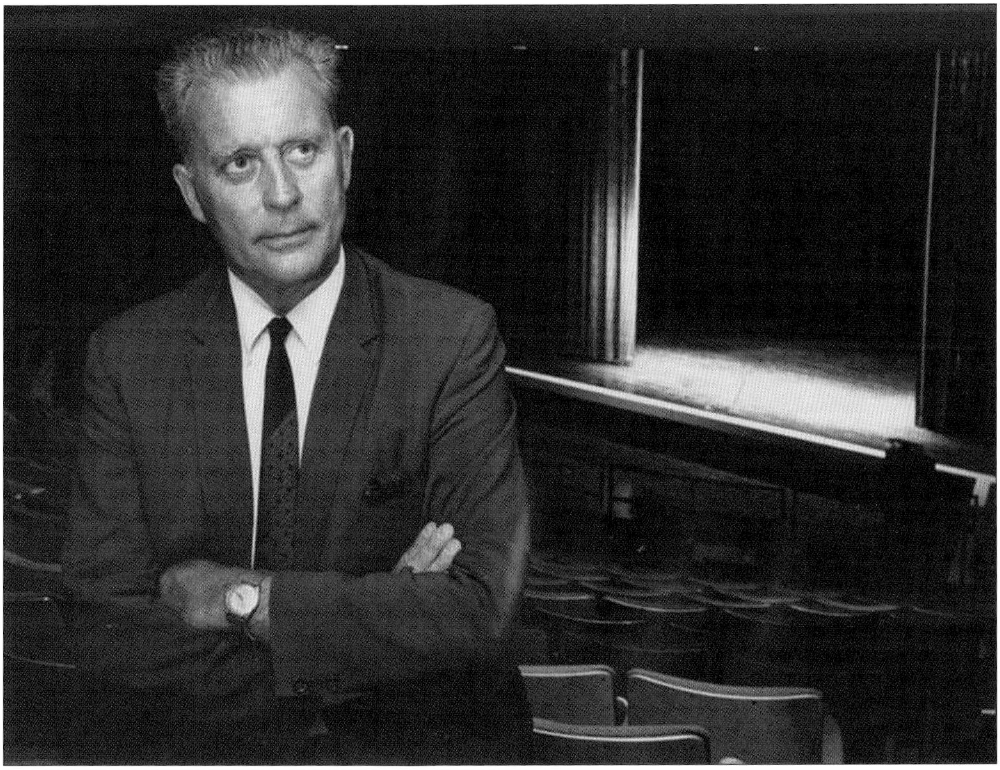

One of Chancellor Varner's key decisions was to recruit John Fernald, the former head of the Royal Academy of Dramatic Art (RADA) in England, to establish a professional theatre on campus. (OUL.)

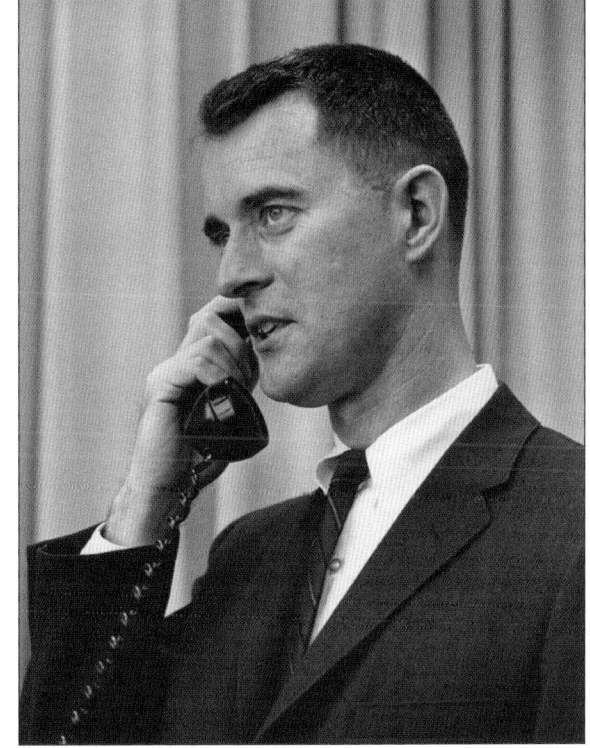

Donald O'Dowd was provost at OU in the 1960s and became president in 1970. While Woody Varner initiated the effort, O'Dowd was the man responsible for convincing John Fernald to bring his company of actors to Rochester, Michigan. He began his quest over Thanksgiving break in 1965. (OUL.)

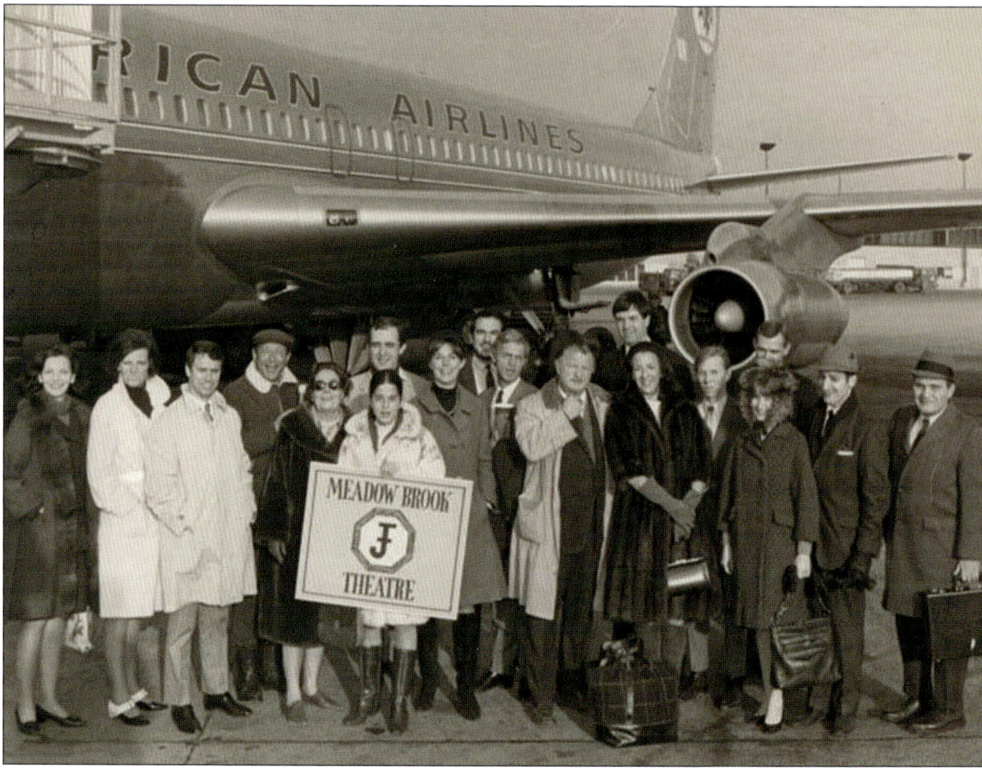

The John Fernald Company landed in Michigan in 1966, and the scene was set for creating a professional theatre at Oakland University. Meadow Brook Theatre would join Meadow Brook Music Festival as a center for performing arts on the OU campus. (OUL.)

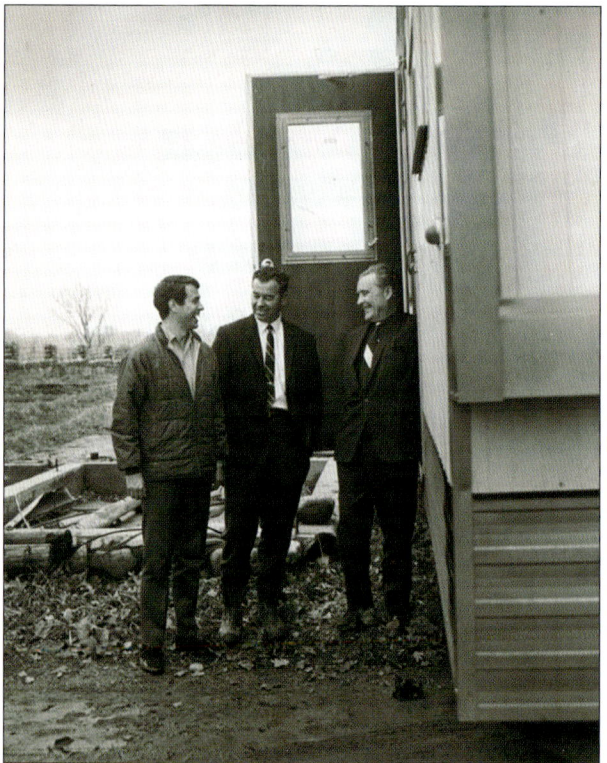

One of the first tasks was to determine how to house a troupe of actors, since they would be performing for the whole season. The solution was to bring in 14 trailers, which were located behind Hannah Hall of Science. The trailers, shown here with George Karas (center) and John Fernald (right), had two bedrooms, a living room, and a kitchen. (OUL.)

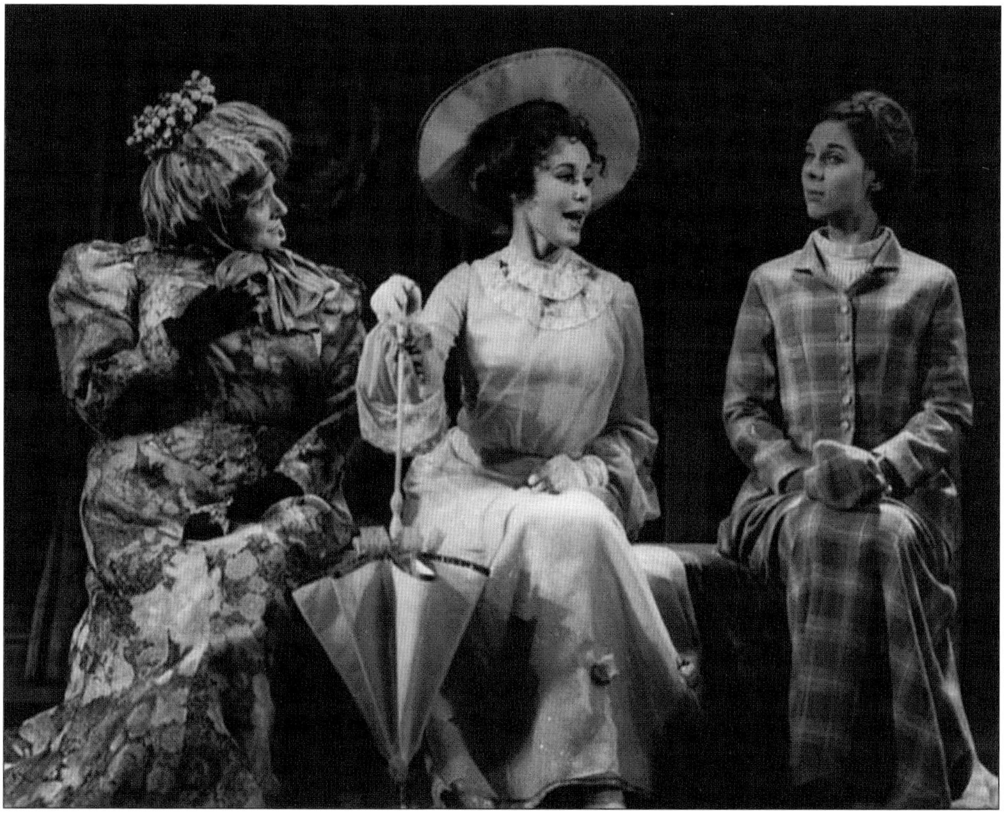

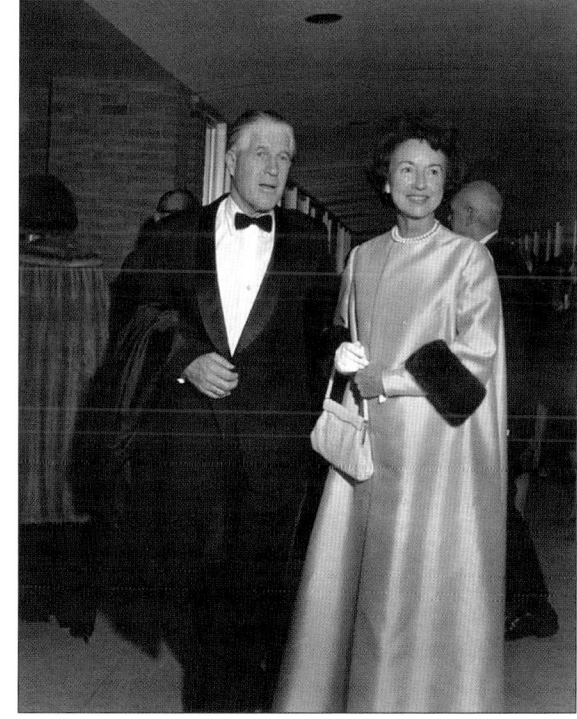

The John Fernald Company was comprised of former RADA actors and teachers, because Fernald strongly believed that the best actors were trained at RADA. *Pygmalion* in 1969 included Fernald actors Elisabeth Orion (left), Karen Fernald (center), and Bonnie Hurren. (MBT.)

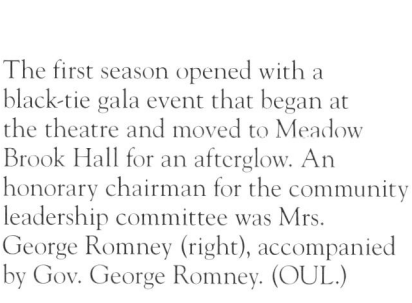

The first season opened with a black-tie gala event that began at the theatre and moved to Meadow Brook Hall for an afterglow. An honorary chairman for the community leadership committee was Mrs. George Romney (right), accompanied by Gov. George Romney. (OUL.)

Matilda Wilson (right), whose enthusiastic support of the arts initially focused on MBMF, shifted to Meadow Brook Theatre when she became an honorary chairman with Mrs. Romney. Speaking in the theatre lobby with Paula Varner during the January 3 premiere, she is holding the first season's program. (OUL.)

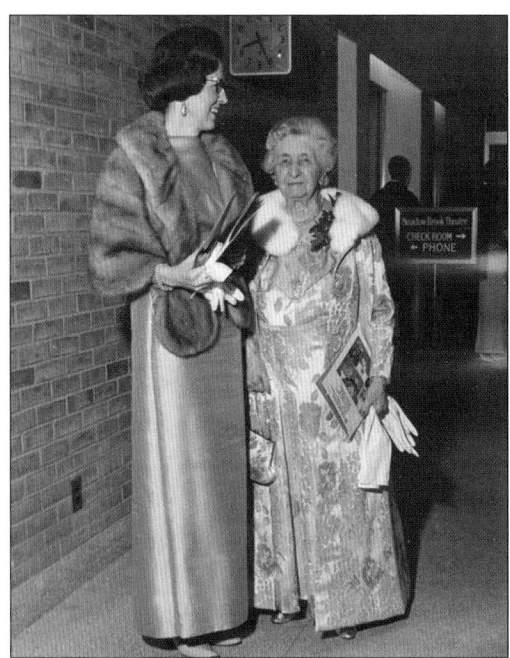

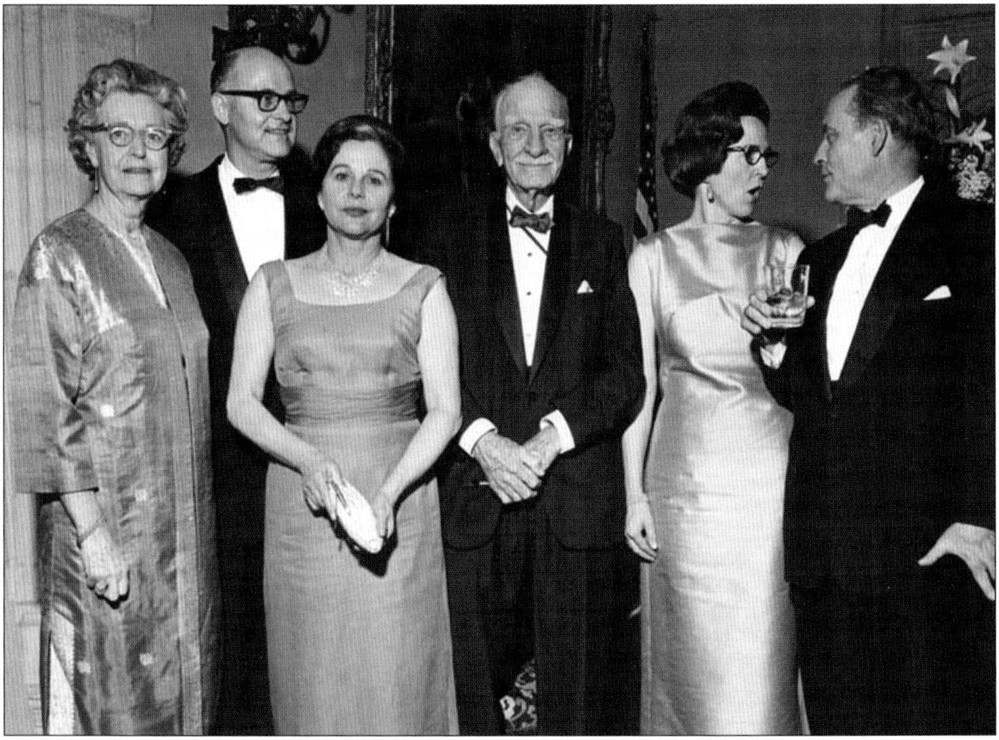

The formal party at Meadow Brook Hall was attended by many key donors, including philanthropist Charles Mott, who has buildings at the University of Chicago and Kettering University named after him. The C.S. Mott Children's Hospital opened in 1969 and is part of the University of Michigan Health System. Pictured from left to right are Mrs. Mott, Chancellor Varner, Jenny Laird, Charles Mott, Mrs. Varner, and John Fernald. (OUL.)

The main event for the 1967–1968 season was to be a formal premiere-night gala for *The Importance of Being Earnest* (pictured) at Meadow Brook Hall on October 5. The event was canceled when Mrs. Wilson passed away in Europe. In its place was a black-tie event in the theatre lobby with members of the cast and staff. (OUL.)

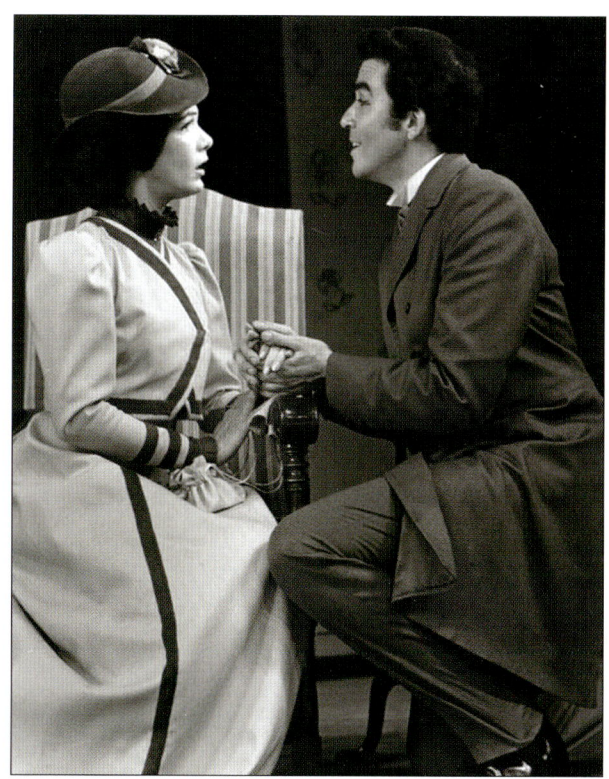

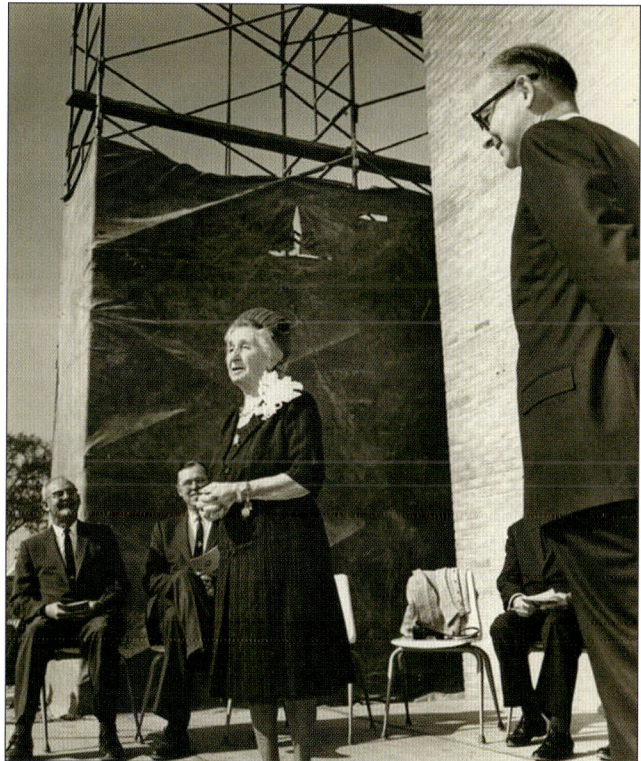

The decision to move forward with MBT happened quickly, and there were no plans to build a theatre on Oakland's campus. Wilson Hall, under construction, included a large lecture hall. Mrs. Wilson (center) and Chancellor Varner (right) are seen at the ground breaking for Wilson Hall. (OUL.)

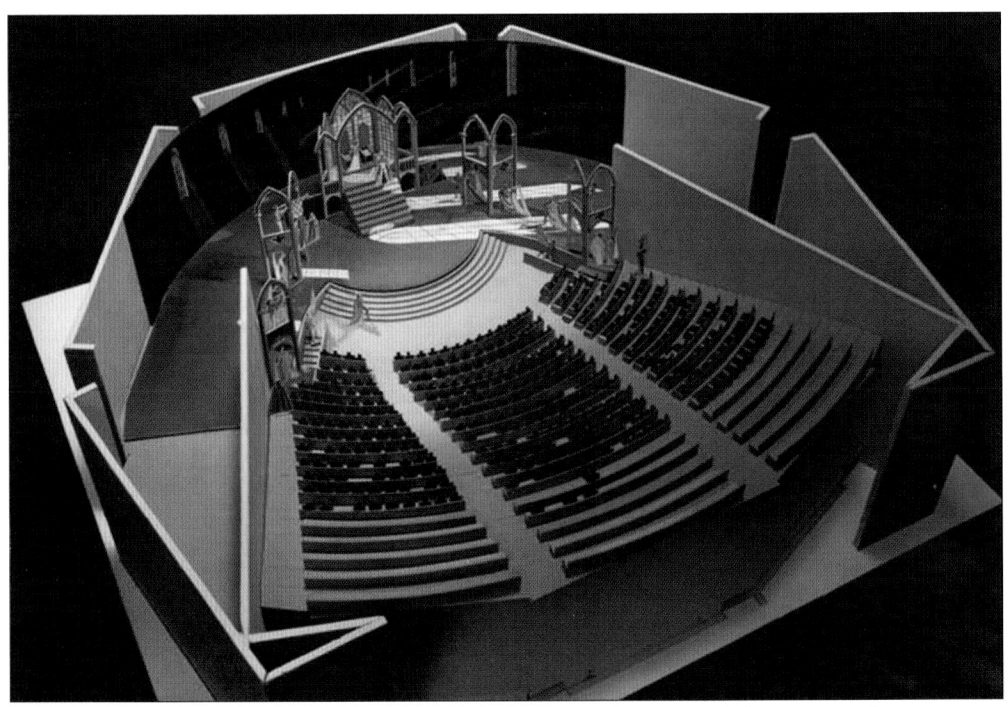

Modifications to the original plan were made by Wilbur W. "Bud" Kent, an associate professor of music, to accommodate the needs of a theatre. This is a conceptual model of the theatre area. (OUL.)

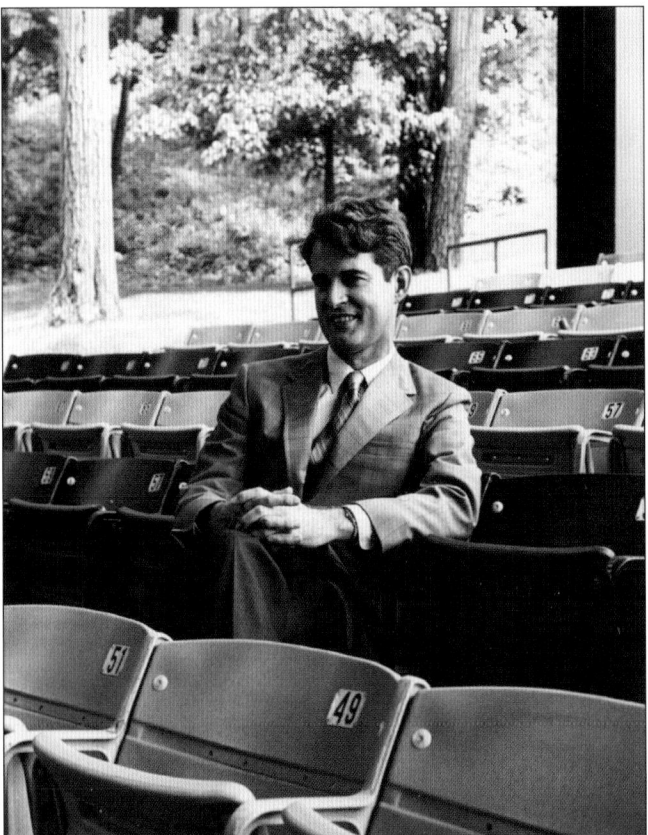

Don O'Dowd (pictured) was able to visit schools with associated professional theatres, courtesy of a grant from the Carnegie Corporation. Stops at Princeton, UCLA, the University of Washington, and others helped develop the initial strategy for MBT and OU. Part of the final plan was to form a new Oakland Academy of Dramatic Arts, led by John Fernald. (OUL.)

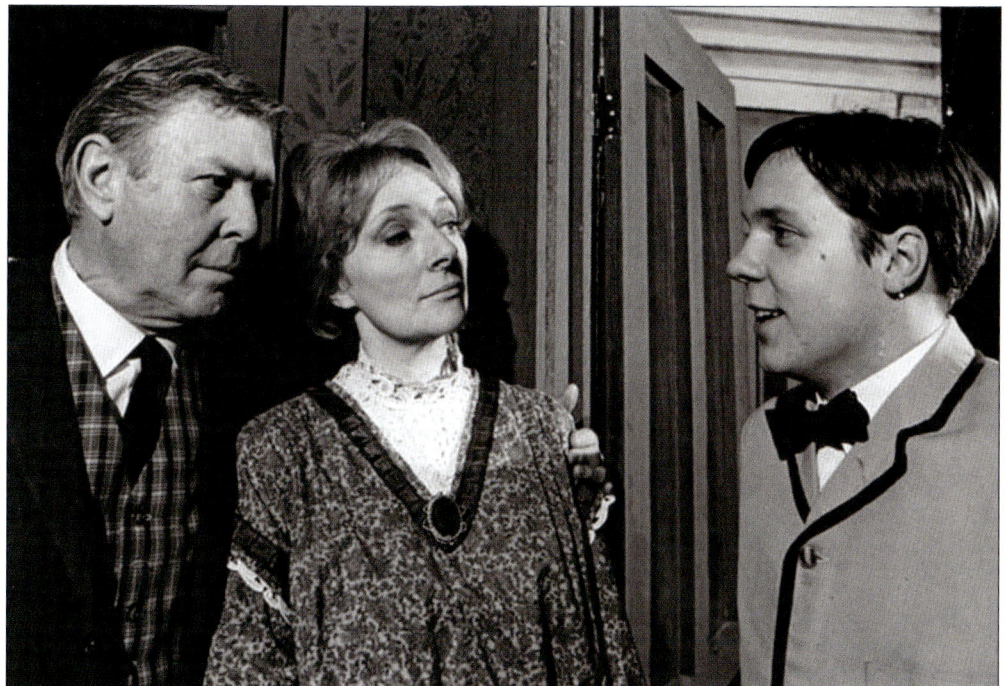

The Academy of Dramatic Arts (ADA) became a key part of Varner's focus on establishing a "center for the arts" in Southeast Michigan. Promising young actors were given the opportunity to work with the John Fernald Company on the Meadow Brook stage. *Ah, Wilderness!* actors included Harry Ellerbe (left), Elisabeth Orion (center), and Jeffery Winner, an ADA graduate. (OUL.)

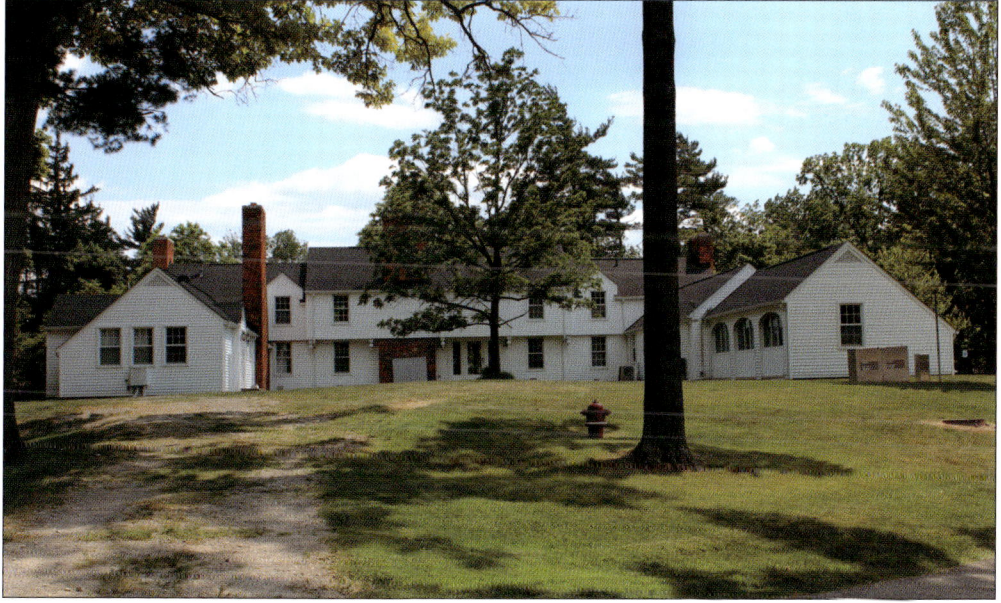

The ADA started with 14 students in the fall of 1967. The teaching staff, mostly members of the Fernald Company, took up residence on the Seyburn estate in Pontiac Township. It was built as the residence for Wesson Seyburn, who married Winifred Dodge, Matilda Wilson's stepdaughter. The building is currently part of the City of Auburn Hills offices. (Courtesy of CAH.)

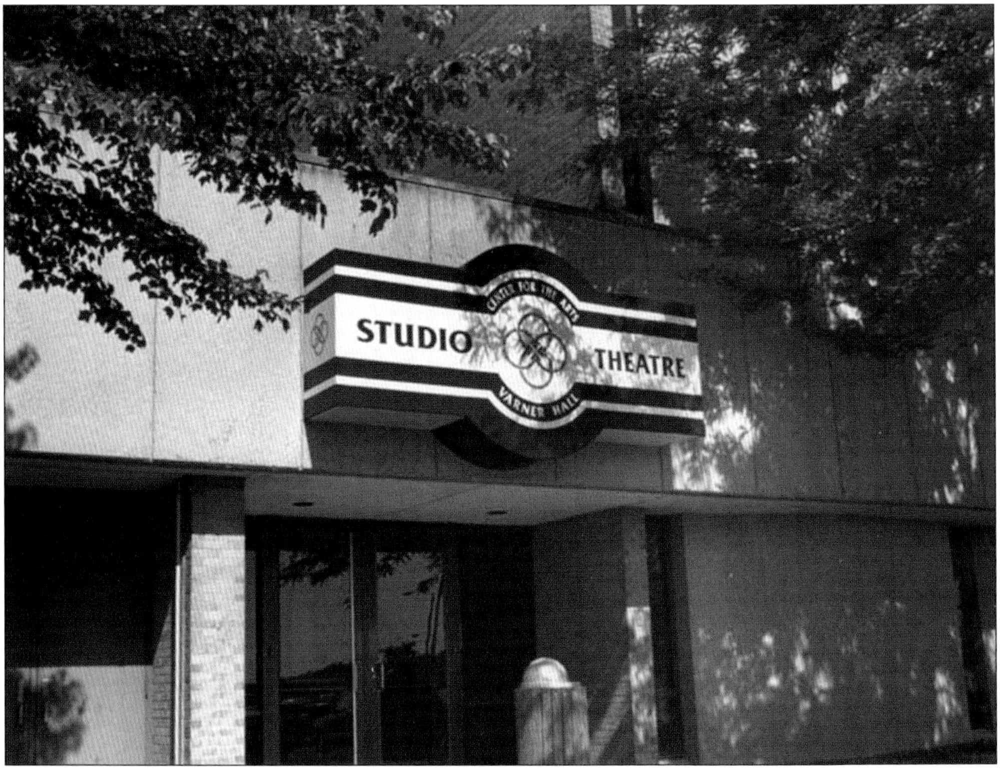

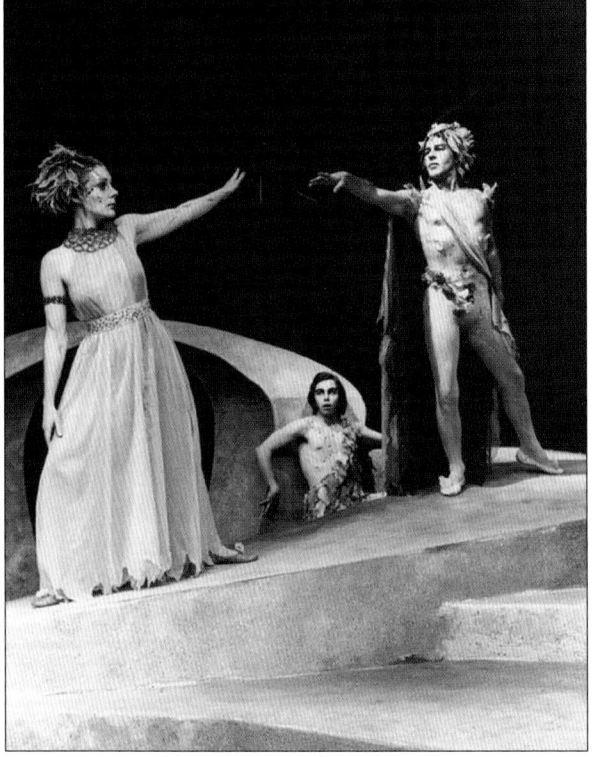

The ADA was organized as the Studio Company and had its own season. Initially, the plays were performed on the MBT stage between Fernald Company productions. The Studio Company moved to the new Performing Arts Building, now Varner Hall, in 1970. John Fernald felt that young actors benefited more in major roles with the Studio Company than bit parts with MBT. (OUL.)

The ADA was not part of OU and did not offer academic credit. It was more of a journeyman program, with classes taught by professional actors and technical personnel. It initially was very successful, with ADA graduates such as Curtis Armstrong (center), shown here on stage with Eric Tavares (right) and Suzanne Peters (left) performing *A Midsummer Night's Dream* in 1975. (MBT.)

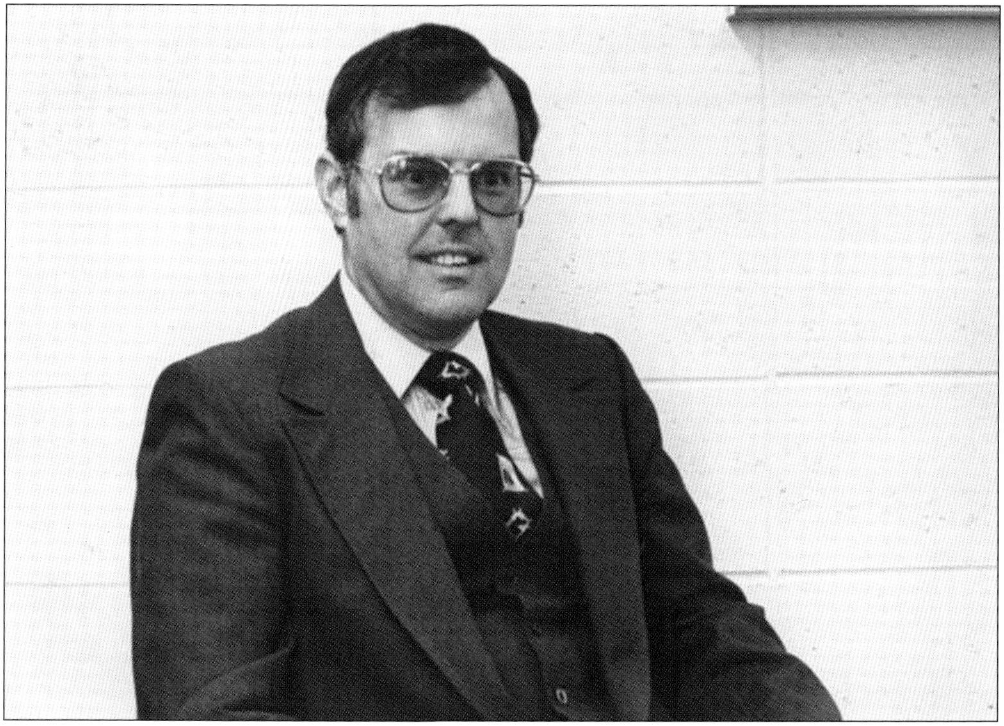

The ADA lasted until the mid-1970s, when the recession caused by the oil embargo hit the automobile industry and the Detroit area. Provost Frederick S. Obear was tasked with identifying ways to reduce budgets. He met with the ADA faculty, and they felt the program had declined. While the program was dropped, the faculty moved on to successful careers here and abroad. (OUL.)

Early play selection was based on John Fernald's belief that well-known plays, specifically those that had gained acclaim in Europe, such as *King Lear* by William Shakespeare, along with classics, were the only plays worth producing. Very few American playwrights met Fernald's standards. Shown here is the program for the 1968 production. (OUL.)

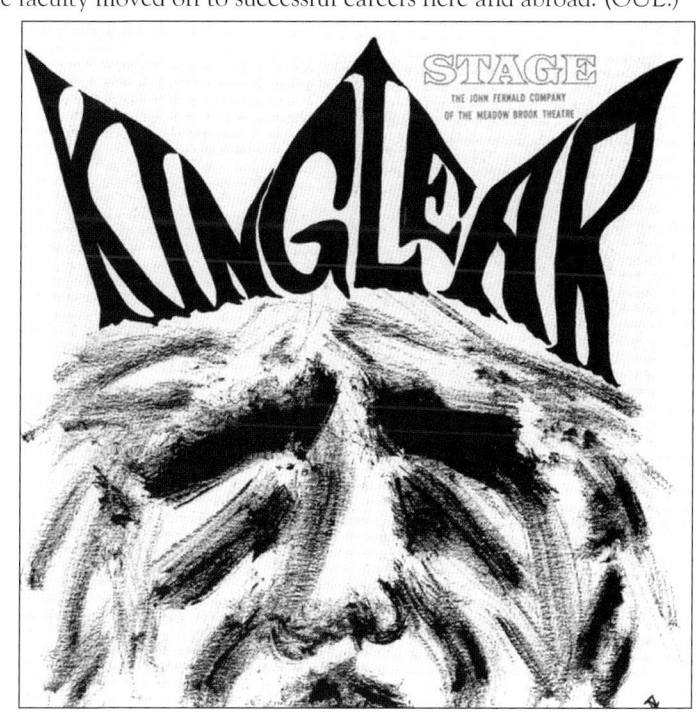

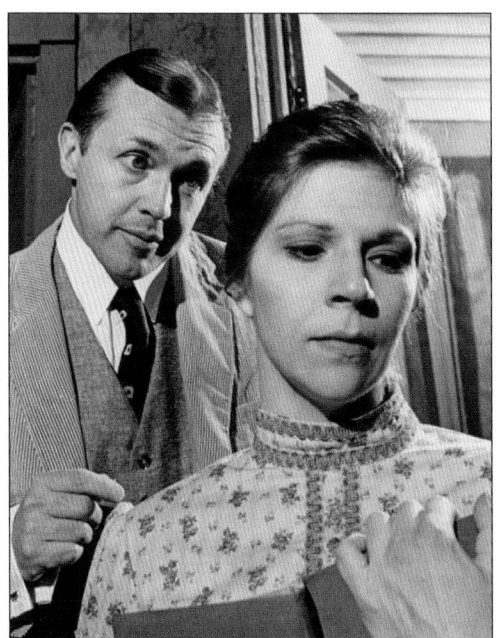

Terence Kilburn (left) was on the ADA faculty and directed two plays for John Fernald in the fourth season. He directed and played a major role in *Ah, Wilderness!* by Eugene O'Neill. It became the highest-grossing play during the Fernald Company years, as the audience found in it a play they could relate to. Diane Bugas is on the right. (OUL.)

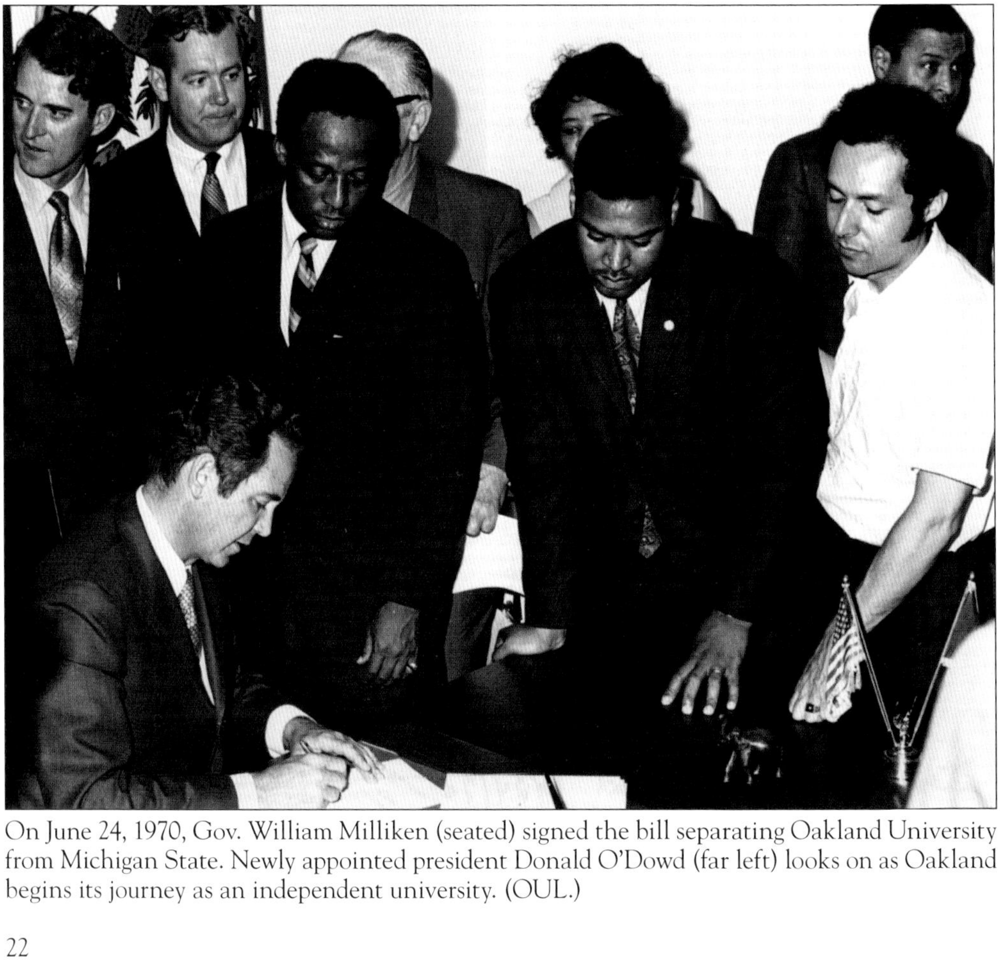

On June 24, 1970, Gov. William Milliken (seated) signed the bill separating Oakland University from Michigan State. Newly appointed president Donald O'Dowd (far left) looks on as Oakland begins its journey as an independent university. (OUL.)

Two
Building a Legacy

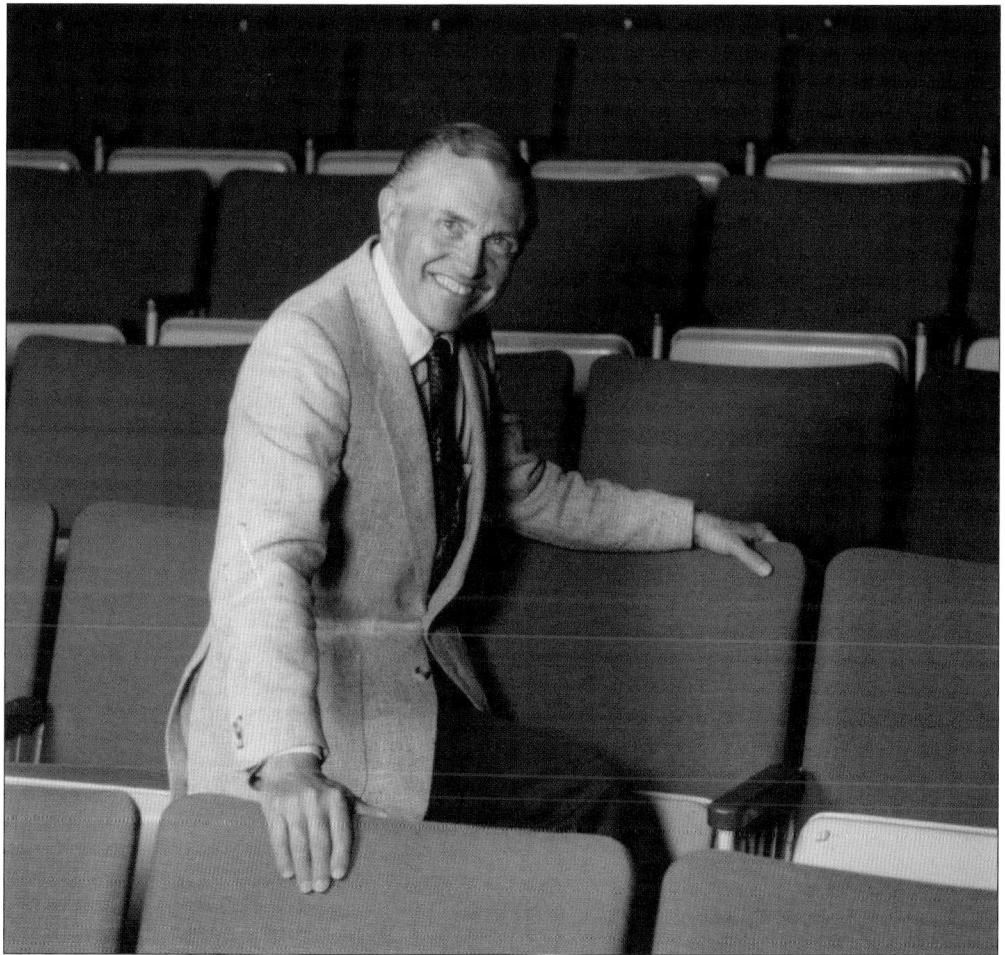

MBT and John Fernald parted ways in the summer of 1970. Fernald left MBT in debt, with an upcoming season that included some costly productions. Fortunately, Terence "Terry" Kilburn (pictured) was made interim artistic director and was able to modify the season to make it more cost effective. (OUL.)

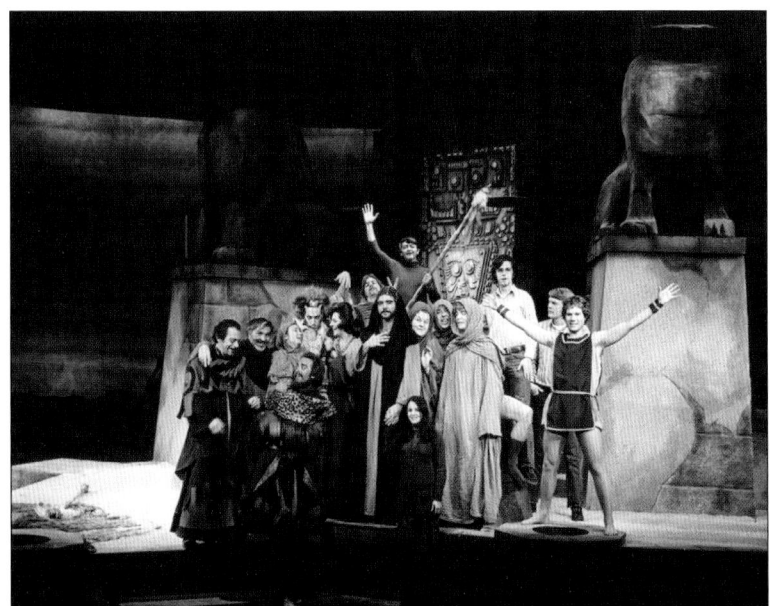

Oedipus Rex by Sophocles, a classic play requiring a large cast, was typical of Fernald's seasons. While MBT continued to include classics in its lineup, newer works were added as part of Terry Kilburn's strategy to increase appeal to local audiences. (MBT.)

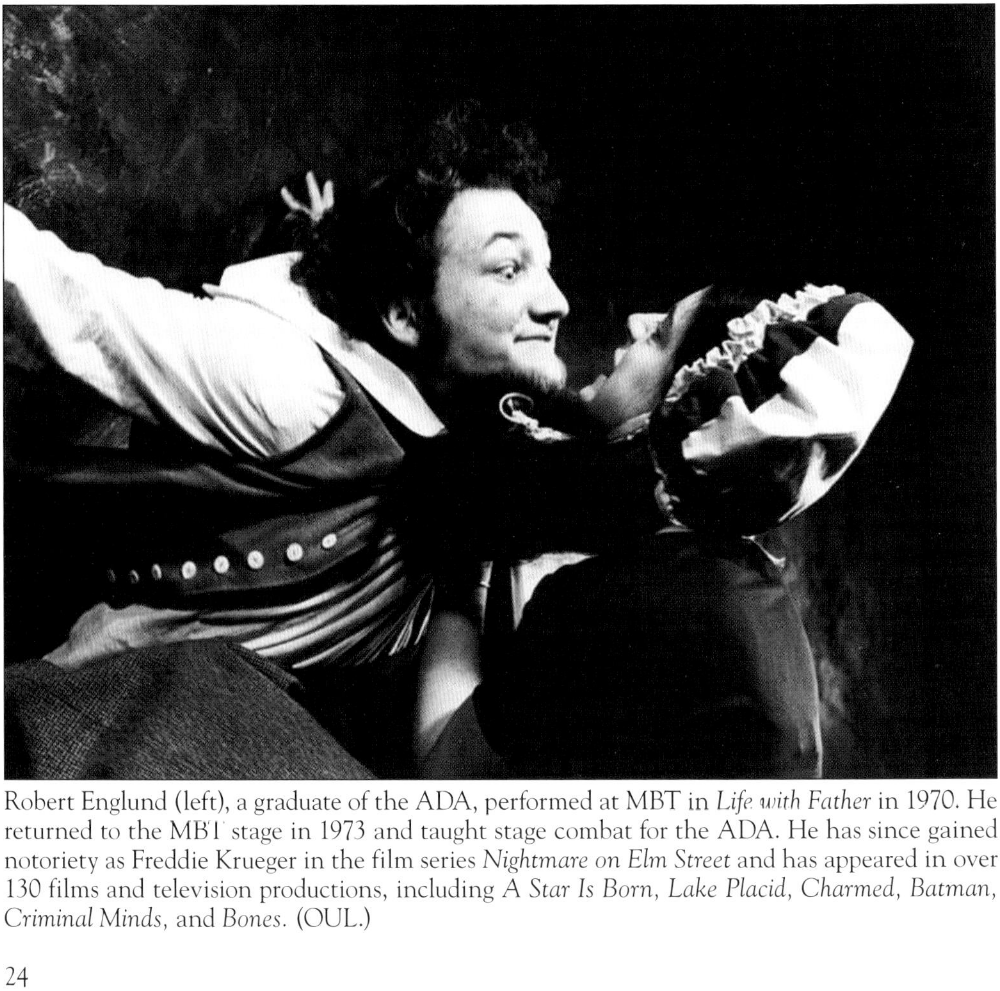

Robert Englund (left), a graduate of the ADA, performed at MBT in *Life with Father* in 1970. He returned to the MBT stage in 1973 and taught stage combat for the ADA. He has since gained notoriety as Freddie Krueger in the film series *Nightmare on Elm Street* and has appeared in over 130 films and television productions, including *A Star Is Born*, *Lake Placid*, *Charmed*, *Batman*, *Criminal Minds*, and *Bones*. (OUL.)

MBT spring touring shows traveled across Michigan from 1974 to 1987. This truck, shown outside the Detroit Institute of Arts (DIA), is similar to one driven by Curtis Armstrong for *The Adventures of Scapin* in 1979, which starred George Gitto and Eric Tavares. (OUL.)

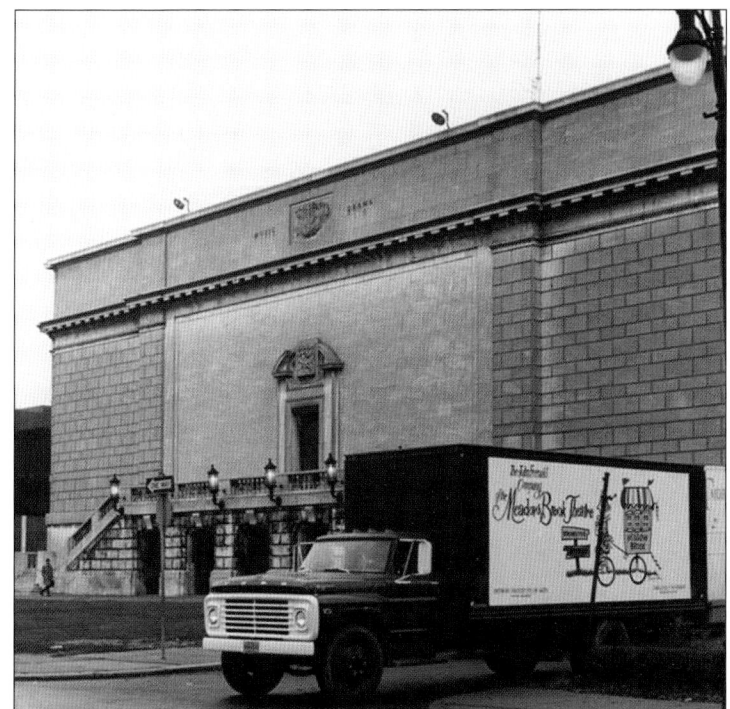

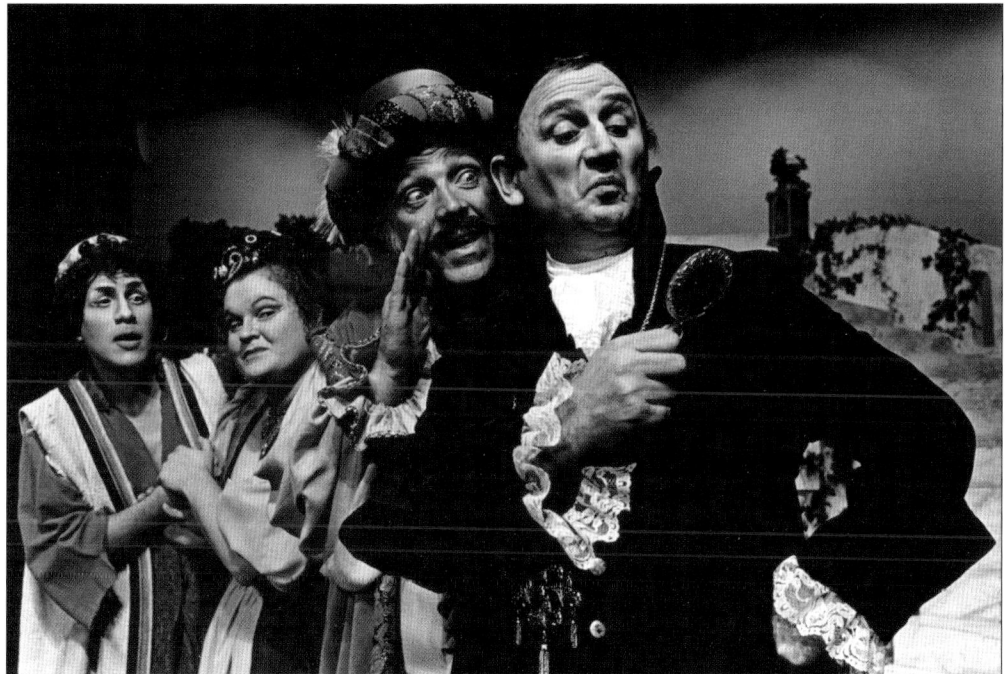

In 1974, the *Twelfth Night* cast included Marianne Muellerleile (second from left). In six seasons at MBT, she appeared in 25 plays. She also worked in New York City and has been in over 80 commercials and over 350 television episodes. She is most remembered as "Gloria" in *Life with Bonnie* and "Norma" in *Passions*. Her film credits include *Return to Me* and *The Terminator*. She recently appeared in *The Sound of Music* at the Hollywood Bowl. (MBT.)

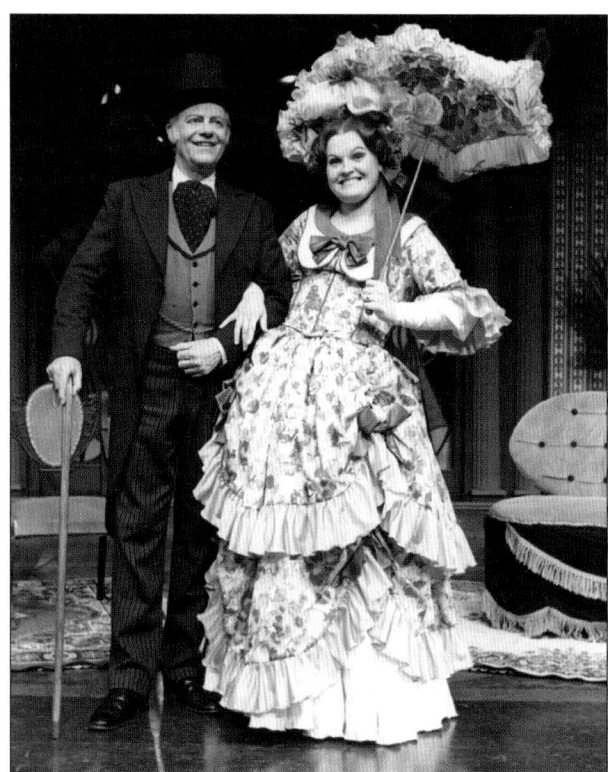

In 1977, Max Showalter (left) and Marianne Muellerleile starred in *Yankee Ingenuity* by Jim Wise and Richard Bimonte. This American musical comedy, which takes place just before the Civil War, is representative of Terry Kilburn's brilliant ability to choose plays with wide audience appeal. (MBT.)

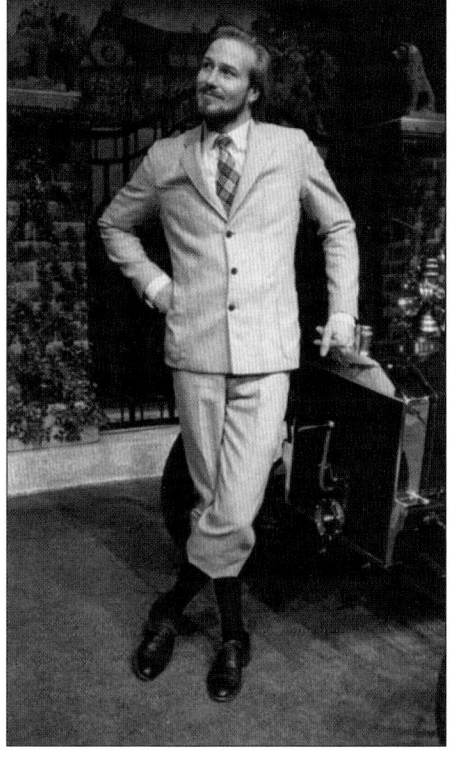

William Hurt attended Tufts University and the Juilliard School. He played John Tanner in *Man and Superman* by George Bernard Shaw at MBT in 1976. A longtime stage and screen veteran, Hurt won an Academy Award for Best Actor for *Kiss of the Spider Woman* in 1985. He also received Oscar nominations for his roles in *Broadcast News* and *A History of Violence*. (OUL.)

At an executive committee meeting on February 21, 1978, Kilburn reported that *The Tempest* was setting an all-time record for attendance. This, despite the opening-night cancellation due to "the Blizzard of 1978." Shown here are, from left to right, Gilbert Cole, G. Wood, and Richard Hilger. (OUL.)

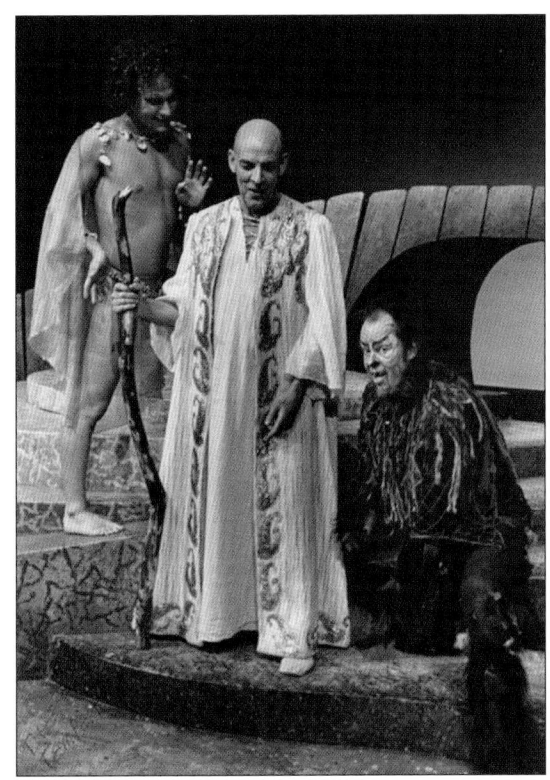

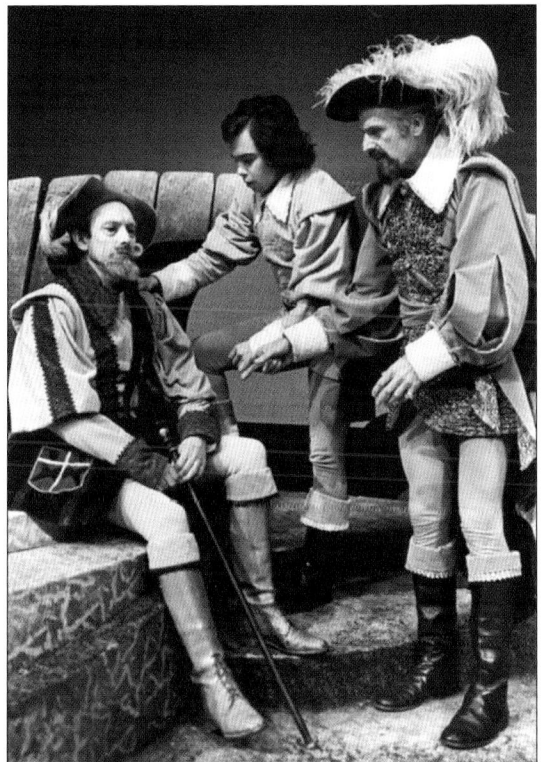

Curtis Armstrong (center) graduated from Berkley High School in Michigan. He then joined the ADA, graduated, and was in seven shows at MBT before making it big as Booger in *Revenge of the Nerds*. He turned to television with a recurring role on *Moonlighting* from 1986 to 1989. Today, he continues to act and produce, with over 30 films and numerous television appearances to his credit. (OUL.)

27

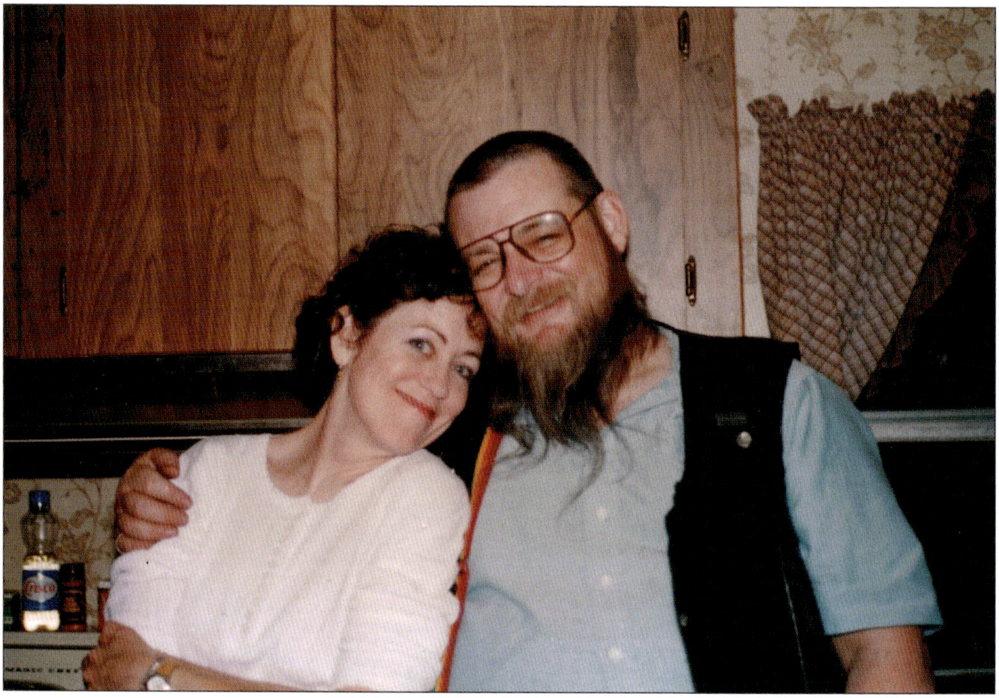

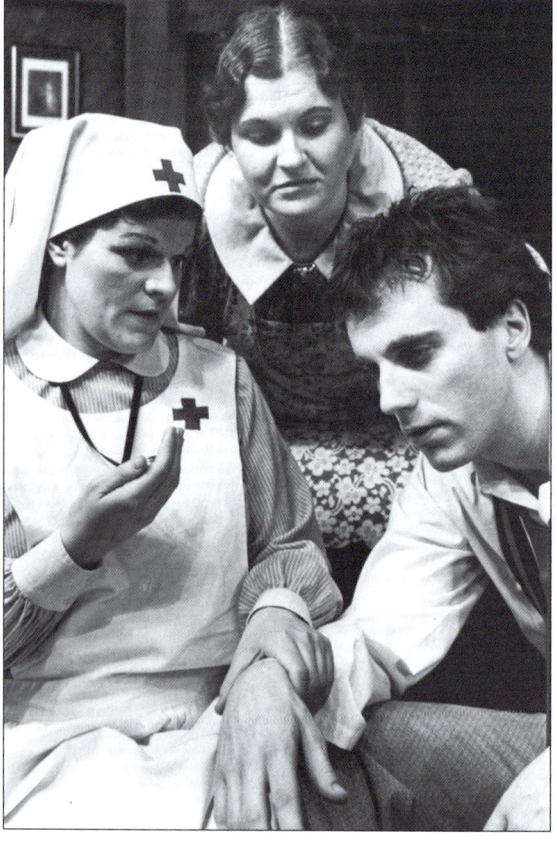

Reid G. Johnson, master electrician, has been at MBT since 1979. He has provided consistently impressive designs for MBT and is a stabilizing force on the staff. Also shown is Karen Sheridan, a professor in OU's Department of Music, Theatre and Dance and an MBT actor and director. (Courtesy of Reid G. Johnson.)

Mary Pat Gleason (left) appeared in *Night Must Fall* with Marianne Muellerleile (center) and Tom Spackman. Besides being a renowned stage, film, and television star, Gleason was awarded a Daytime Emmy Award for her writing on *Guiding Light*. She also received accolades for writing a one-woman show called *Stopping Traffic* and for her philanthropic work. After spending several seasons at Meadow Brook Theatre, she appeared in *The Crucible*, *NCIS*, *Friends*, *Desperate Housewives*, *The Middleman*, and many more shows. (MBT.)

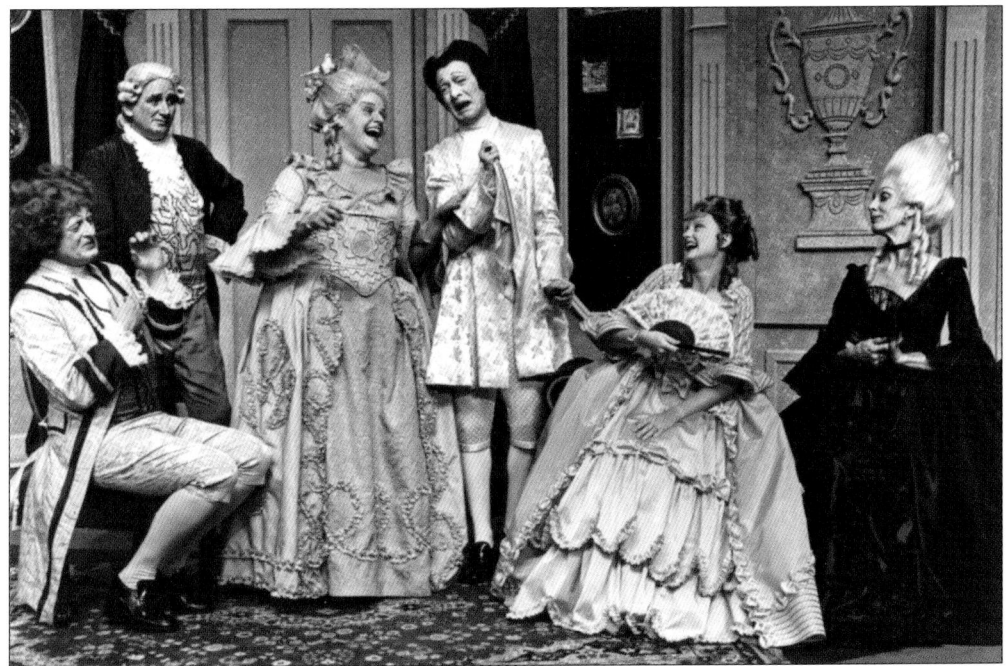

The School for Scandal by Robert Brinsley Sheridan is a good example of the popular comedies of Kilburn's tenure. For this 1979 production, Kilburn designed the magnificent costumes, and Mary Lynn Bonnell constructed them. Pictured from left to right are A.D. Cover, Donald Ewer, Marianne Muellerleile, David Kroll, Erika Peterson, and Jillian Lindig. (MBT.)

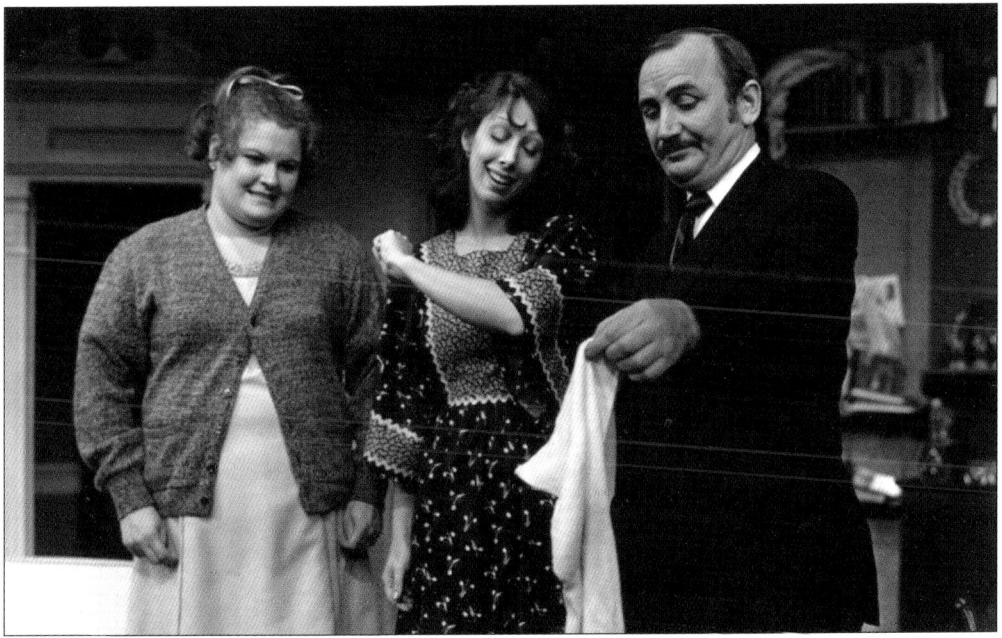

British film and stage actor Donald Ewer, seen here in *How the Other Half Loves* in 1973, was a longtime favorite of MBT audiences. He earned an Obie Award for his role in *Saved* in 1971. He was in the Off-Broadway show *Billy Liar* and spent four seasons at the Stratford Festival of Canada. Appearing here with Ewer are Marianne Muellerleile (left) and Marilyn Meyers. (MBT.)

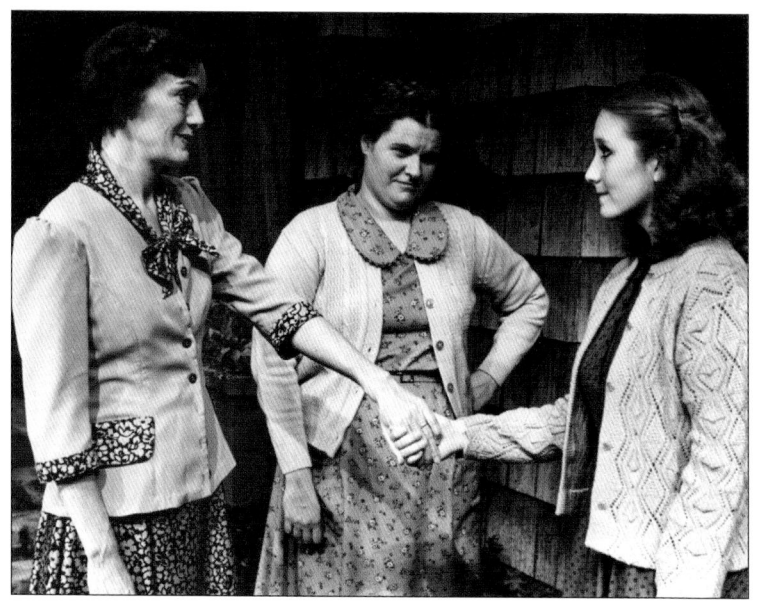

For 30 years, Charles Nolte directed some of Meadow Brook's most distinguished productions, among them *The Andersonville Trial*, *A Streetcar Named Desire*, and *Inherit the Wind*. His own plays, *A Summer Remembered* (shown here) and *The Last Days of Mr. Lincoln*, and his adaptation of *Oedipus Rex*, also premiered at MBT. (MBT.)

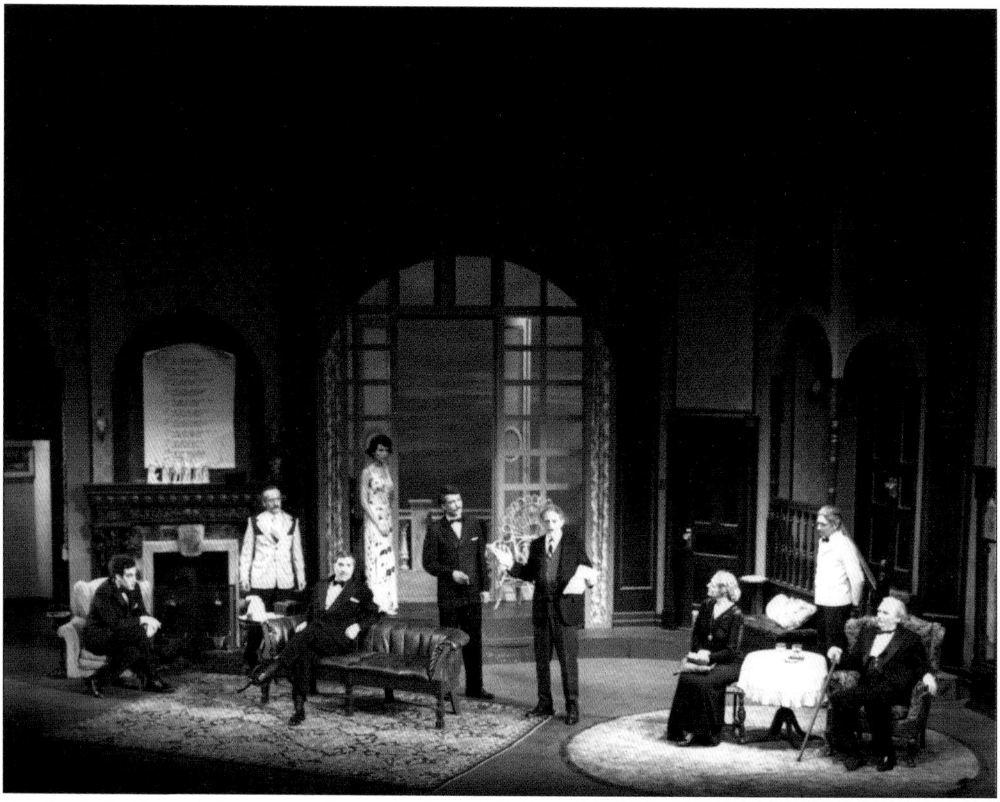

Ten Little Indians' elaborate set design by Peter W. Hicks and beautiful costumes are exactly what MBT audiences came to expect under Terry Kilburn's direction. (MBT.)

Terry W. Carpenter, longtime associate director, has been one of MBT's stage managers since 1981. He has overseen over 140 productions, including several that toured Michigan. He directs the annual presentation of A Christmas Carol and, for many years, taught stage management for Oakland University's Department of Music, Theatre and Dance. (MBT.)

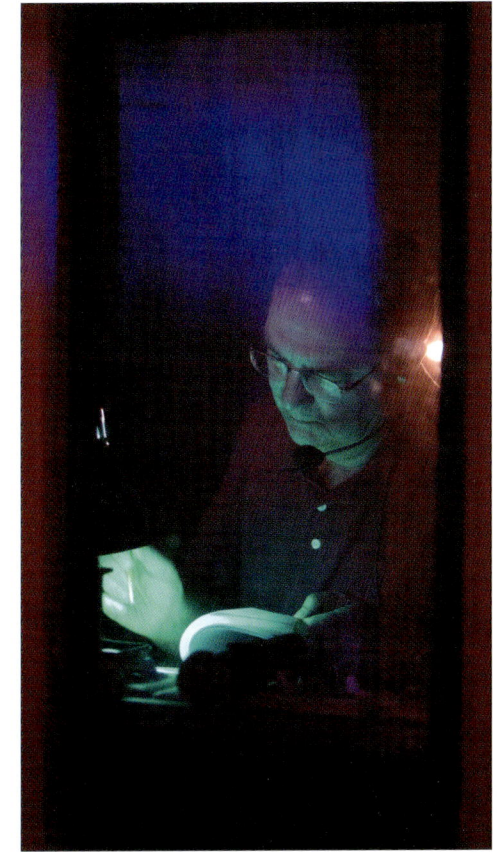

Grace Alexandra Aiello (left), Kevin Skiles (center), and Thom Haneline appeared in the first presentation of A Christmas Carol in 1982. Attending this beloved classic has become an annual event for many local families. The 30th anniversary production was in 2011, and many former actors were in attendance on opening night. (OUL.)

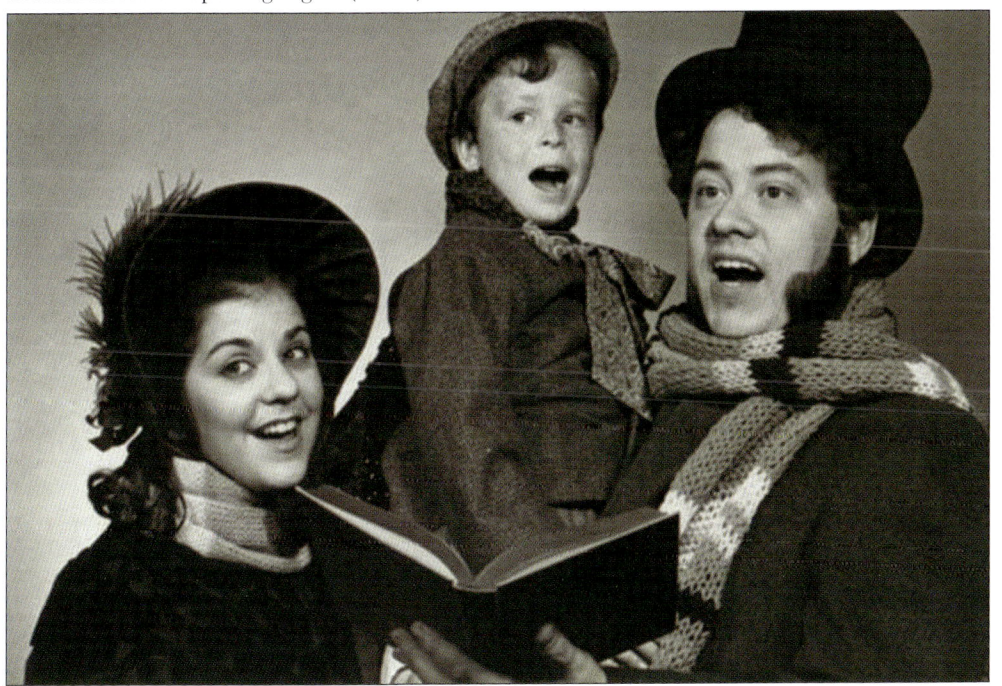

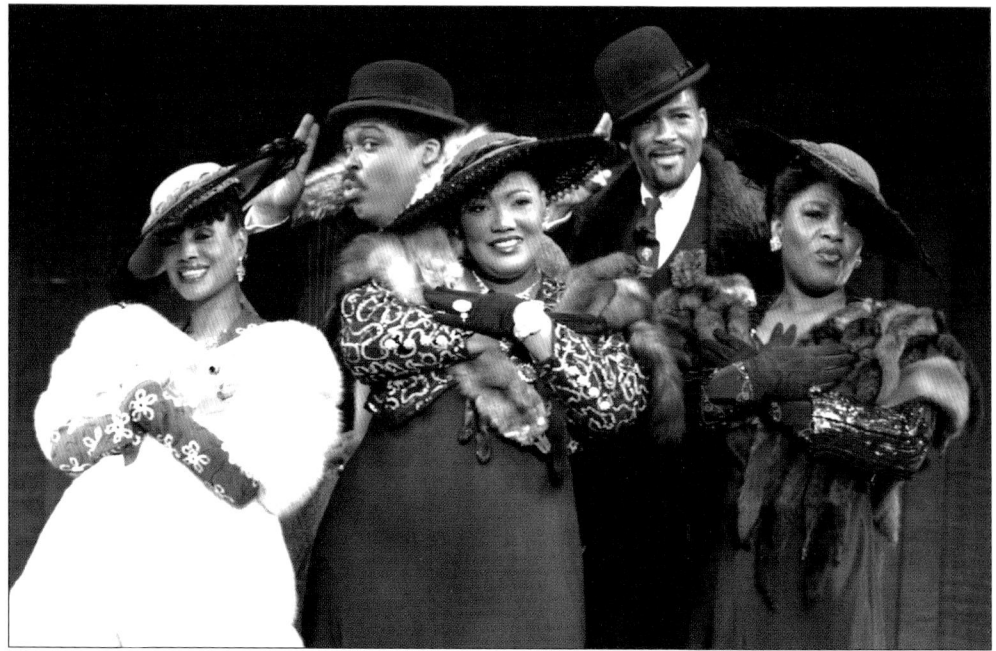

Tony Award winner *Ain't Misbehaving* by Richard Maltby Jr. was a tribute to black musicians of the 1920s and 1930s. MBT director Arthur Faria recreated the magic in 1992; Peter W. Hicks designed the set. Pictured from left to right are Julia Lema, Clent Bowers, Cynthia Thomas, Gene Barry-Hill, and Terri White. (MBT.)

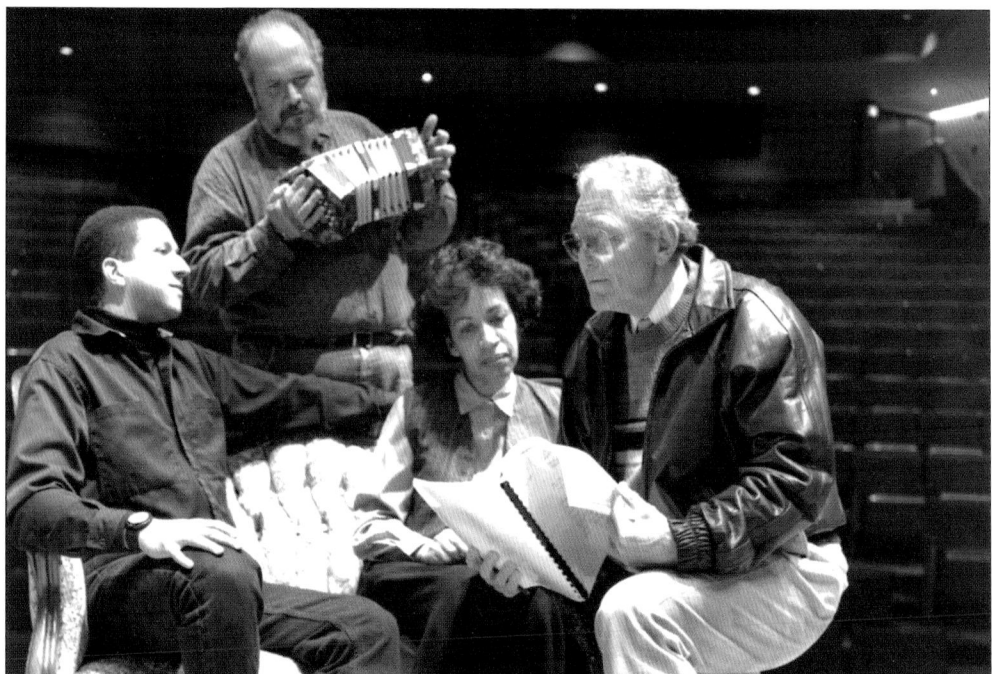

The Last Days of Mr. Lincoln was written and directed by Charles Nolte in 1994. Shown here rehearsing for the world premiere at Meadow Brook Theatre are, from left to right, Morgan Duncan, Joseph Reed, Alma Washington, and Nolte. (MBT.)

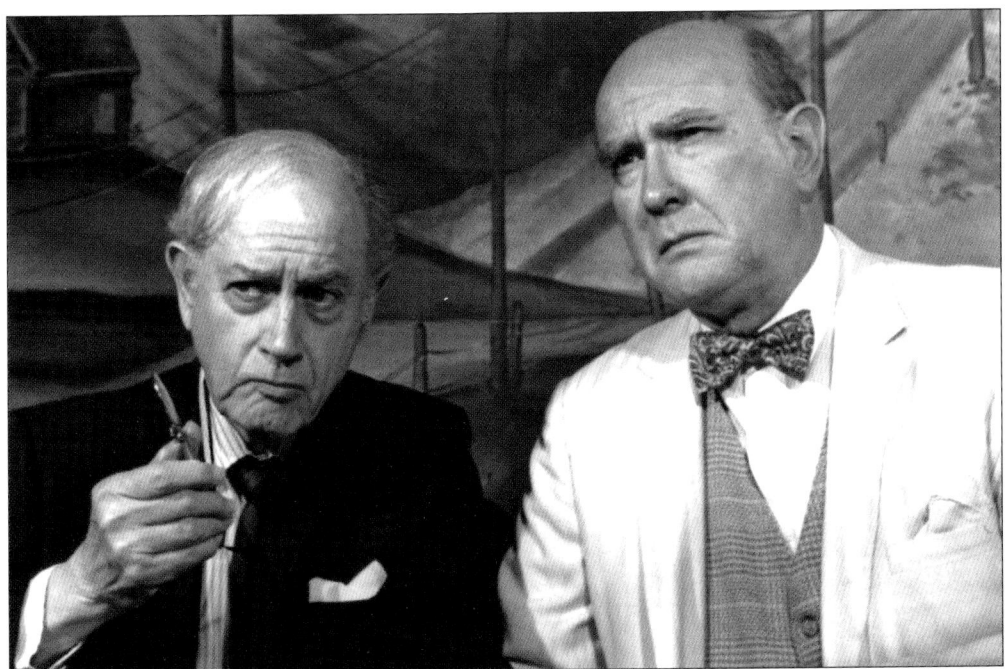

Booth Colman (left) and Arthur J. Beer appear in *Inherit the Wind* by Jerome Lawrence and Robert Lee. It was directed by Charles Nolte in 1991. This courtroom drama put Darwinism on trial and was controversial at the time. (MBT.)

In *A Christmas Carol*, Adam Carpenter (left) portrayed Tiny Tim in 1990, 1991, and 1993. He is the son of associate director Terry W. Carpenter. His younger brother, Joel, who later also played Tiny Tim, was being born during the 1992 production, preventing Adam's appearance that year. He is shown here with Booth Colman, who played Ebenezer Scrooge for 13 years. (MBT.)

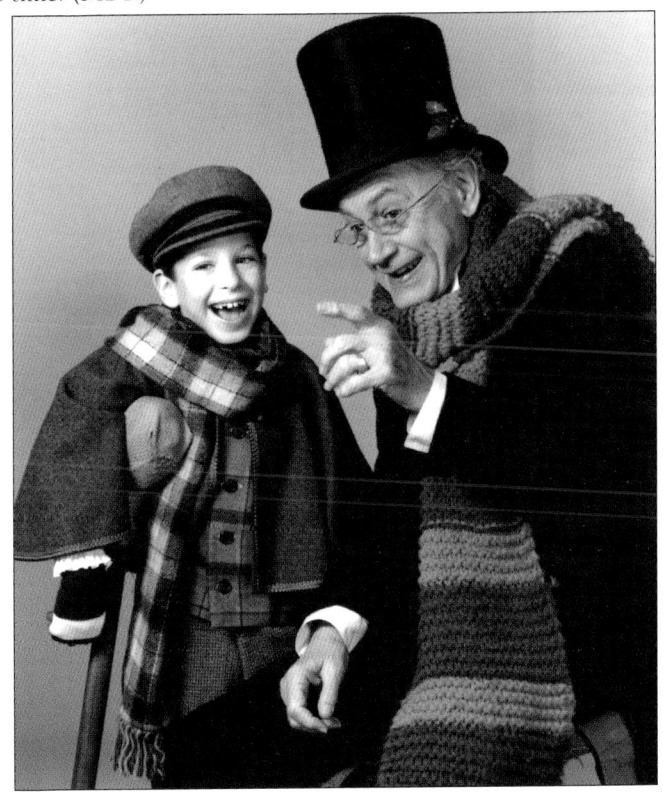

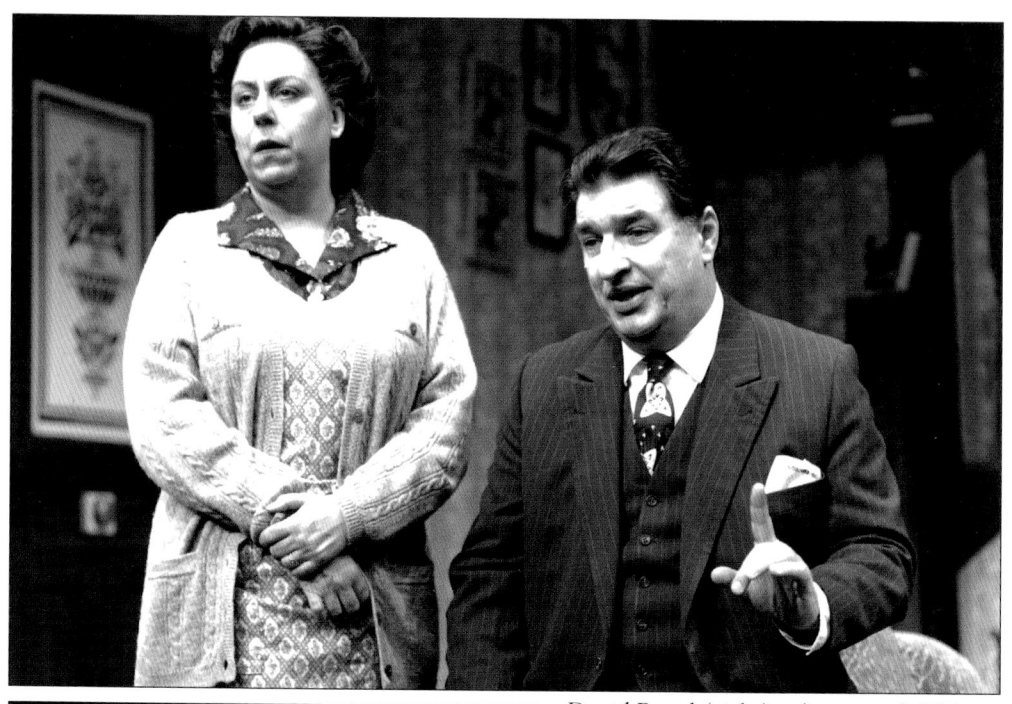

David Regal (right), a longtime MBT actor and artistic director from 2003 to 2007, was responsible for the initial direction for the Theatre Ensemble. He is currently an associate professor at the University of Detroit–Mercy Theatre Company. He appeared in *Broadway Bound* by Neil Simon in 1994 with Jayne Houdyshell (left). (MBT.)

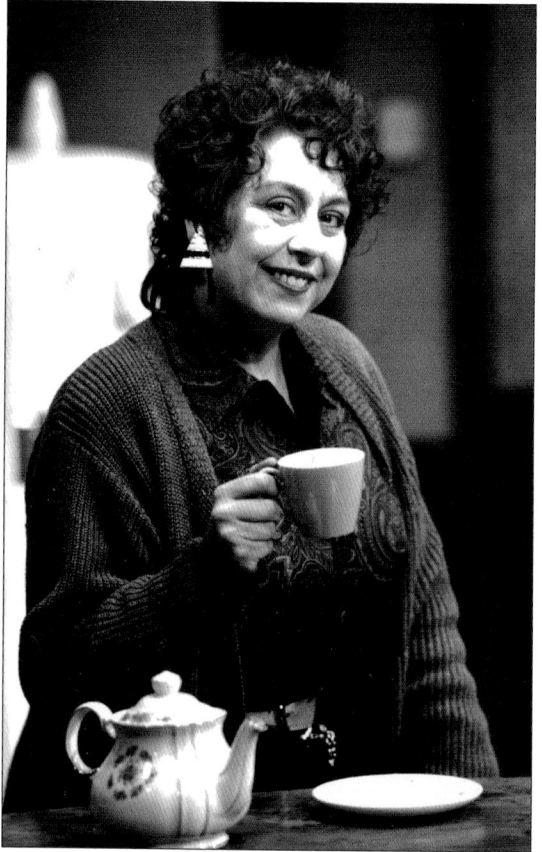

Jayne Houdyshell, a 1974 ADA graduate, was featured in the 1994 production of *Shirley Valentine*, a one-character play written by Willy Russell. A MBT favorite for several seasons, Houdyshell earned a Tony nomination for her role as Ann Kron in the Broadway production of *Well* by Lisa Kron in 2006 and performs regularly on Broadway. (MBT.)

To Kill a Mockingbird by Harper Lee, dramatized by Christopher Sergel, captivated MBT audiences in 1994. Maggie Keenan-Bolger (left) was on national tours of *The Music Man*. Mike Kopera (center) became CEO of Lakeview Pictures. Andrew Keenan-Bolger (right) was in Broadway productions of *Seussical, Newsies,* and *Beauty and the Beast*. (MBT.)

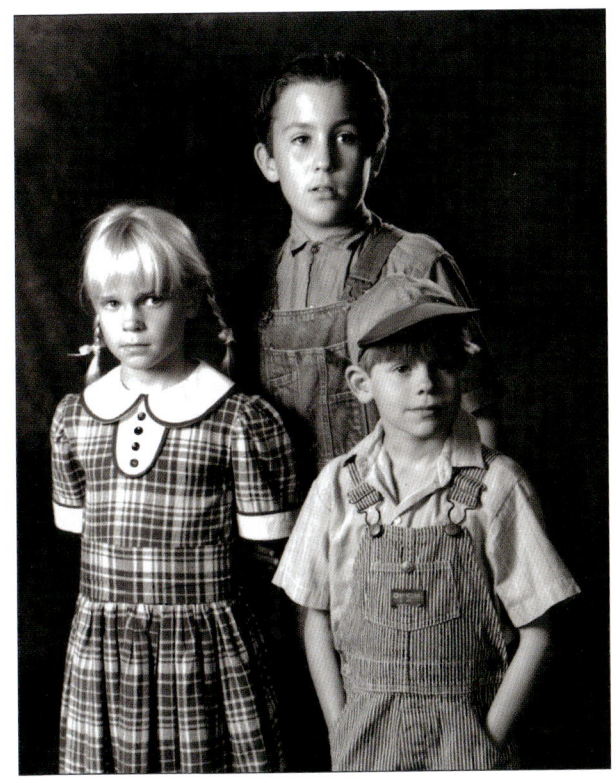

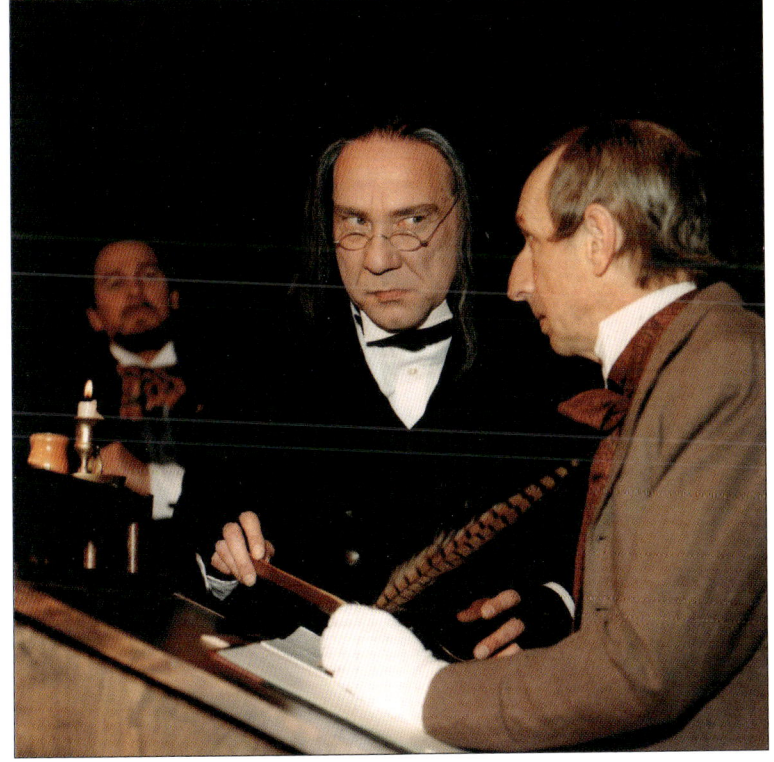

Geoffrey Sherman adapted *A Christmas Carol* in 1995. His version was narrated by Charles Dickens, played by Richard A. Schrot (left). Philip Locker (center) played Ebenezer Scrooge, and Thomas D. Mahard played Bob Cratchit. Locker, a longtime actor, also directed for Meadow Brook Theatre. (MBT.)

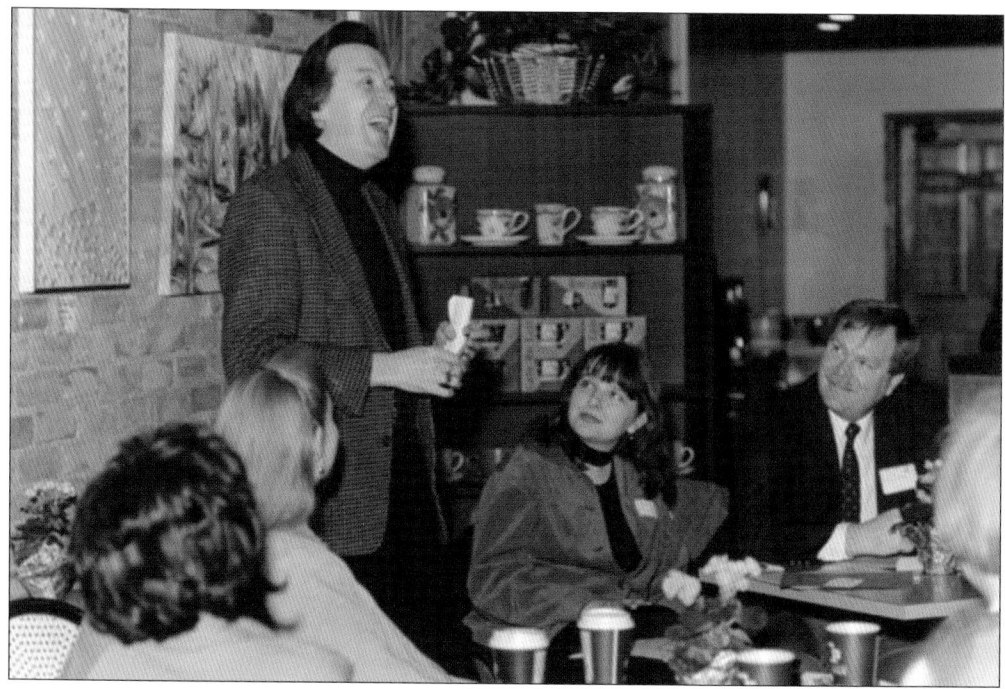

Geoffrey Sherman (standing) is the featured speaker at a Rochester Downtown Development Authority's "Talk of the Town" meeting. Topics included special theatre/shopping packages to attract business to MBT and downtown Rochester. (OUL.)

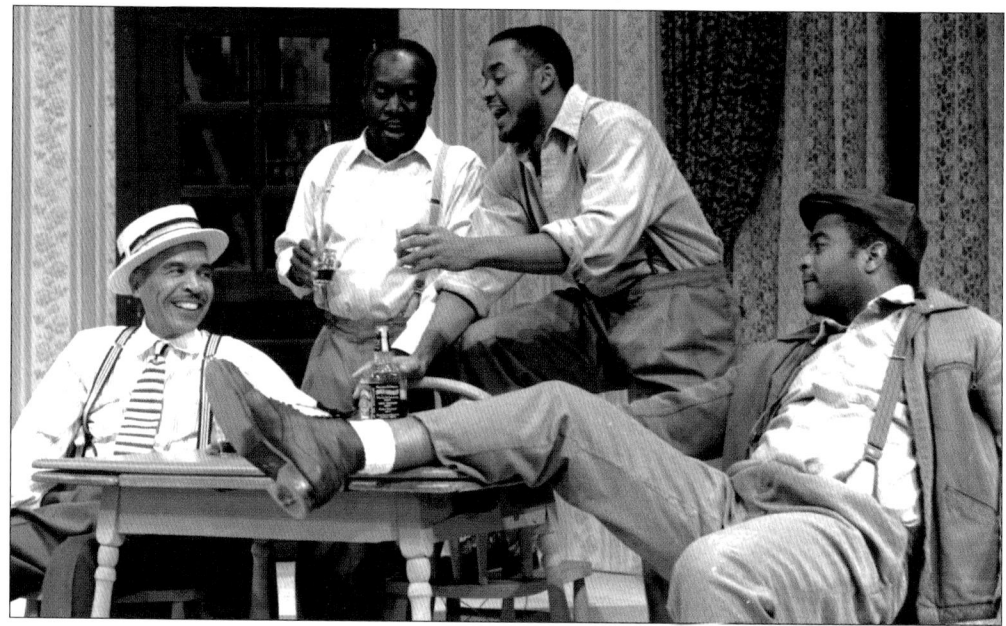

The 1996 Pulitzer Prize winner *The Piano Lesson* by August Wilson portrayed members of an African American family in the 1930s striving to overcome the past. It was directed by Debra Wicks, with set designed by Peter W. Hicks. The actors here are, from left to right, Danny Robinson Clark, Ron Bobb-Semple, Anthony Lamont, and Eric A. Payne on the Meadow Brook Theatre stage. (MBT.)

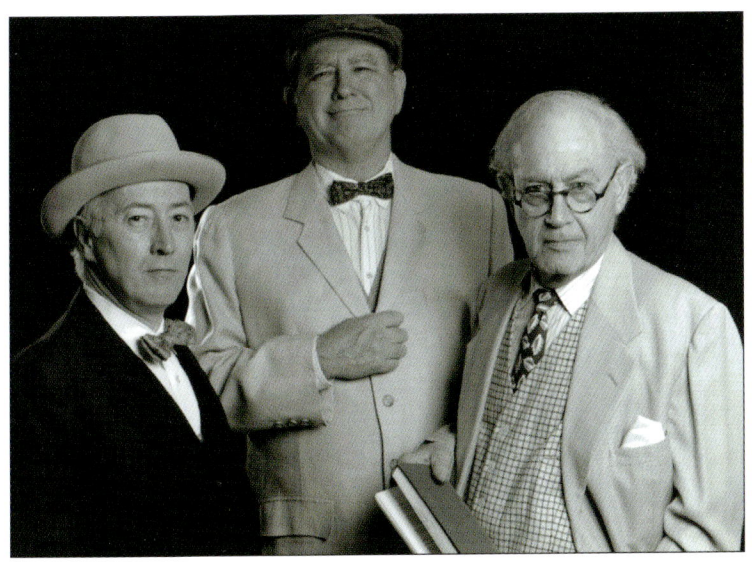

Camping with Henry and Tom, by Mark St. Germaine, was directed by T. Newell Kring in 1996. The play was based on an actual camping trip taken in 1921 by Henry Ford, Warren G. Harding, and Thomas Edison. Pictured from left to right are William J. Norris (Ford), Arthur J. Beer (Harding), and Booth Colman (Edison). (MBT.)

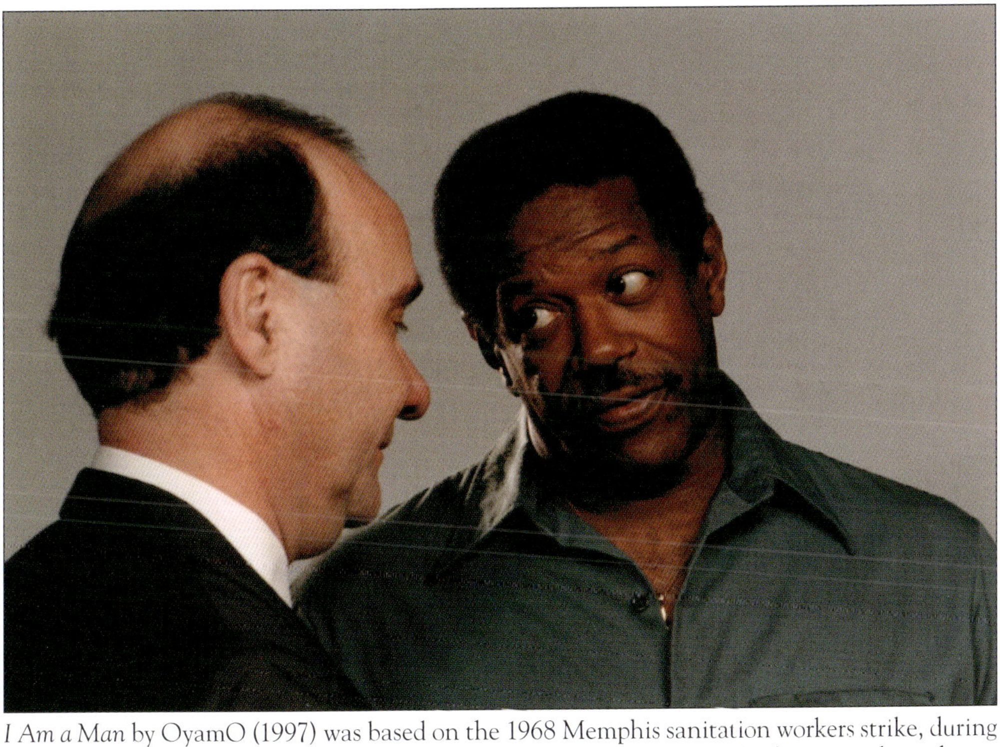

I Am a Man by OyamO (1997) was based on the 1968 Memphis sanitation workers strike, during which Martin Luther King Jr. was assassinated. It was directed by Gary Anderson, with set design by Peter W. Hicks. Actors included Phillip Locker (left) and Lou Beatty Jr. as T.O. Jones. Beatty has appeared in numerous television episodes and the movie *Hard to Kill*. Locker, a film and stage actor, appeared in *Poltergeist*. (MBT.)

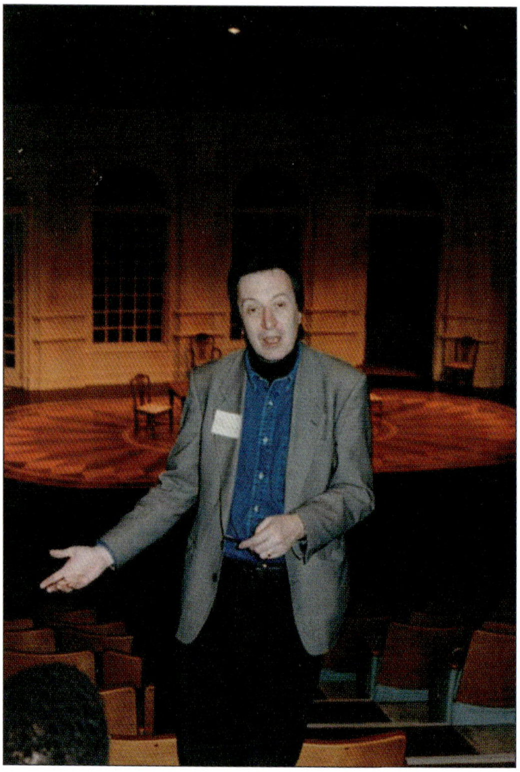

An interesting Sherman initiative was to establish a space and opportunity to do "edgier" works not necessarily appropriate for the MBT stage. The solution was to form the New Studio Company, a combination of MBT Equity actors and OU students, which used the stage in Varner Hall for performances. (OUL.)

Thunder Knocking on the Door, by Keith Glover, featured Luray Cooper (left) as Marvell Thunder and Keesha Fleth as Glory in this 1999 blues musical. The music and lyrics were written by three-time Grammy winner Keb' Mo'. (MBT.)

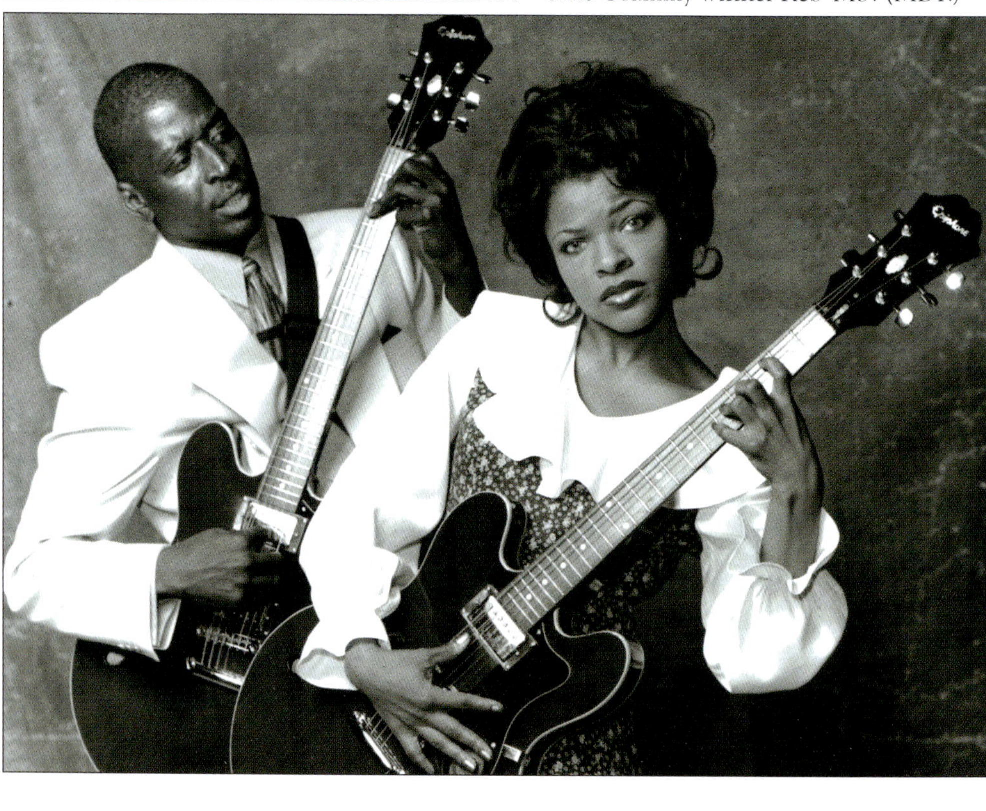

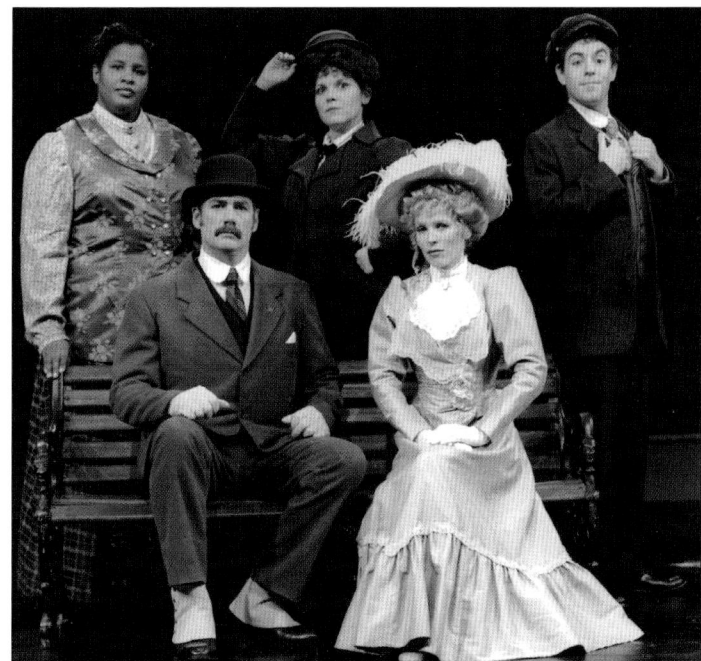

The Tony-nominated *Tintypes* (1999), by Mary Kyte with Mel Marvin and Gary Pearle, featured popular tunes from the Great American Songbook. Pictured from left to right are (first row) Christopher Howe and Leisa Way; (second row) Lea Charisse Woods, Stacy White (director of the Peanut Gallery Players), and Bart Philip Williams. (MBT.)

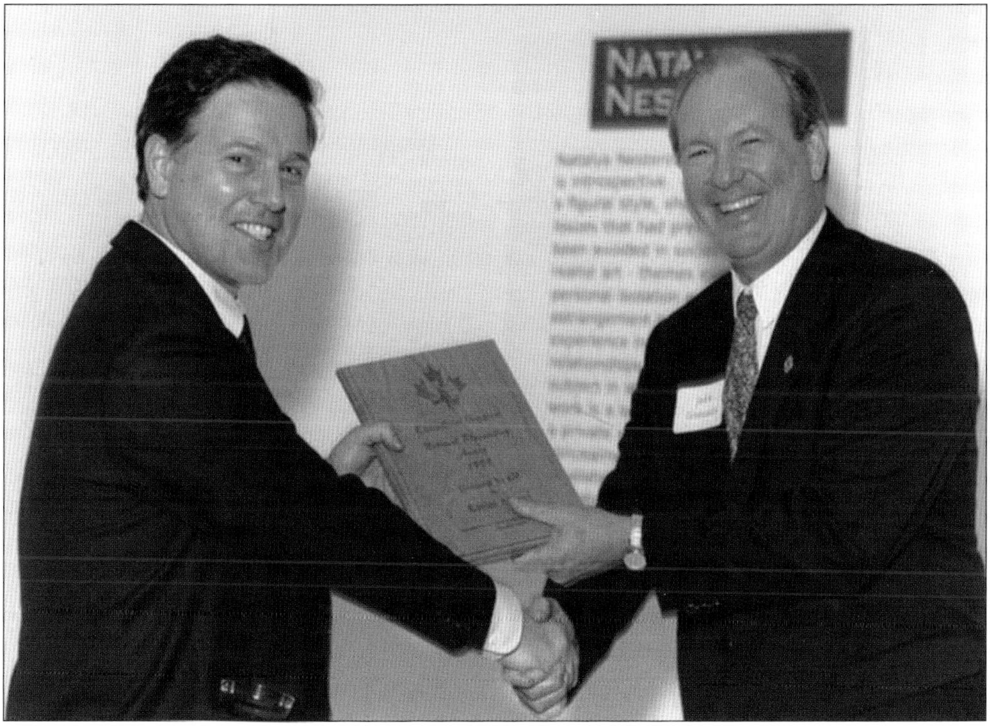

Karim Alrawi (left), playwright-in-residence for three seasons at Meadow Brook Theatre, is pictured receiving the Canadian Theatre National Playwriting Award from John Tennant (right) in 1999 for *Killing Time*. This controversial play, which deals with the right to die, received national attention because of the trial of Dr. Jack Kevorkian in Michigan. This play also received the International 2000 Playwriting Award. (OUL.)

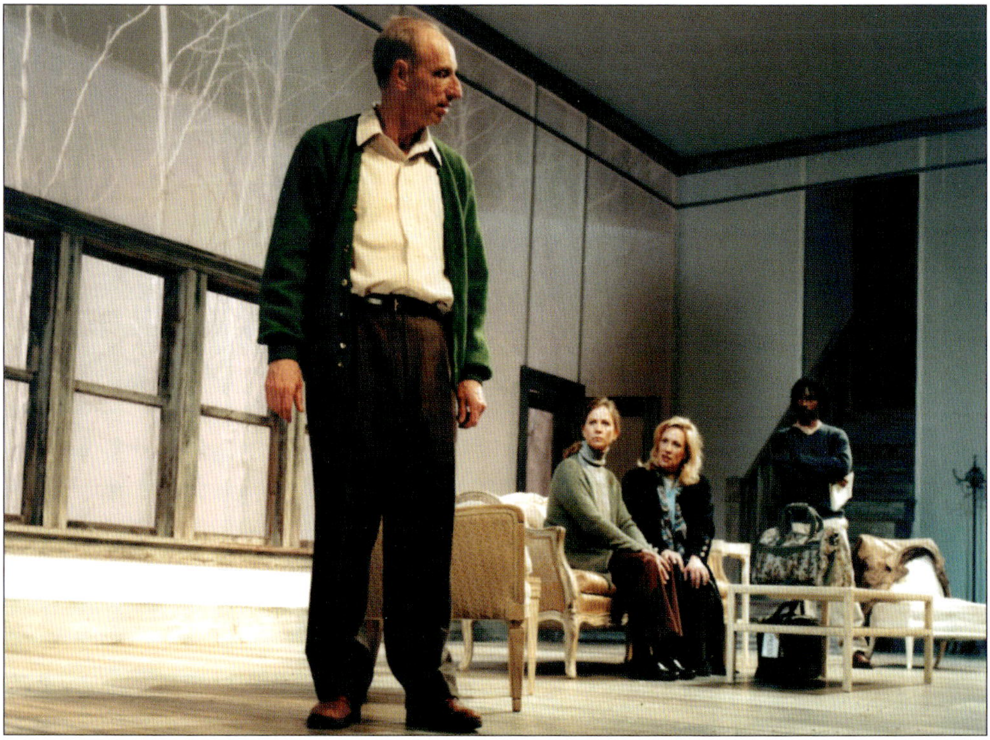

Killing Time by Karim Alrawi opened at Meadow Brook Theatre in 2001. Thomas D. Mahard (left) portrayed Dr. Jack Kevorkian and has appeared in over 70 MBT productions since 1979. He is approaching 30 years in *A Christmas Carol*, six of which were as Scrooge. Mahard appeared in over a dozen feature films, including *Gran Torino*, *Conviction*, and *Beyond the Mask*. He has taught acting classes at OU for over 20 years. (MBT.)

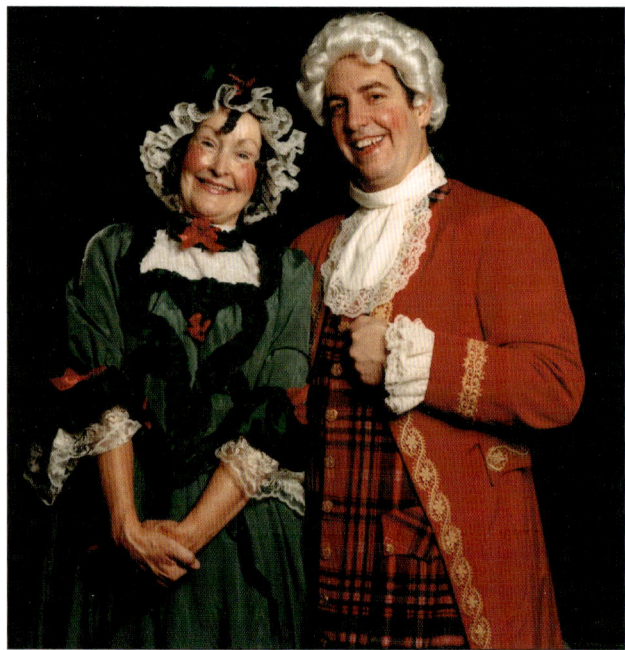

A Christmas Carol in 1996 featured Mary Benson as Mrs. Fezziwig (left) and John Patrick Lowrie as Mr. Fezziwig. Benson's time at MBT spanned over 33 years. She said of her time here, "How blessed I was to get to play on that stage." She is currently living in Portland, Oregon. (MBT.)

Three
MEADOW BROOK THEATRE GUILD

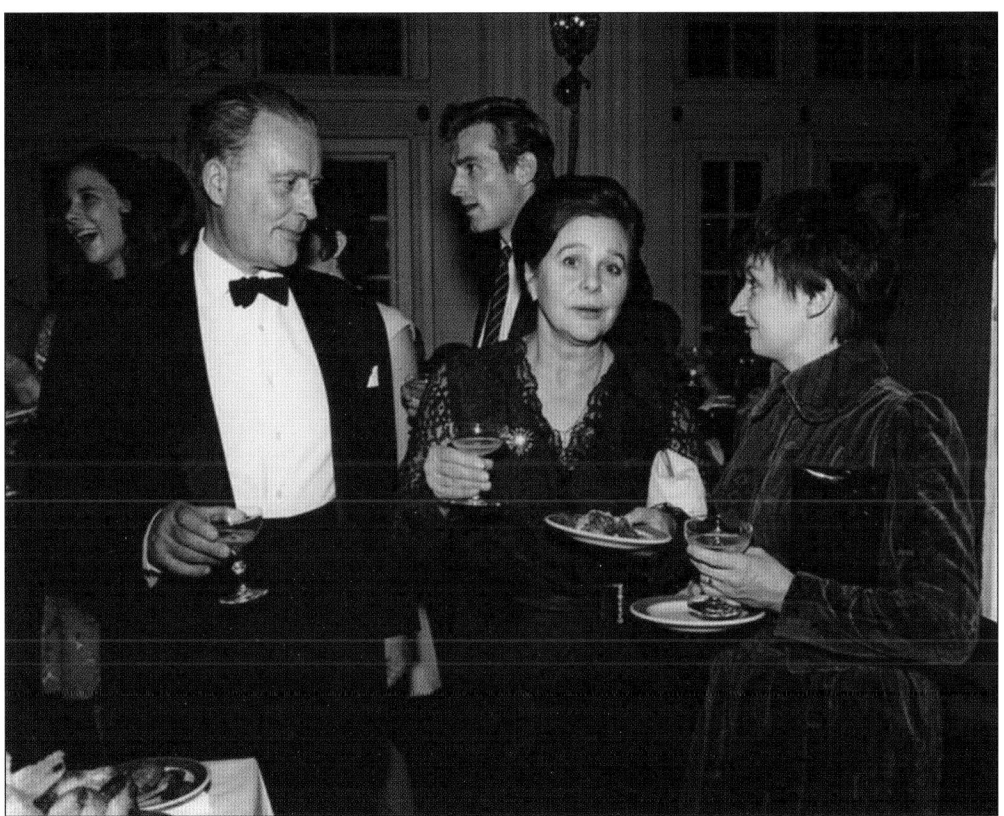

The idea of a guild originated when Mr. and Mrs. Boutell of Bloomfield Hills, who for several years served on the Meadow Brook Executive Committee, acted as hosts for a series of parties for the actors and directors who came to Meadow Brook Theatre. Shown here are John Fernald (left) and Jenny Laird (center). (OUL.)

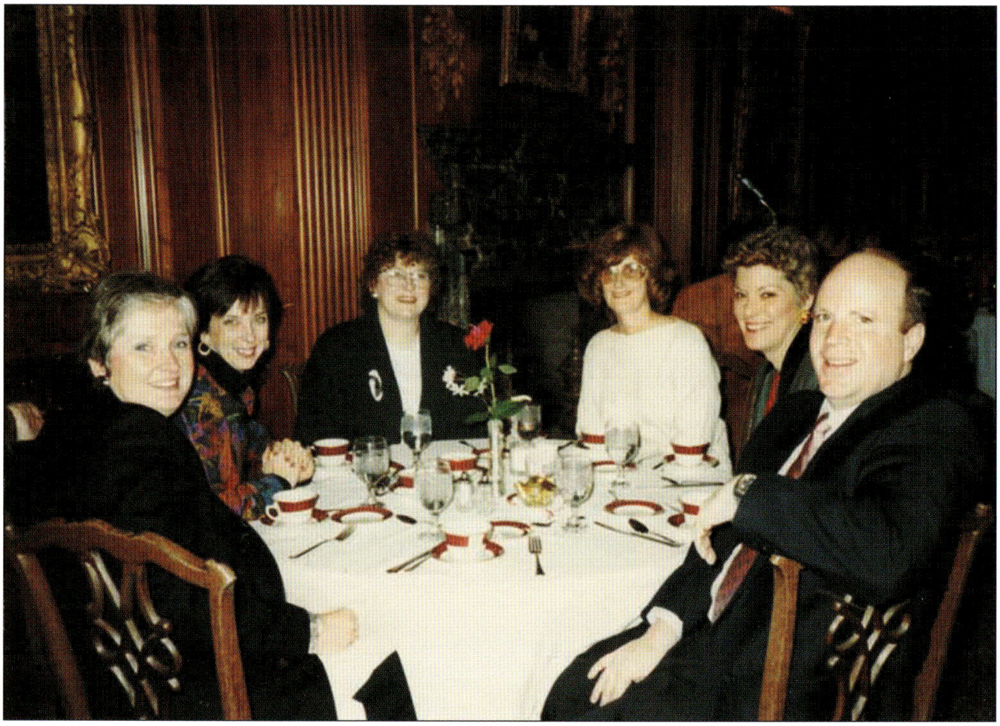

Robert Dearth, director of cultural affairs at Oakland University, suggested a more formal structure that would provide an opportunity to assist the theatre and its staff. The outcome was the development of the Meadow Brook Theatre Guild in 1977. Meetings were held at Meadow Brook Hall. Seated here from left to right are Kathy Kohler, past president Nancy Golick, Diane Gruebnau, past president Claudia Goss, Chris Powell, and Stuart Hyke, the second director of cultural affairs. (OUL.)

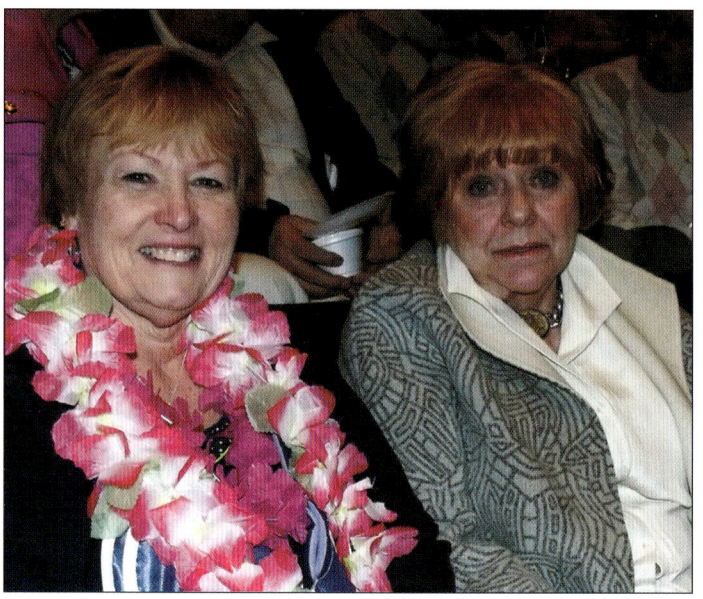

Carol McClure (right) of Rochester served as the first president of the guild. It was during her second term that the guild developed goals, formed bylaws, and undertook a few projects, providing a structure and format that has continued to the present. Mary Caughlin (left) served as president, vice president, treasurer, secretary, Luncheon on the Aisle chairman, parliamentarian, and numerous other chairmanships over the years. (MBT.)

A number of services were initiated in the first years, including the following: tech suppers, afterglow parties, welcome baskets, brunches for the cast, and furnishings for the trailers in which the cast members lived while at Meadow Brook Theatre. Here, Brian Kessler, technical director (center), and Cobey Buckner, scene shop foreman (right), partake of a tech supper. (MBT.)

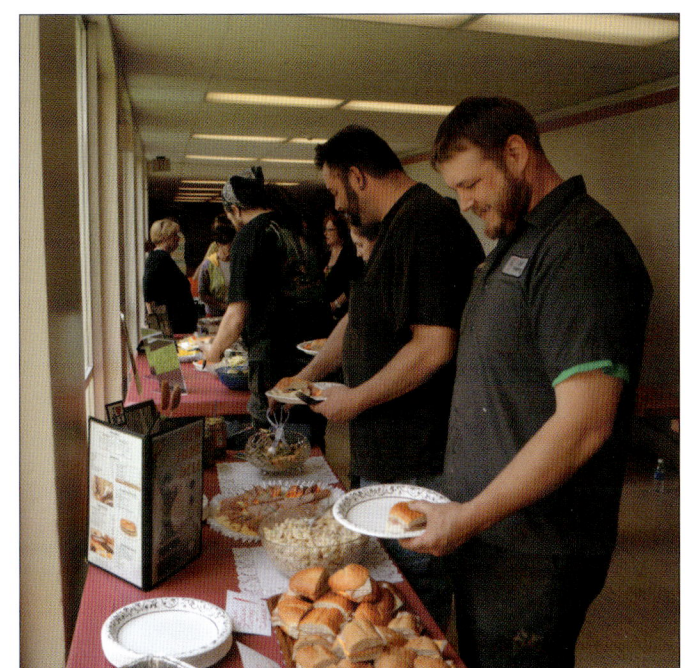

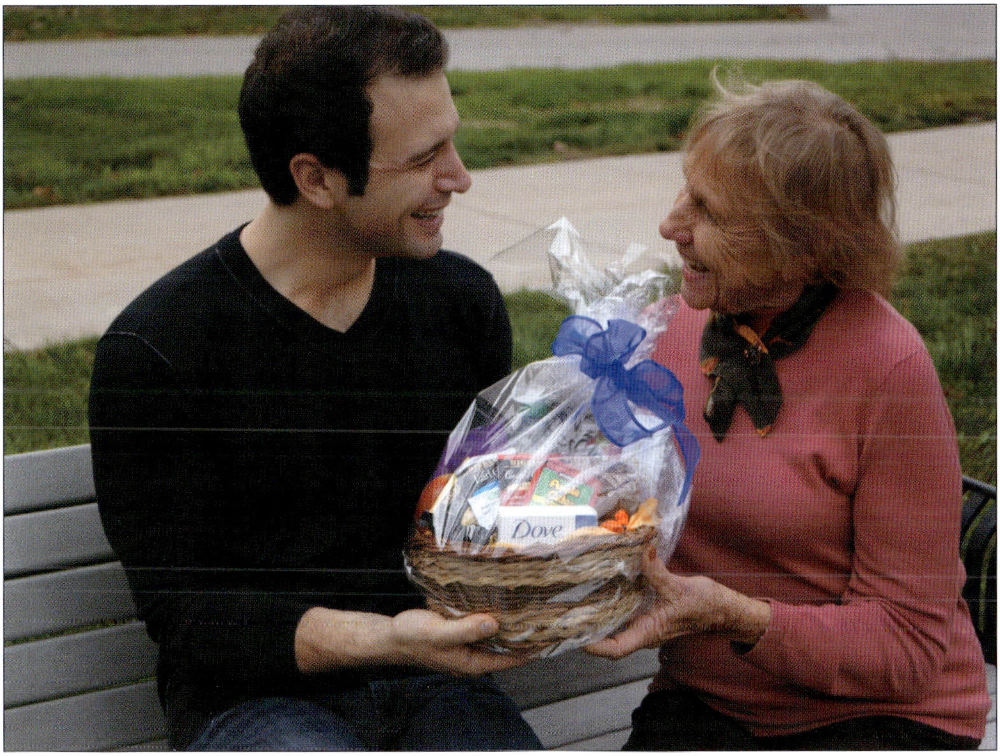

Flo Beck (right), guild president in 1984 and from 2008 to 2010, initiated giving welcome baskets to out-of-town cast members who lived in the trailers. Today, the actors stay at a local hotel. Mathew Schwartz (left) appeared in *Around the World in 80 Days*, *Life Could Be A Dream*, and *Cole Porter's You Never Know* at Meadow Brook Theatre and performs throughout the country. (MBT.)

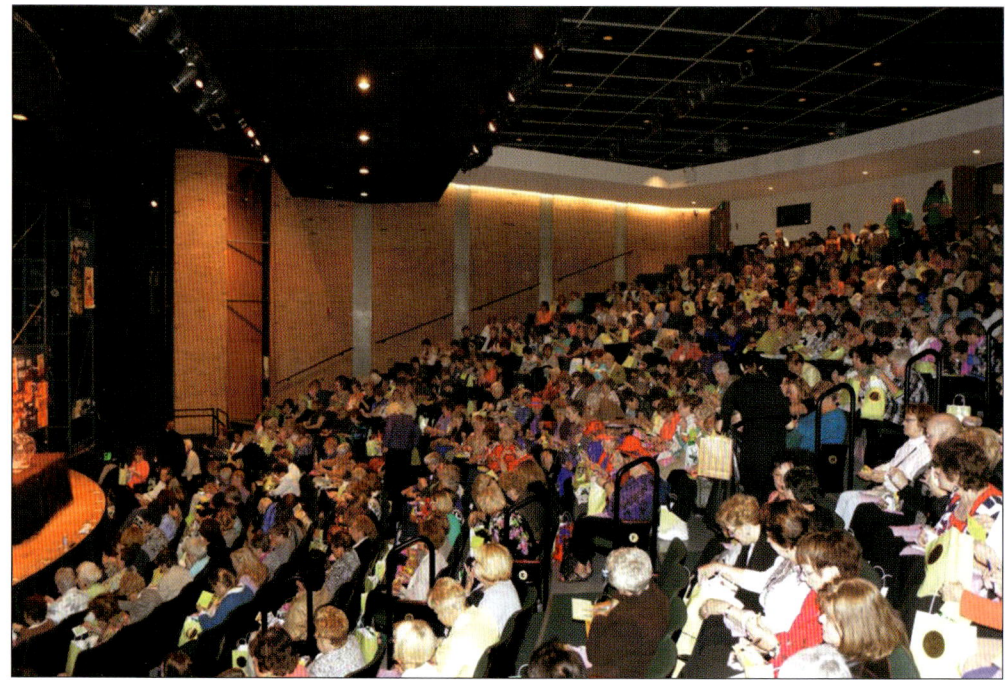

Luncheon on the Aisle was initiated in 1977 by Carol McClure and became an immediate success. Guests were served a gourmet lunch in the theatre, followed by a working rehearsal with discussion by the director. Today, the event also includes boutique shopping, a high-end raffle, costume displays, and selections from the spring musical. (MBT.)

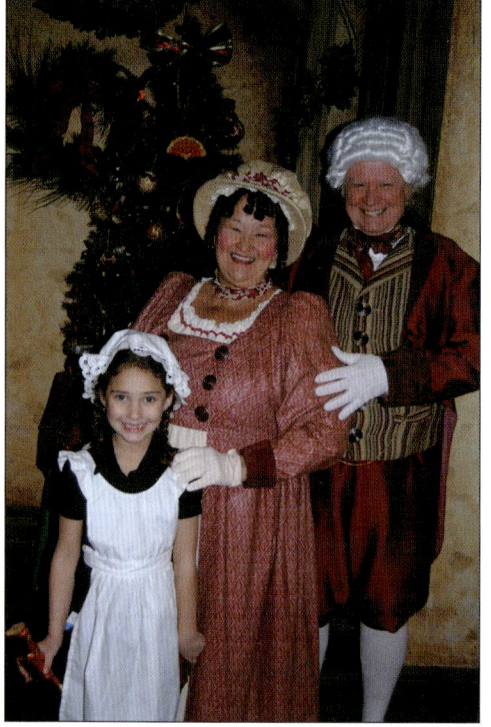

Savannah Foxlee (left), Judy Dery (center), and Paul Hopper donate their time for a "Tea with the Fezziwigs" on the set of *A Christmas Carol*—a memorable Luncheon on the Aisle raffle prize! Dery and Hopper, both longtime MBT favorite actors, have performed in numerous plays locally and throughout the country. Each year, Dery, a guild member, volunteers her storytelling skills at "Spotlights Market" and plays the Fairy Godmother for the guild's Princess Teas. (MBT.)

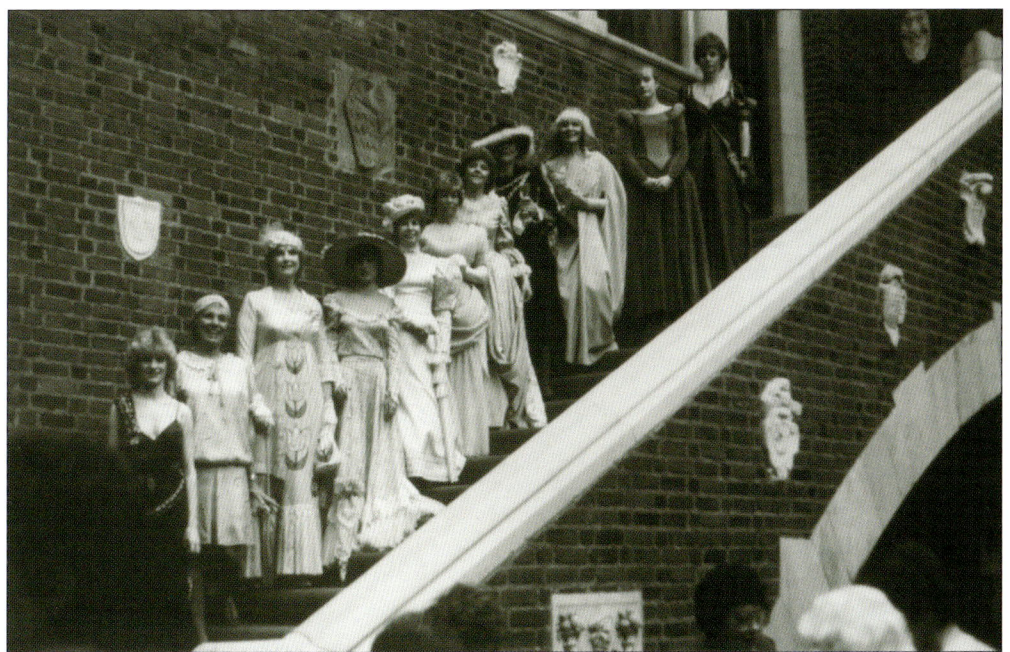

Touring costume shows were started in 1982, and guild members modeled costumes from MBT productions throughout the metro Detroit area. Seen here at the Detroit Institute of Arts are, from left to right, Lea Allen, Flo Beck, Nettajo Morter, Nancy Shock, Kit Sroka, Millie Wallen, Donna Ferry, Lois Matesa, unidentified, Jeni Dahlman, and Doris Atwood. (OUL.)

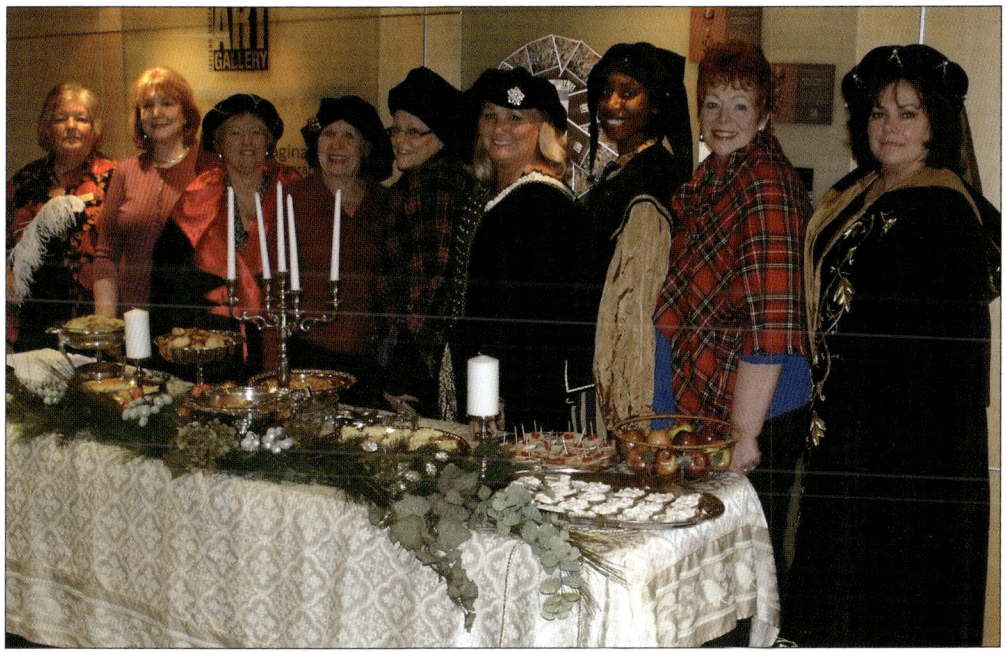

At the "Meet and Greet" on the first day of rehearsal, the guild prepares a themed luncheon for the actors, staff, and crew. Shown here are, from left to right, Karen Kullman, Donna Soule, Mary Caughlin, Flo Beck, Suellen Parkes, Maryann Foxlee, Nicole Davis, Sandy Altemann, and Colleen Brnabic. The actors are dressed in Renaissance attire for *Mary Stuart*. (MBT.)

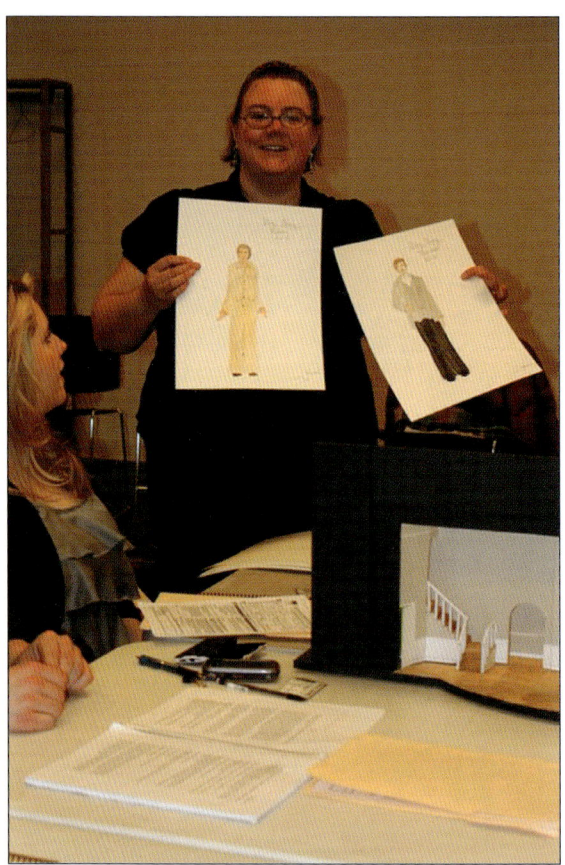

After the "Meet and Greet," guild members are invited to attend a presentation of the costumes and set design, followed by a read-through of the play. Here, costume manager Liz Goodall presents the renderings for *Ding Dong*. Renee Turner looks on. (MBT.)

The guild decorates the theatre lobby for Christmas and fall each year. Shown here assembling the garlands are, from left to right, Colleen Brnabic, Maryann Foxlee, Sheryl Frabotta, Thom Foxlee, Bob Brnabic, and Sara Finney. (MBT.)

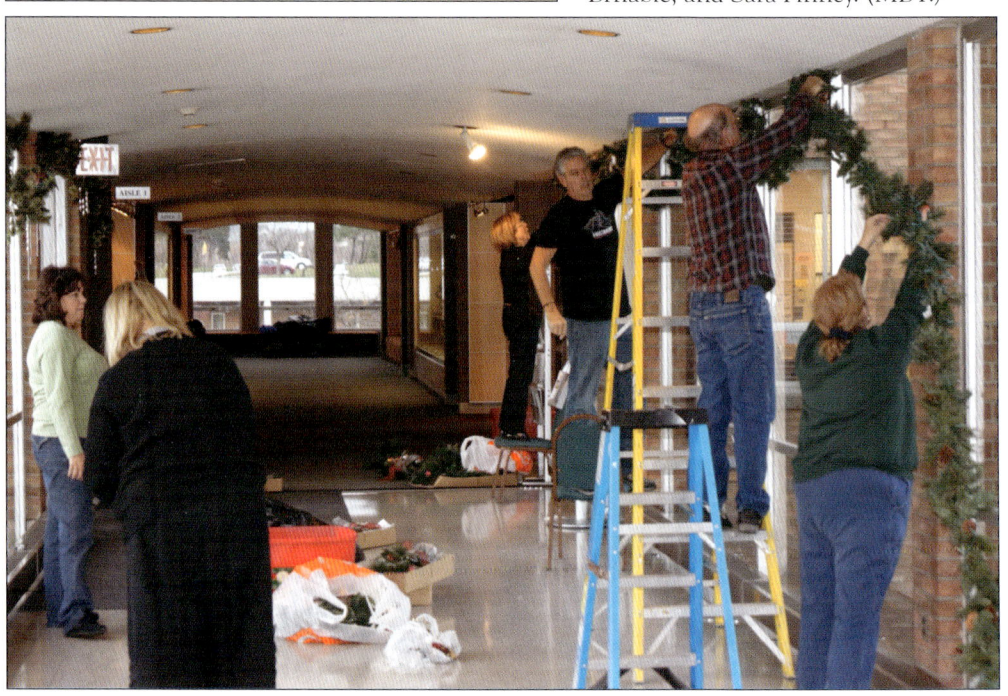

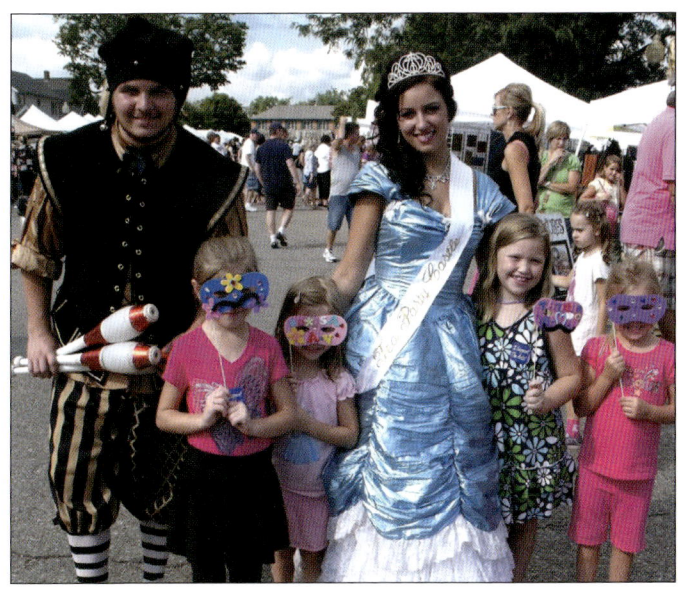

The guild's biggest annual fundraiser has been "Spotlights Market," a juried outdoor art and gift show. For many years, it has been held in the streets of downtown Rochester on the Friday, Saturday, and Sunday following Labor Day. This show has over 120 exhibitors with a variety of original works of art and fun for the whole family. Juggler Dan Baier (left) and Princess Kelly (center) from the Tea Party Castle entertain children, who made masks in the activities tent. (MBT.)

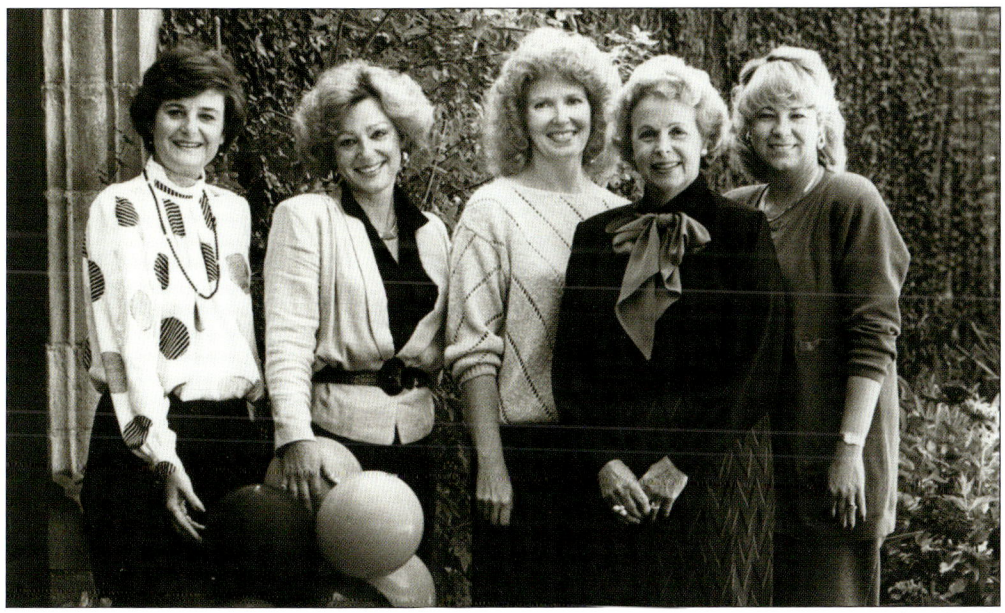

President Cindy Cirar modeled the first "Spotlights" after an art show at Marion High School. It was held in the Shotwell-Gustafson Pavilion on the campus of Oakland University. Shown here are, from left to right, Kathie Eastman, Joan Mac Vay, Karen Williams, Marion Mitchell, and Cirar. (OUL.)

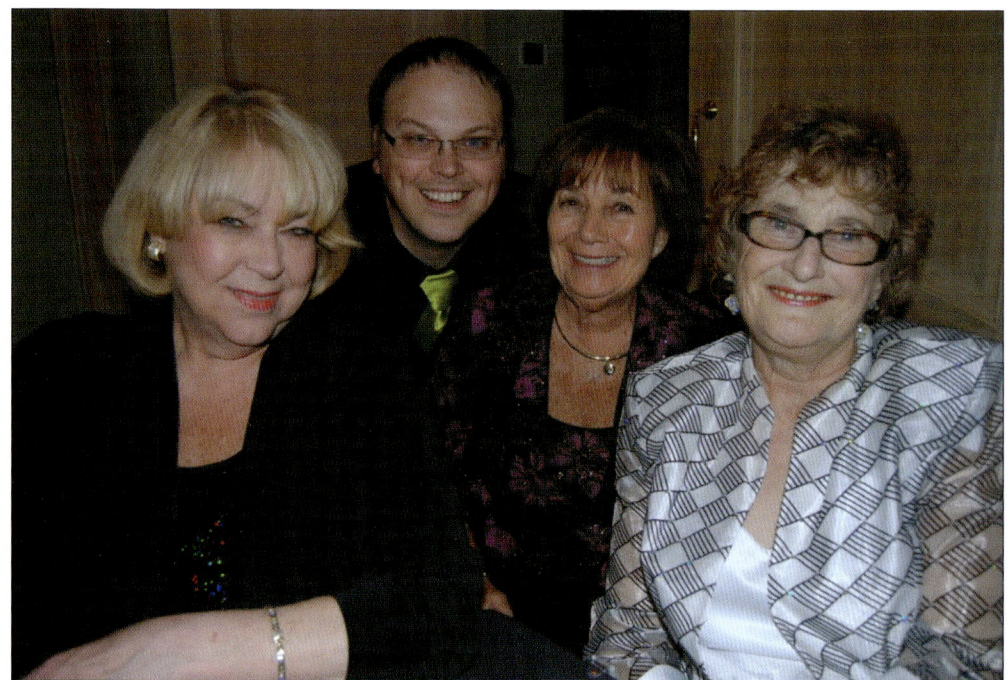

Past guild president and MBT board member Cindy Cirar (far left) and past MBT board president Linda Jarkey chaired the Motown Gala at Great Oaks Country Club in 2012. Longtime guild member Birdie Kutcher (second from right) and past president Claudia Goss (far right) served on the committee. Also pictured is artistic director Travis W. Walter. (MBT.)

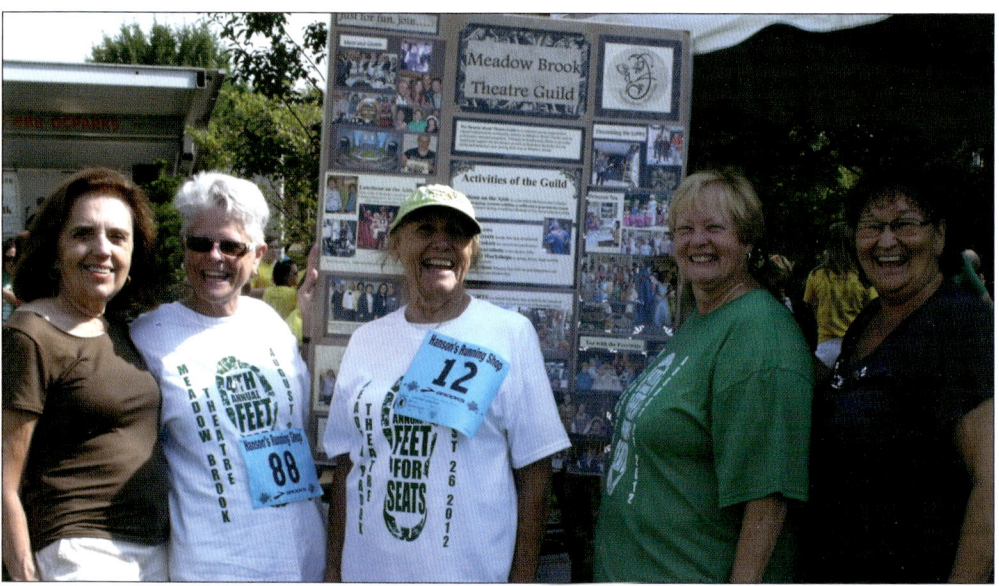

The guild is a yearly sponsor of Feet for Seats. Participating in the fun run and assisting with registration are, from left to right, past treasurer Nancy Schmidt, past president Suellen Parkes, past president and LOA chairman Flo Beck, past president Mary Caughlin, and actress/past secretary Judy Dery. (MBT.)

Prior to the 2003–2004 season, Meadow Brook Theatre separated from Oakland University. Guild president Mary Jo Byrd (right) procured a nonprofit 501(c)(3) status for the guild. Past president Jan Marshall (left) served in 2001 and chaired many committees throughout the years. (MBT.)

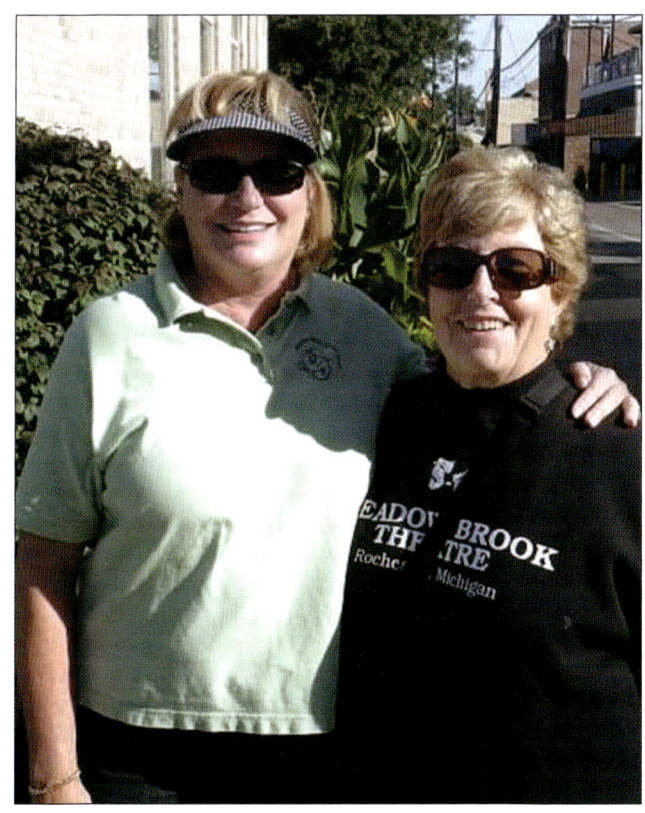

Early guild presidents are, from left to right, Ginny De Steiger, Anne Parsons, Dianne Christman, Doris Atwood, Flo Beck, Millie Wallin, Lois Matesa, Betty Prescott, and Helen Morgan. Not pictured are Carol McClure, Jane Allen, Margorie Brooks, Ernie Pixley, Myska Reeck, Shirley Wells, and Nancy Golick. (OUL.)

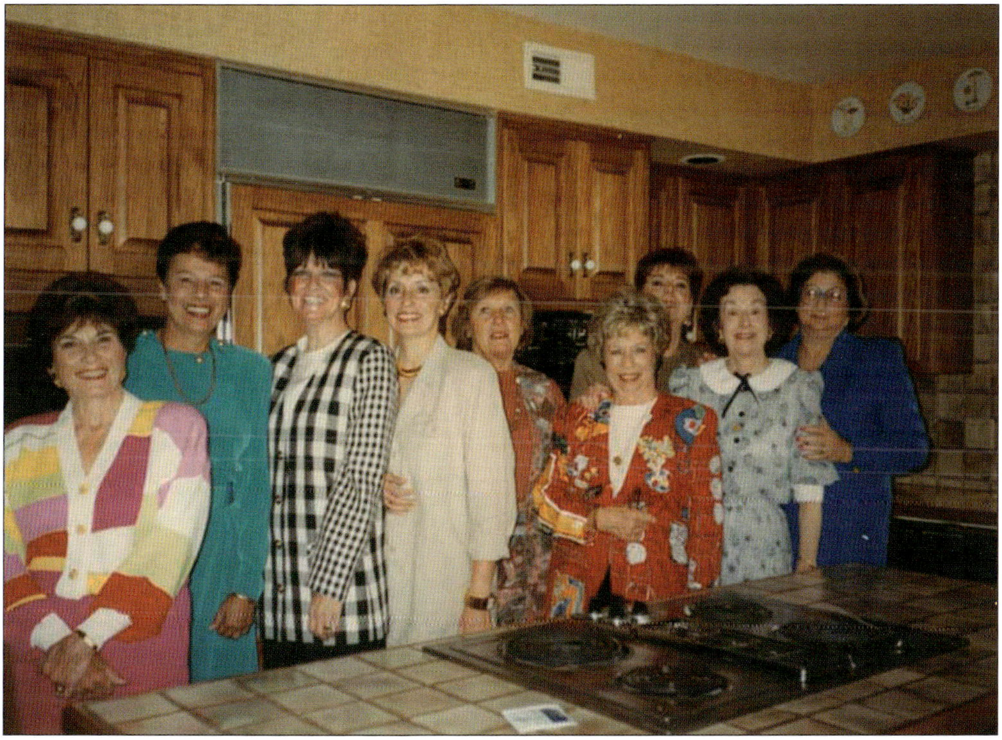

49

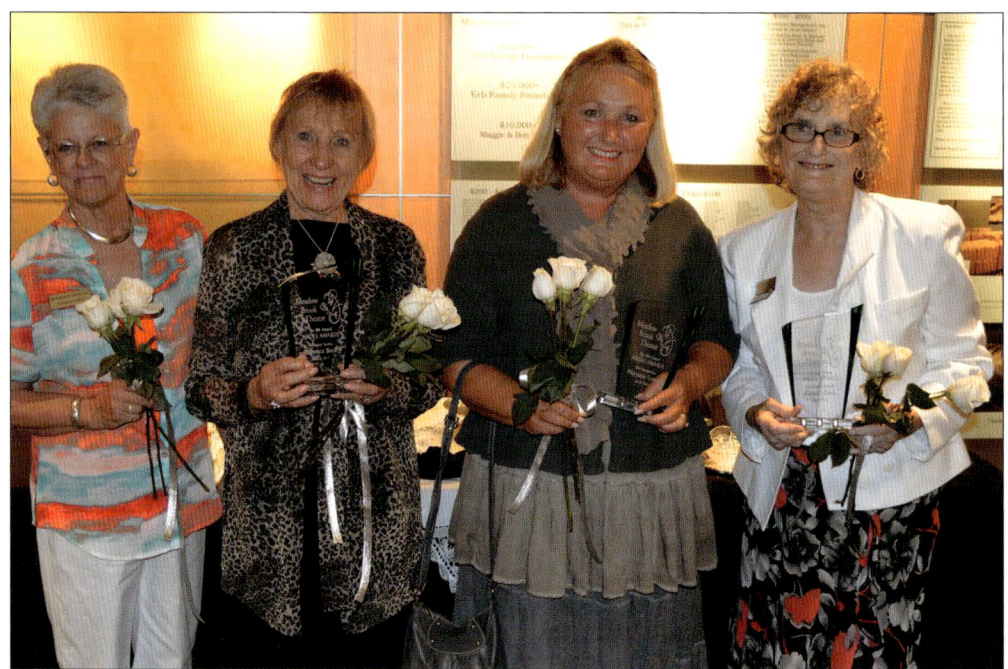

Past guild presidents Suellen Parkes, Flo Beck, Maryann Foxlee, and Claudia Goss were given Andes Awards for outstanding service in 2013. Goss served in 1994, followed by Cindy Cirar, D'rae Freyermuth, Barb Henry, Linda Chayka, Mary Jo Byrd, Karen Lewis, Jan Marshall, Donna Osgood, Mary Caughlin, Lorna Salmon, Doré McGowan, Beck, Foxlee, Suellen Parkes, and Teresa Koempel in 2015. (MBT.)

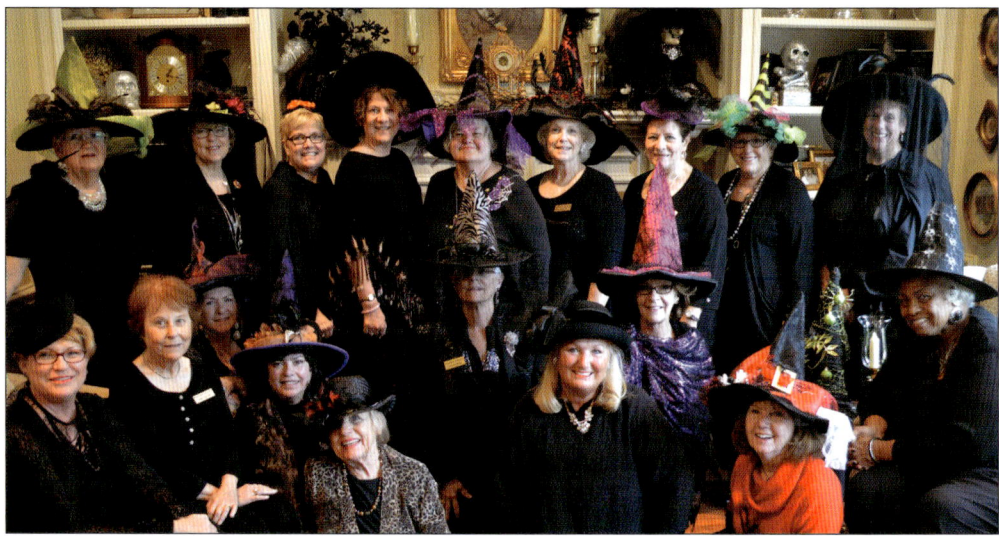

Social events throughout the years have included golf outings, luncheons, teas, trips to see plays, historical sights, and exhibits. For the last several years, members have enjoyed a Witches Tea Party on the Monday before Halloween. (MBT.)

Stage manager and associate director Terry W. Carpenter attends all the guild meetings as theatre liaison. He coordinates the "Meet and Greet" events, welcome baskets, and all special events with the guild. Production manager and assistant stage manager Sarah Lin Warren also works closely with the guild, organizing intern work schedules for Luncheon on the Aisle and helping coordinate the welcome back picnic and tech suppers. Warren has worked in New York, Texas, at Second City, Cirque du Soleil, and the Shaw Festival of Canada. (MBT.)

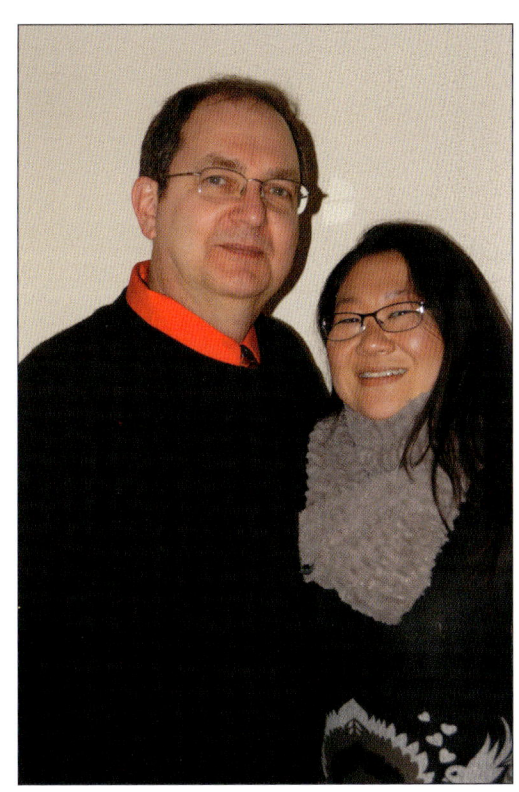

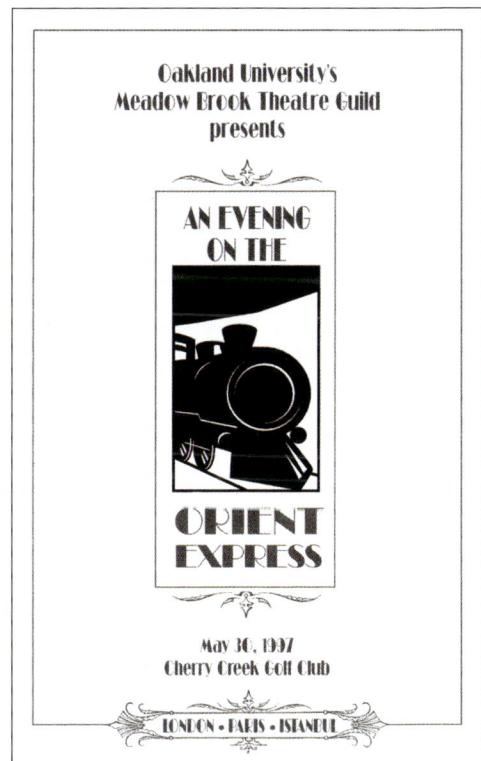

In 1997, Cindy Cirar chaired the successful and glamorous gala, An Evening on the Orient Express, at Cherry Creek Golf Club. MBT actor Phil Locker portrayed Hercule Poirot at the extravaganza, which included dinner, dancing, and an amazing silent auction. The committee included Claudia Goss, Linda Chayka, Birdie Kutcher, Kathy Diewald, Diane Gruebnau, Kathy Koler, Lynn Mack, Alice Walker, Kathie Eastman, Nancy Golick, Lois Matesa, Doris Atwood, and Donna Winkleman. (Courtesy of Claudia Goss.)

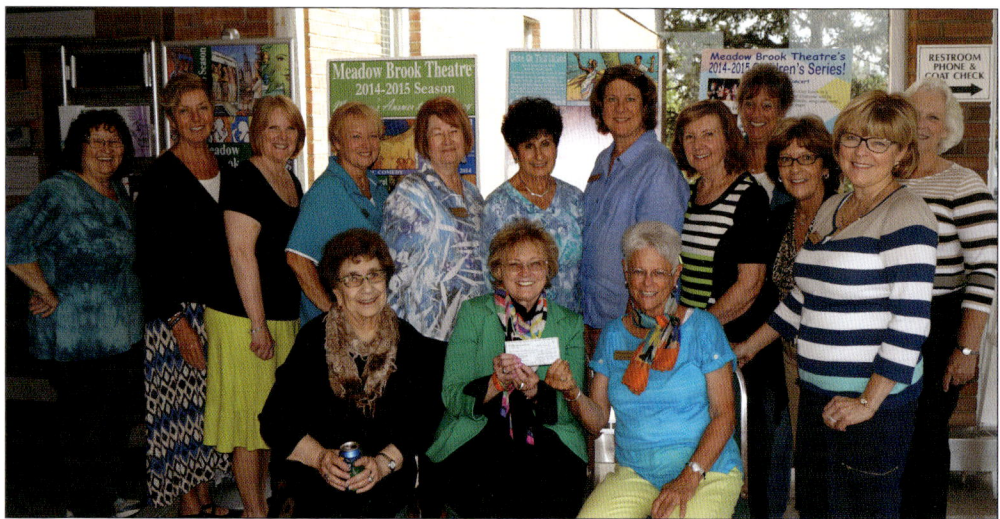

Meadow Brook Theatre Guild has donated over $800,000 in goods and services to MBT since its inception in 1977. Pictured from left to right are (first row) Antoinette Brubaker, MBT managing director Cheryl L. Marshall, and guild president Suellen Parkes; (second row) Judy Dery, Patty Hazen, secretary Karen Calavenna, past president Mary Caughlin, past president Donna Osgood, Corrine Alonso, vice president Teresa Koempel, Mila Bednarz, Speedy Bates, Lynn Jendrzejewski, treasurer Sheryl Frabotta, and Jan Shotwell. (MBT.)

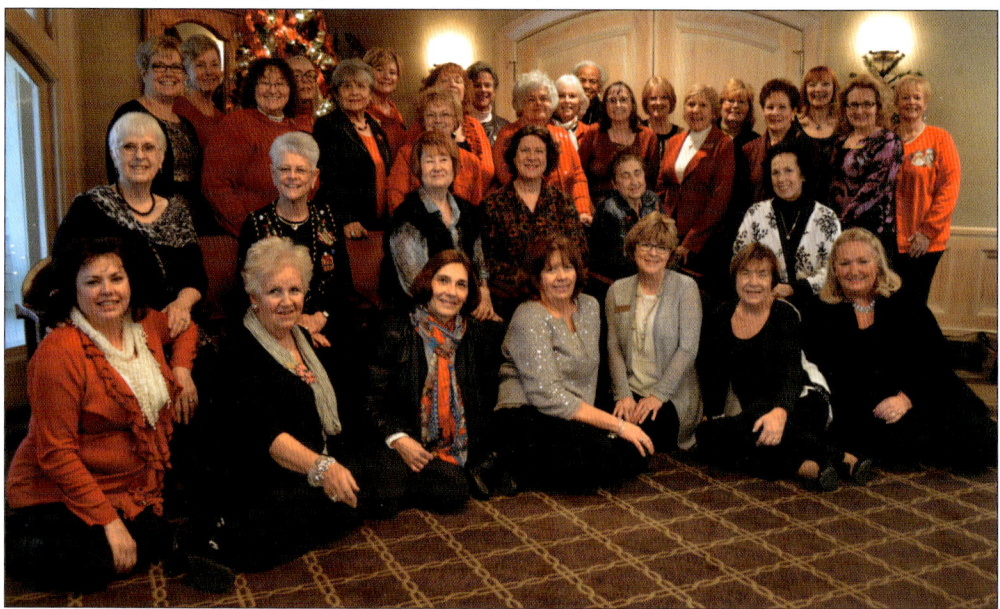

Today, 54 dedicated women continue the work of the many amazing women who came before them. From left to right are (first row) Colleen Brnabic, Mary Jo Cerget, Sue Steltenkamp, Debbie McInerny, Sheryl Frabotta, Dorothy LaBay, and Maryann Foxlee; (second row) Lucille Walla, Suellen Parkes, Donna Osgood, Teresa Koempel, Josie Fritz, and Romayne Stapleton; (third row) Maureen Nakonek, Patty Hazen, Judy Dery, Shirley Sikov, Carol Tomasi, Jan Marshall, Cheryl Marshall, Linda Boehmer, Speedy Bates, Gail Bothwell, Jan Shotwell, Gwen Ray, Chris May, Karen Calavenna, Flo Beck, Rae Cubba, Theresa Meegan, Kim Kusnier, Sue Benson-Pridemore, and Mary Caughlin. (MBT.)

Four
BEHIND THE SCENES

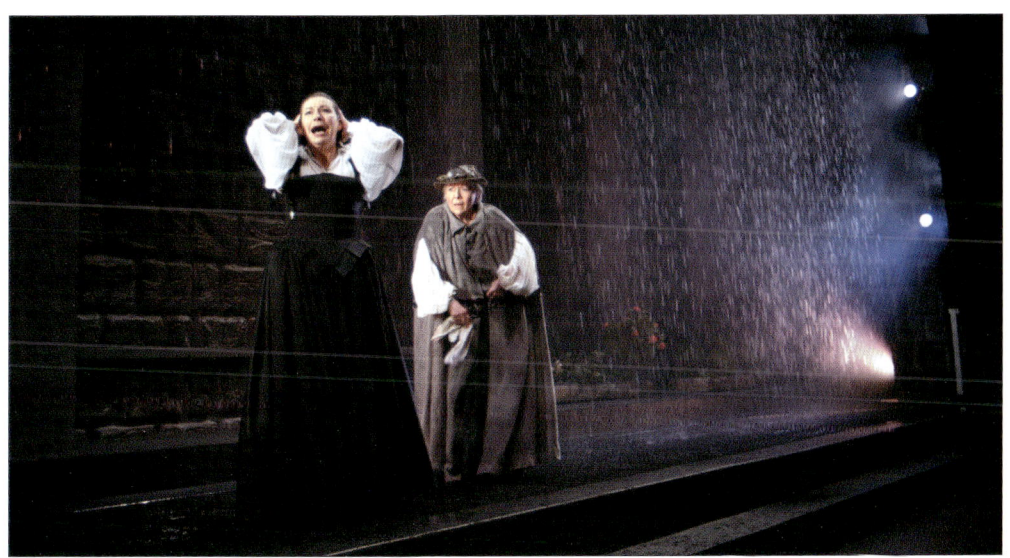

The set for *Mary Stuart* included a 1,000-gallon, fully contained, heated rain system that covered a 6-foot-by-20-foot area of the stage. The rain fell for eight minutes, and Julia Glander (left) and Trudy Mason wore wet suits under their costumes to keep warm. The set design by Brian Kessler impressed audiences. (MBT.)

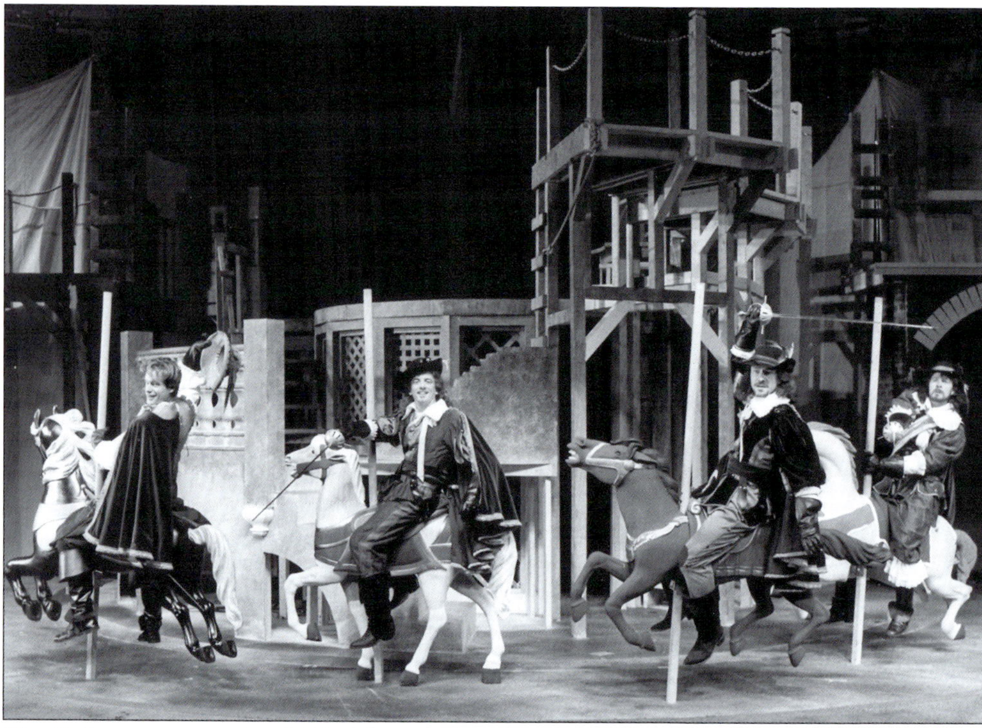

The 30th season opened with *The Three Musketeers*, adapted by Charles Morey, based on the book by Alexandre Dumas. The musketeers appeared to ride across the stage as the set revolved on a large turntable. The musketeers are, from left to right, Timothy Altmeyer, Christopher Mixon, Matthew Loney, and Richard A. Schrot. (MBT.)

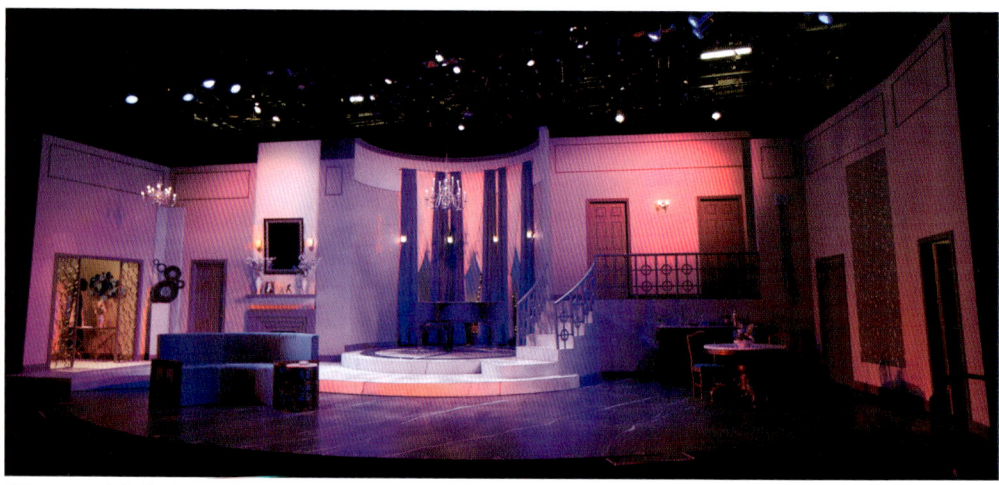

The set of *Cole Porter's You Never Know* was designed to be graphically elegant, but the neutral colors looked very bland under normal lighting conditions. Note the number and variety of lights above the set. The various pastels and spotlighting proved to be very striking and were a key part of a great set design by Kristen Gribbin. (MBT.)

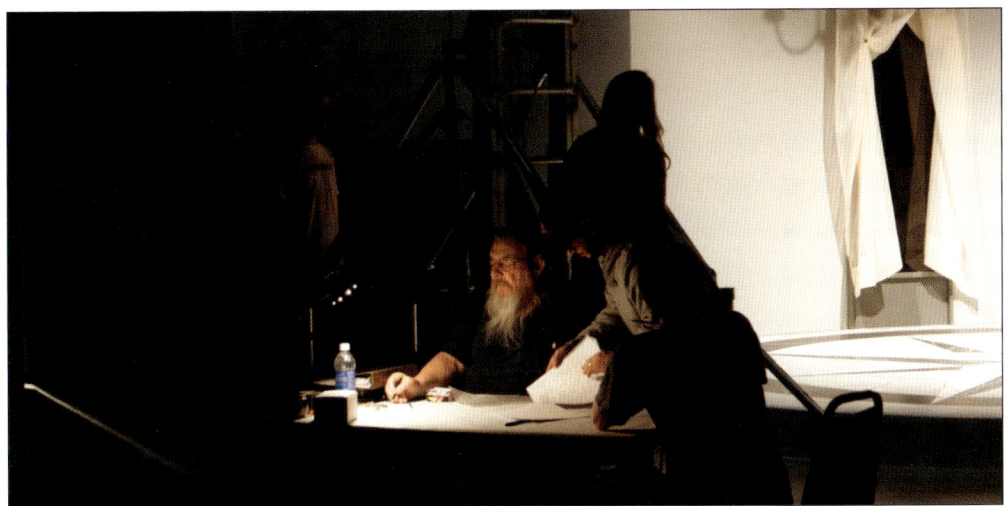

Master electrician Reid G. Johnson (center) executes the light scheme for *Cole Porter's You Never Know*, designed by Matthew J. Fick. Reid has designed the lighting for more than 150 productions at Meadow Brook Theatre. A native Detroiter, he earned his degree in design and technical theatre at Wayne State University. (MBT.)

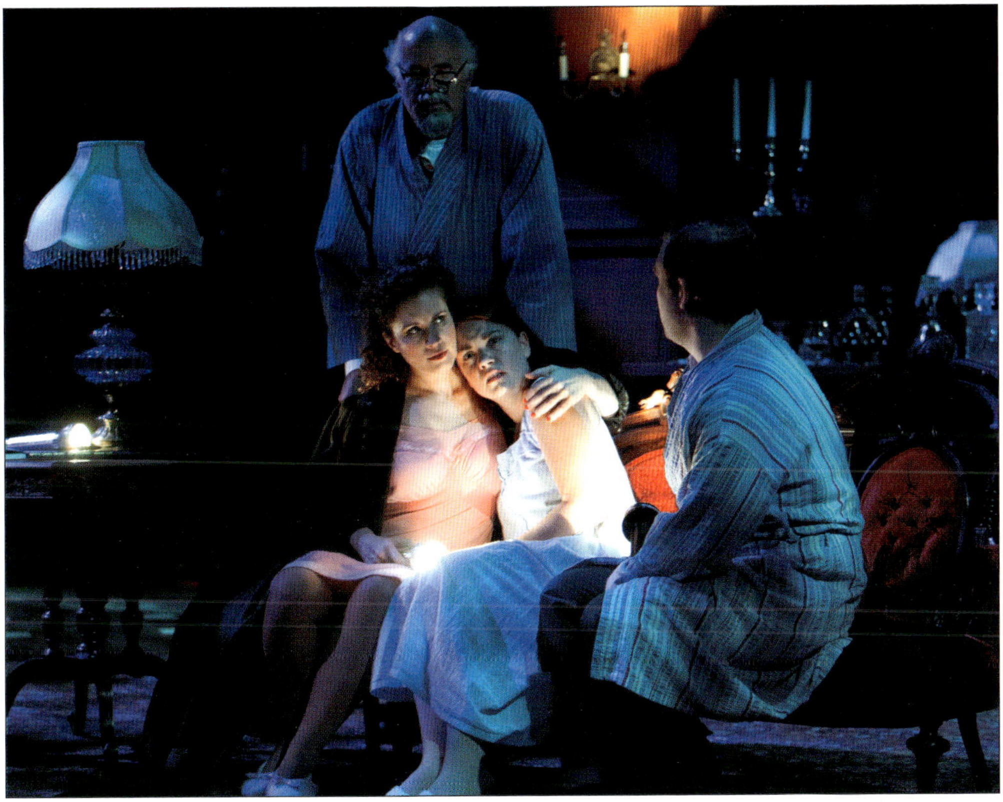

Light design by Reid G. Johnson provided a "spooky" atmosphere to this scene from *The Haunting of Hill House*. It was achieved by strategically pointing three flashlights to create a focal point in the center of the actors. Seated here are, from left to right, Leslie Ann Handleman, Robyn Lipnicki, and Peter C. Prouty. Hugh Maguire stands in the background. (MBT.)

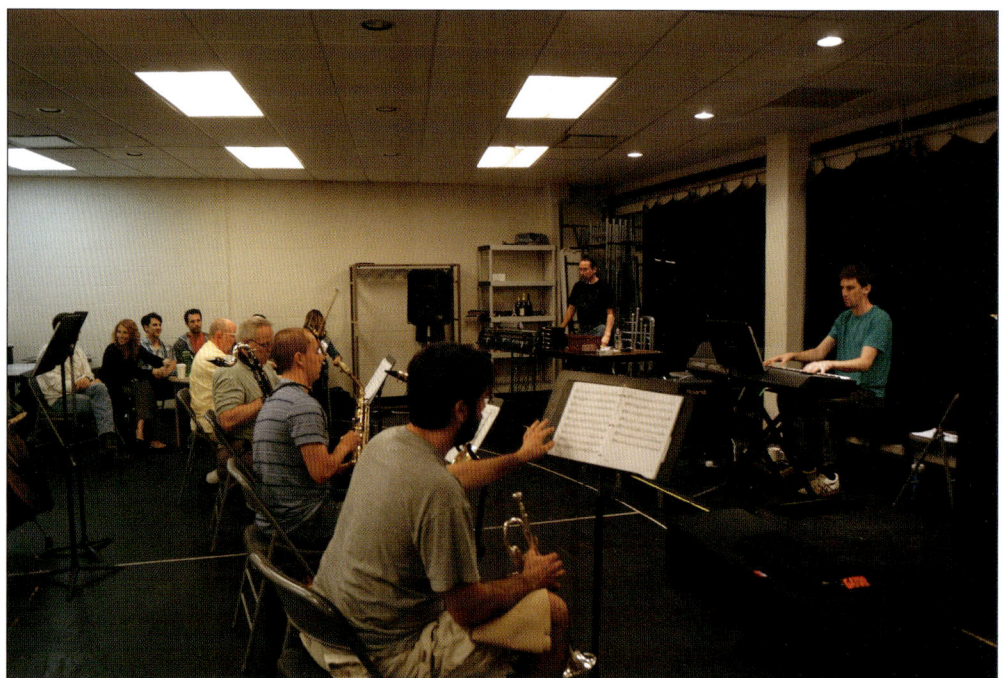

This is an inside look at a sitzprobe, when the actors hear the musicians for the first time in the rehearsal room. Greg Kenna (right) is the musical director for *Cole Porter's You Never Know*. The actors are seated on the left at the far side of the room. An eight-piece band provides the "big band sound" typical of Cole Porter musicals. (MBT.)

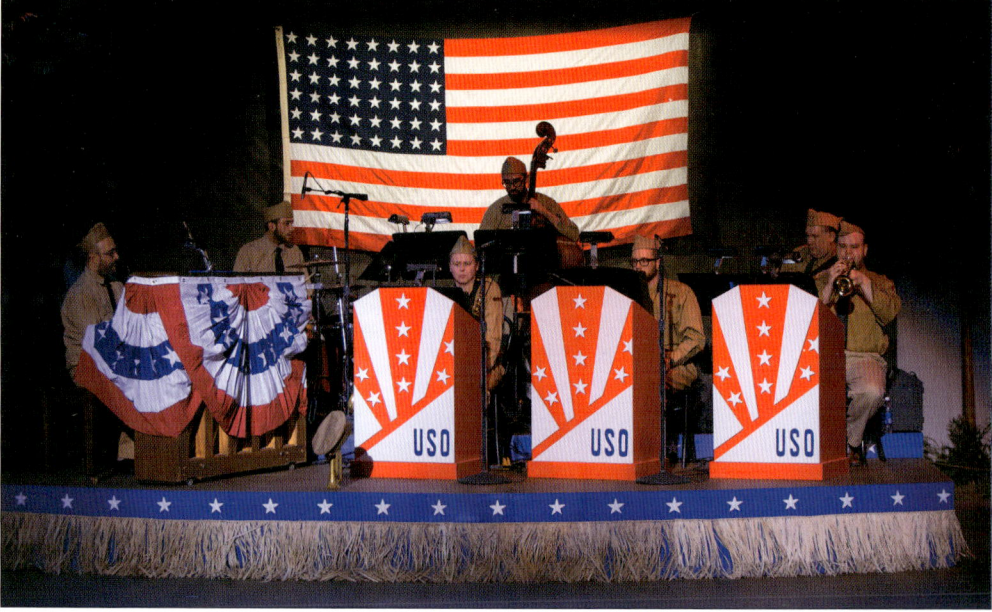

The Michigan premiere of *The Andrews Brothers*, by Roger Bean, featured the songs made famous by the Andrews Sisters. The band was able to reproduce the 1940s swing sound for this show. They are led by music director Daniel Feyer (left) at piano. MBT always uses live music in its musicals. (MBT.)

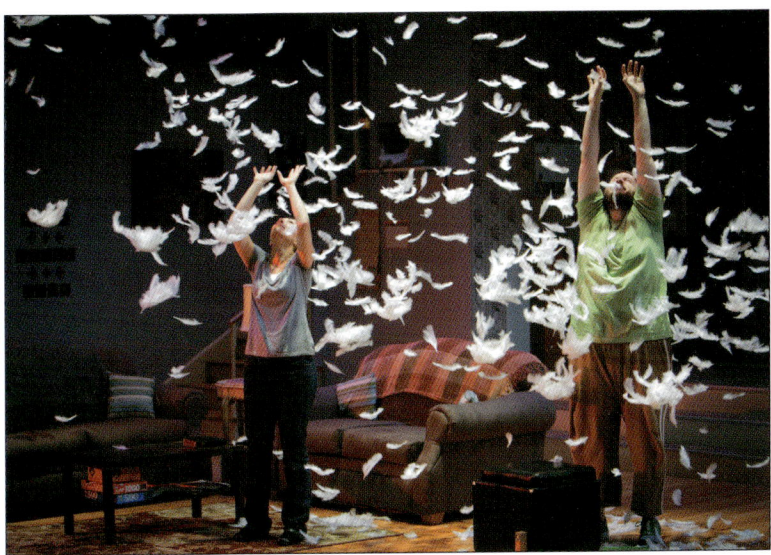

The last scene of *Falling* required building a feather drop to complete the emotion of the show. In the scene, the mom, played by Sarab Kamoo (left), makes a tough decision. This effect was created at the theatre by MBT's technical staff and lit beautifully by lighting designer Reid G. Johnson. (MBT.)

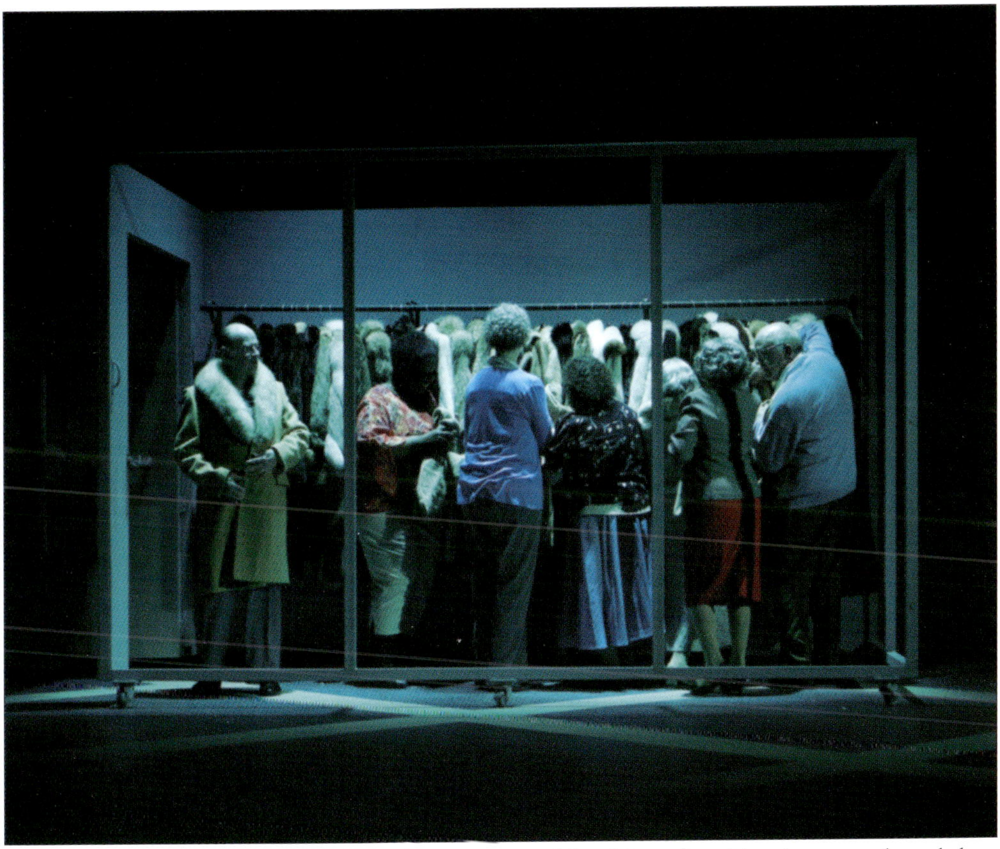

One challenge in *70, Girls, 70* was to show a group of fur thieves breaking into a vault and then seeing their reactions when they get locked in. Building a vault that was open on one side was the solution provided by designer Kristen Gribbin. The actors seen here are, from left to right, Paul Hopper, Tamara Anderson, Candace M. Coleman, Judy Dery, Trudy Mason, Mary Robin Roth, and Hugh Maguire. (MBT.)

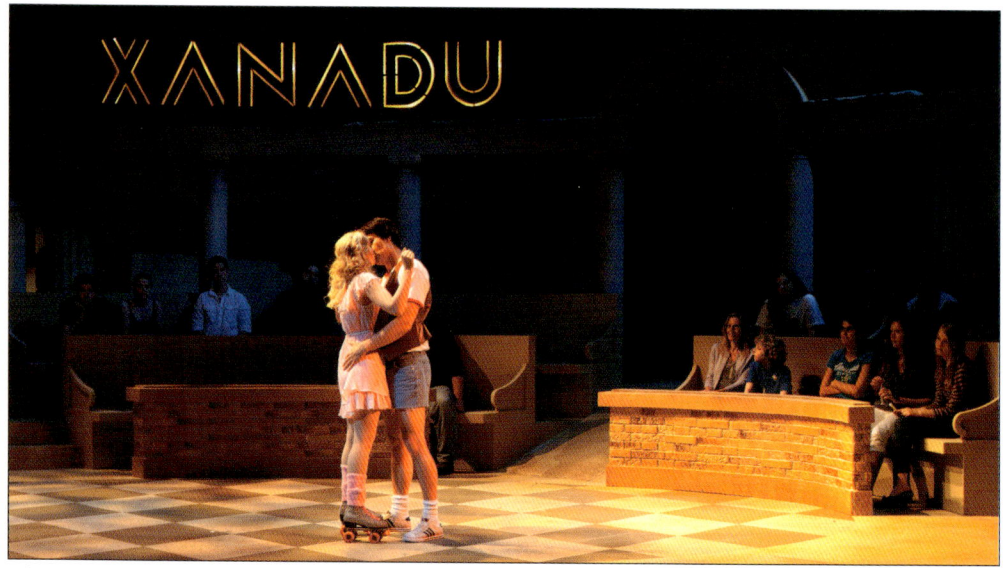

The presence of a Greek chorus in *Xanadu* provided a rare opportunity to include the audience on stage. Allison Hunt (Kira) and David Havasi (Sonny Malone) are surrounded by audience members seated in bleachers on Mount Olympus. The set design is by Kristen Gribbin. (MBT.)

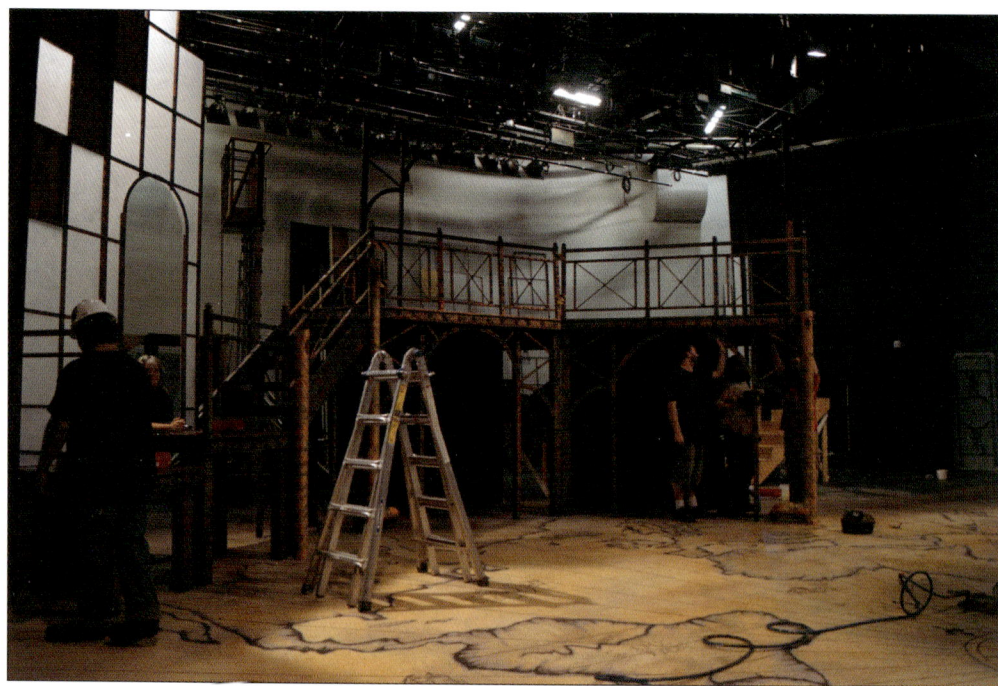

Typically, the set for a given show is broken down on Sunday after the final matinee. The technical team has a week to build the set (*Around the World in 80 Days*, in this case), position the lights, and set up the sound system. The following Sunday is tech rehearsal, when actors are on the set, and final adjustments to the technical elements are made. (MBT.)

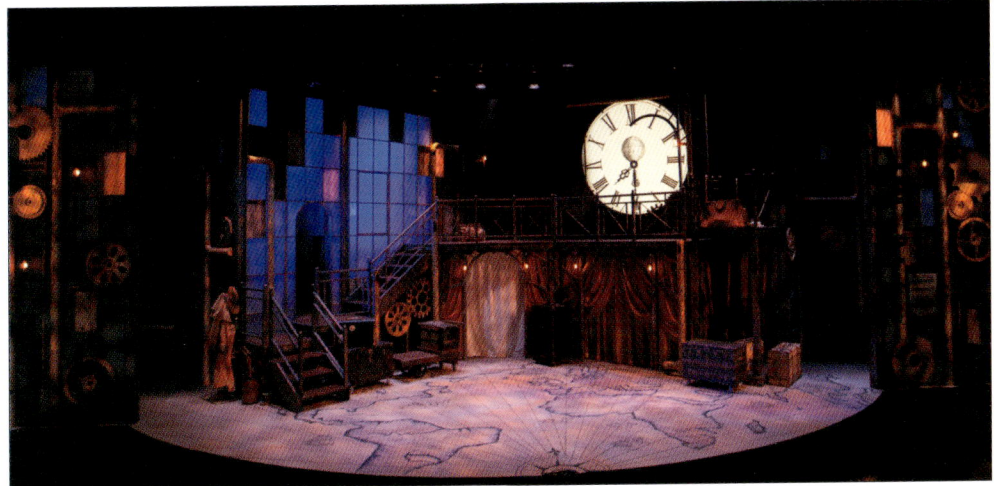

Around the World in 80 Days took place in 1872, just as it became possible to travel the world by steam-powered locomotives and ships. Set designer Jen Price Fick executed a "Steampunk" theme, including a Victorian clocklike structure that lighting designer Reid G. Johnson used for projections to identify locations. (MBT.)

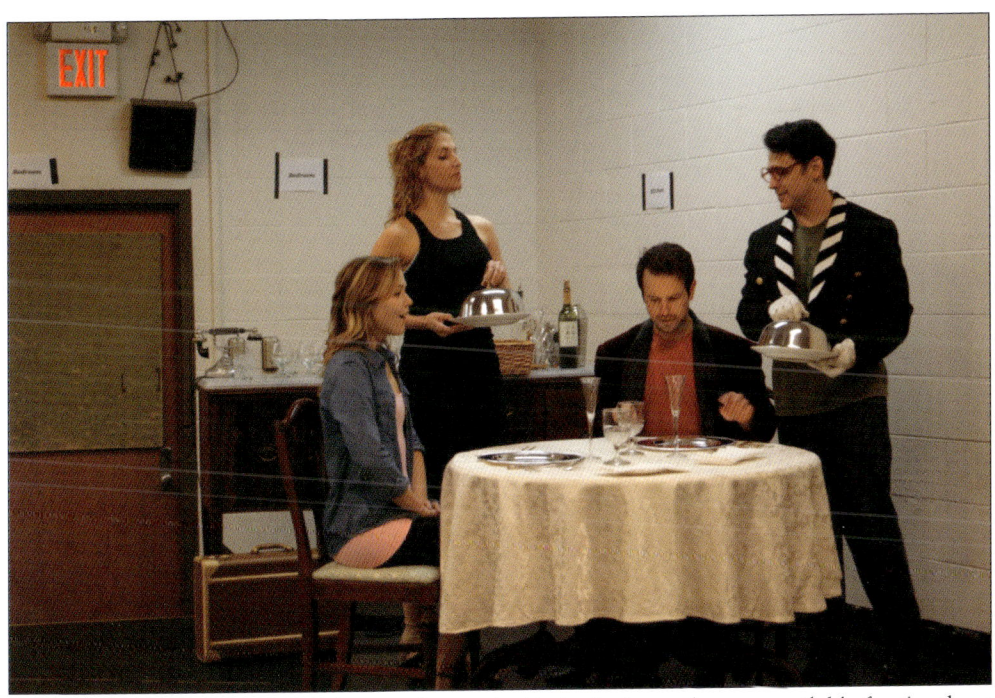

One challenge the directors and actors face is the limited rehearsal space available for the three weeks leading up to a show. Here, actors Sarah Parnicky and Mathew Schwartz (seated) and Stephanie Wahl and Ron Williams (standing) rehearse for *Cole Porter's You Never Know* in the rehearsal room at Meadow Brook Theatre. (MBT.)

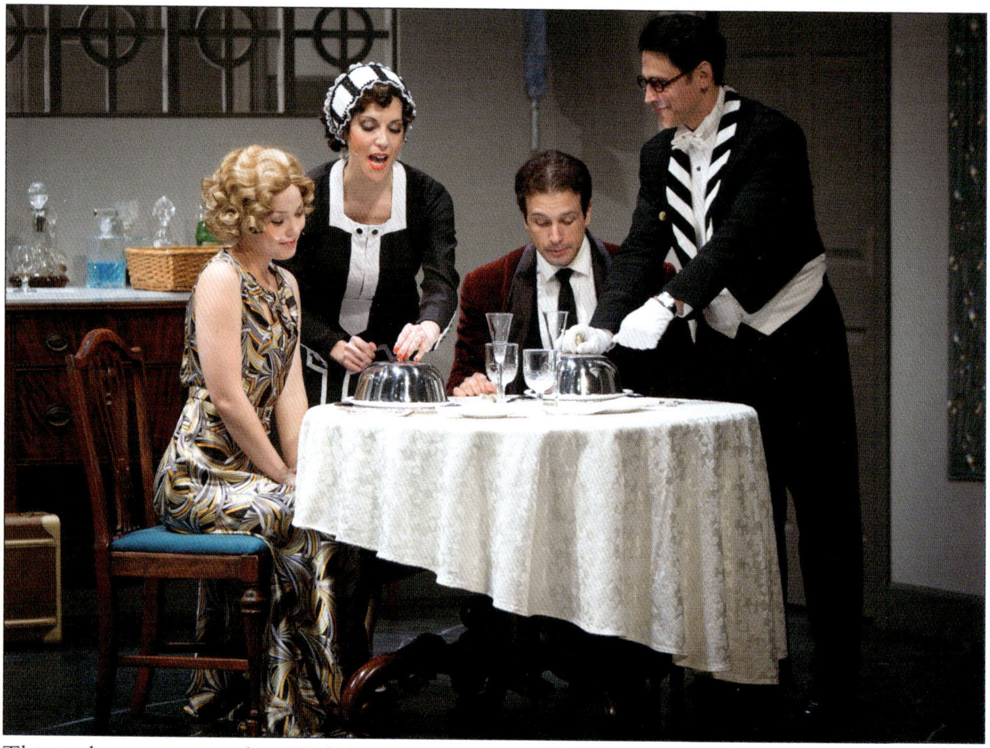

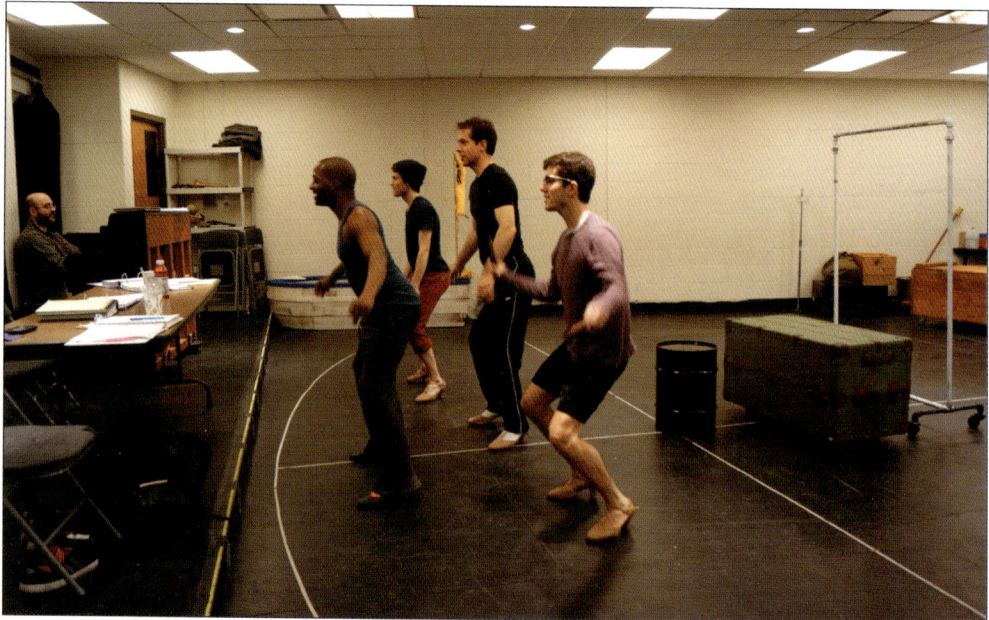

This is the same scene from *Cole Porter's You Never Know* on stage with full costumes by Corey Globke and lighting by Matthew J. Fick. The first time the actors have access to the stage is on restage day, and they have only two additional tech days before the first preview night. (MBT.)

In a rehearsal for *The Andrews Brothers*, choreographer Tyrick Wiltez Jones teaches the men of the cast how to dance in heels. On the floor are, from left to right, Tyrick Wiltez Jones, Lucas Wells, Joe Lehman, and Ben Garrett. Musical director Dan Feyer is at the piano. (MBT.)

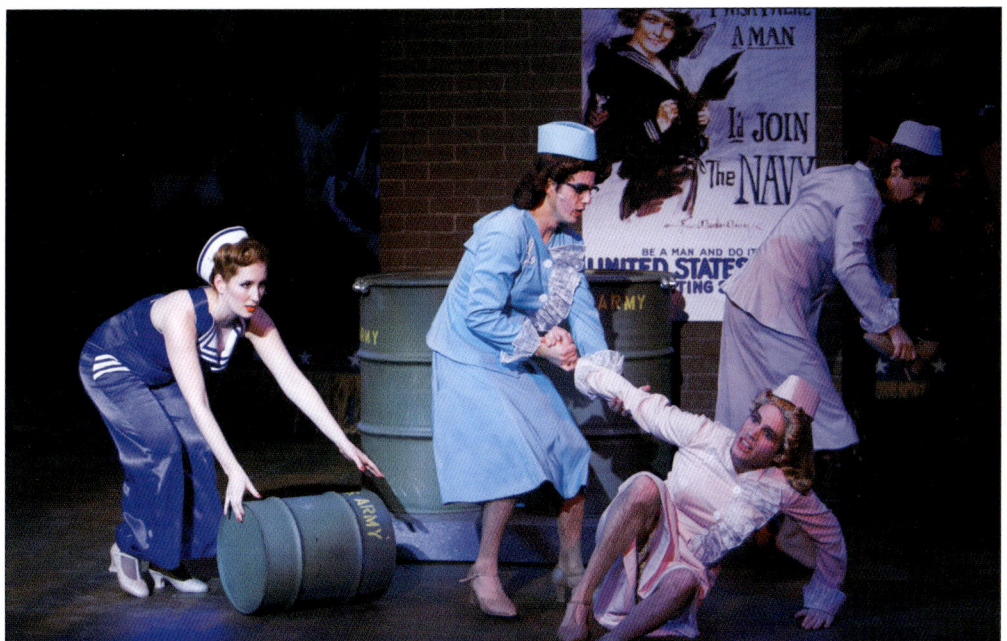

The Andrews Brothers was a challenging show for the male leads. The roles called for great voices and dancing skills, as well as a high level of conditioning. Dressed as the Andrews Sisters, the men had to perform in dresses and heels. Seen here on stage are, from left to right, Allison Hunt, Ben Garrett, Lucas Wells, and Joe Lehman. (MBT.)

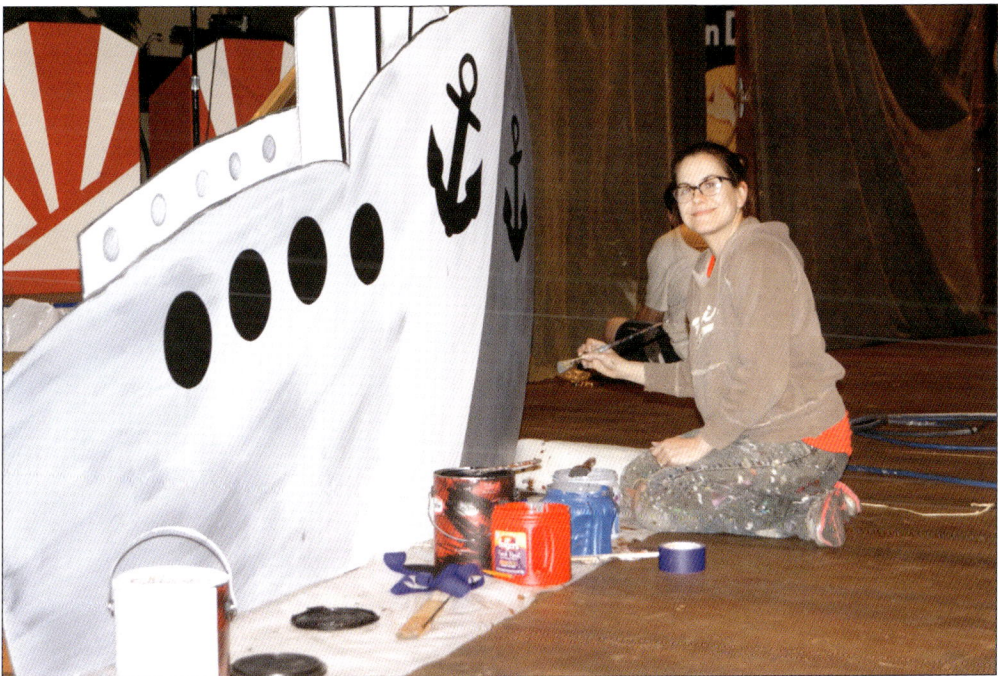

The scenic designer for *The Andrews Brothers*, Jen Price Fick, does some finishing paint touches to a ship flat for the show. The boat was pulled out by the Andrews Brothers, recreating a scene from *In the Navy*, an Andrews Sisters movie. (MBT.)

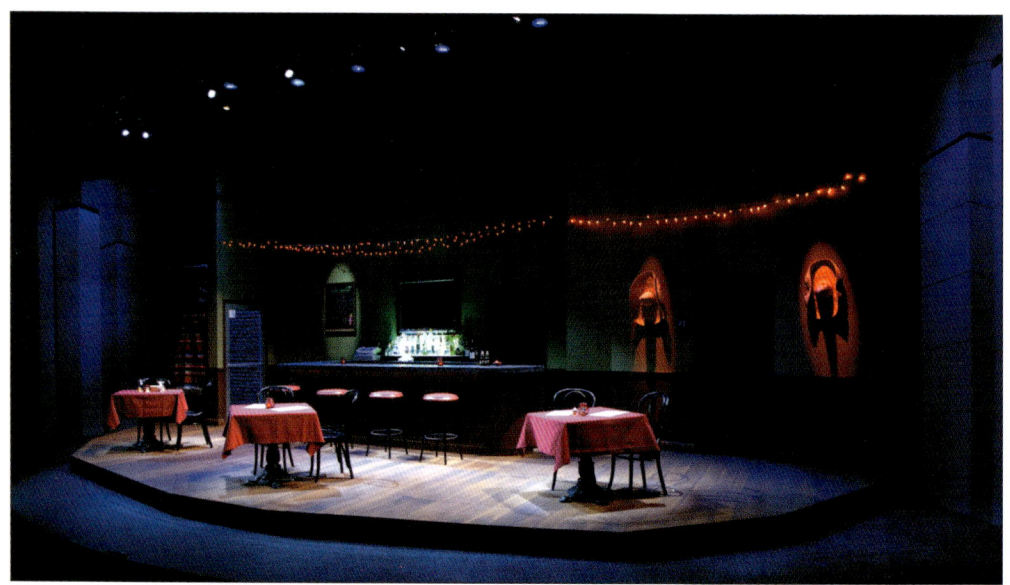

Brian Kessler's set design for *White's Lies* was unique in several ways. The entire set revolved on a giant turntable so that two complete and unique scenes were possible. The bar scene (pictured) was designed to be reconfigured as several differently themed bars. Perhaps the most unusual feature was the dressing area, contained in a four-foot space between the two sets. (MBT.)

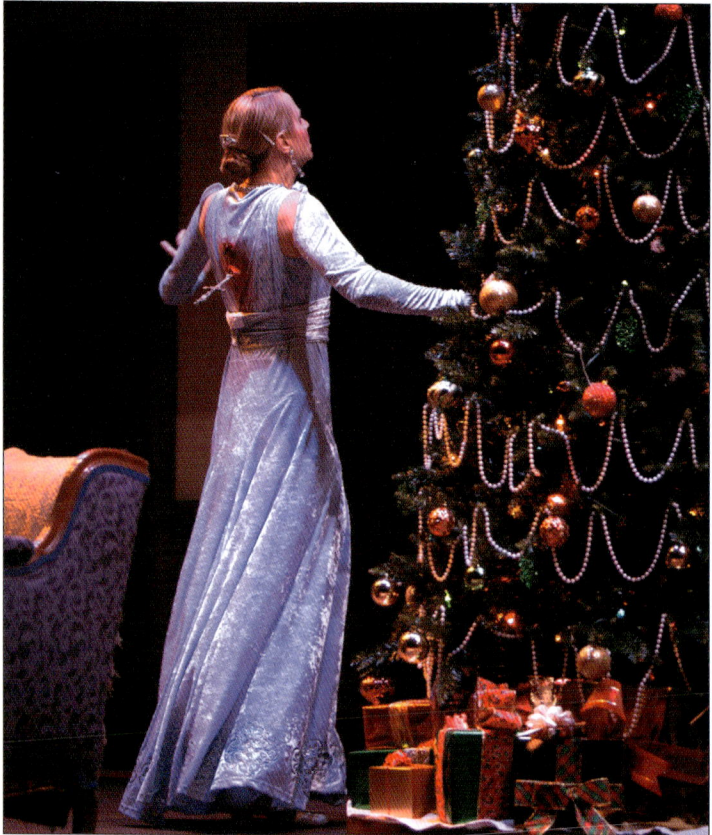

The elegant dress worn by Cheryl Turski in *The Game's Afoot*, designed by costume shop manager Liz Goodall, has one unique feature: a murder weapon. As sometimes happens in live theatre, a wardrobe malfunction occurred, and the knife was revealed in the scene leading up to the murder. Another actor was able to fix her costume on stage, in full view of the audience. Feedback after the performance was very positive; playgoers clearly enjoyed the unexpected. (MBT.)

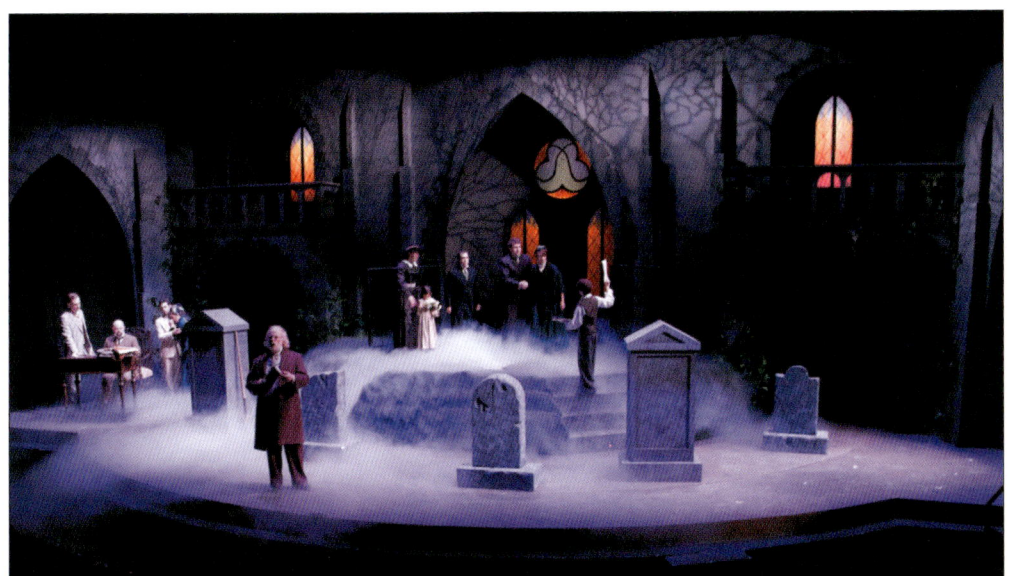

The set design for *Dracula, A Rock Opera* was a challenge because of the many complex elements required for the multiple scenes. The center arch housed a church and crypt at different times. The tombstones were on a rotating ring that moved the coffins, a boat, and a horse and buggy in various scenes. Brian Kessler won a Wilde Award for this set design. (MBT.)

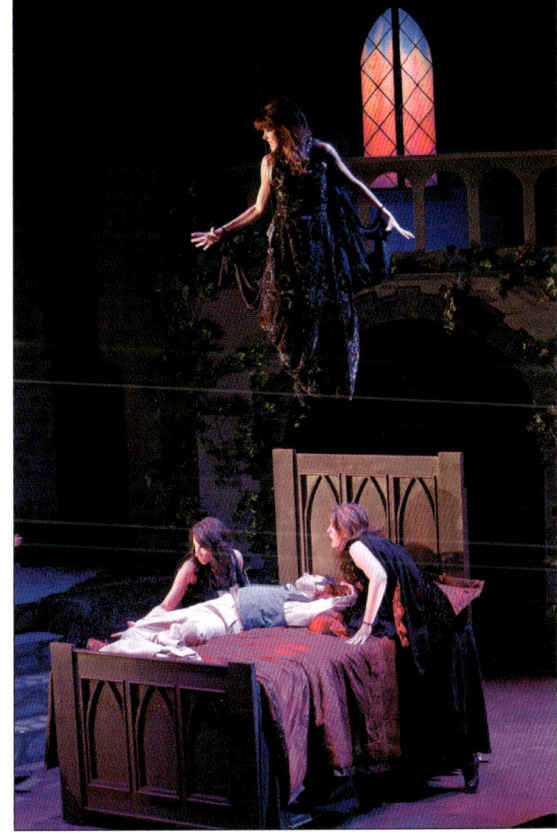

The 45th season started with the Michigan premiere of *Dracula, A Rock Opera*, by John R. Briggs and Dennis West. For this interpretation of the classic novel, Meadow Brook Theatre hired ZFX, a professional flying company. Shown here on stage are Jennifer George-Consiglio (left), Eric Gutman (center), and Ann O'Brien. Janet Caine flies above. (MBT.)

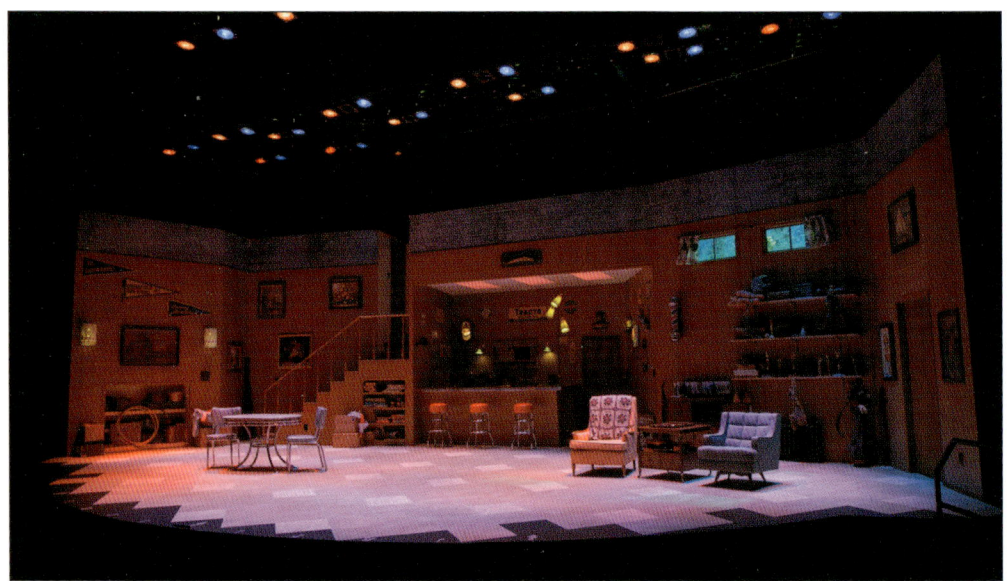

The set for *Life Could Be a Dream* was designed by Brian Kessler and resembled a 1960s wood-paneled basement. It featured an intercom, a staircase to the kitchen, and basement windows (upper right). Actors walked by these windows and looked through them into the basement. (MBT.)

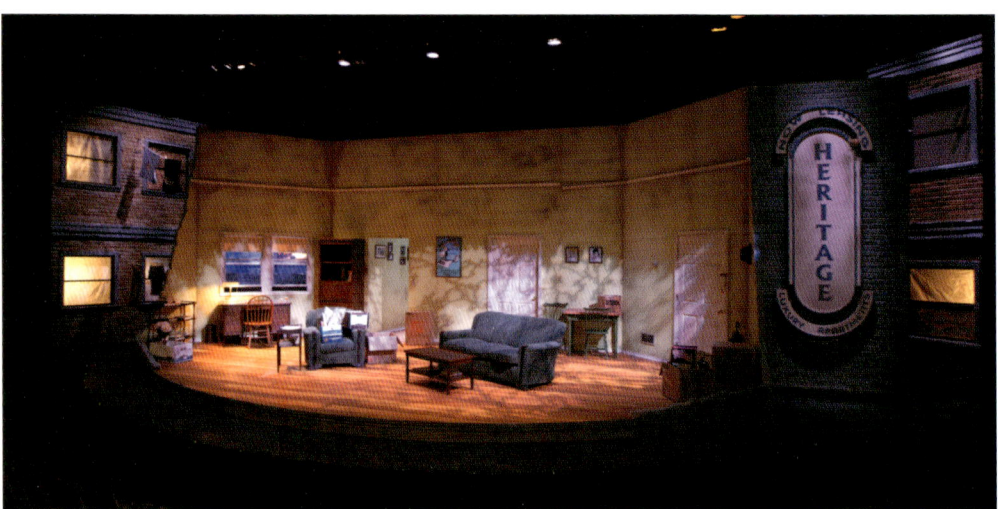

Harris Cashes Out!, by Londos D'Arrigo, had its world premiere at Meadow Brook Theatre in January 2014. Brian Kessler's set depicted a broken-down apartment in a seedy neighborhood. He created a small, cramped apartment and conveyed a sense of the neighborhood around it. (MBT.)

Five
FAMILY AND COMMUNITY

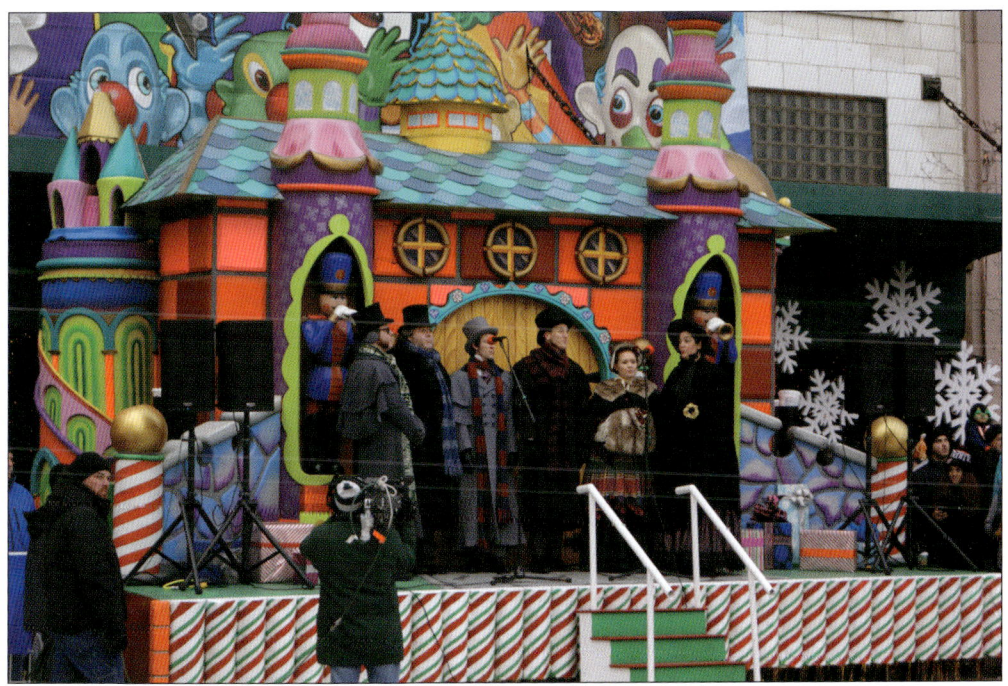

The MBT Christmas Carolers participate in many community celebrations, including downtown Rochester's annual Lagniappe event and the annual America's Thanksgiving Day Parade through downtown Detroit (pictured). (MBT.)

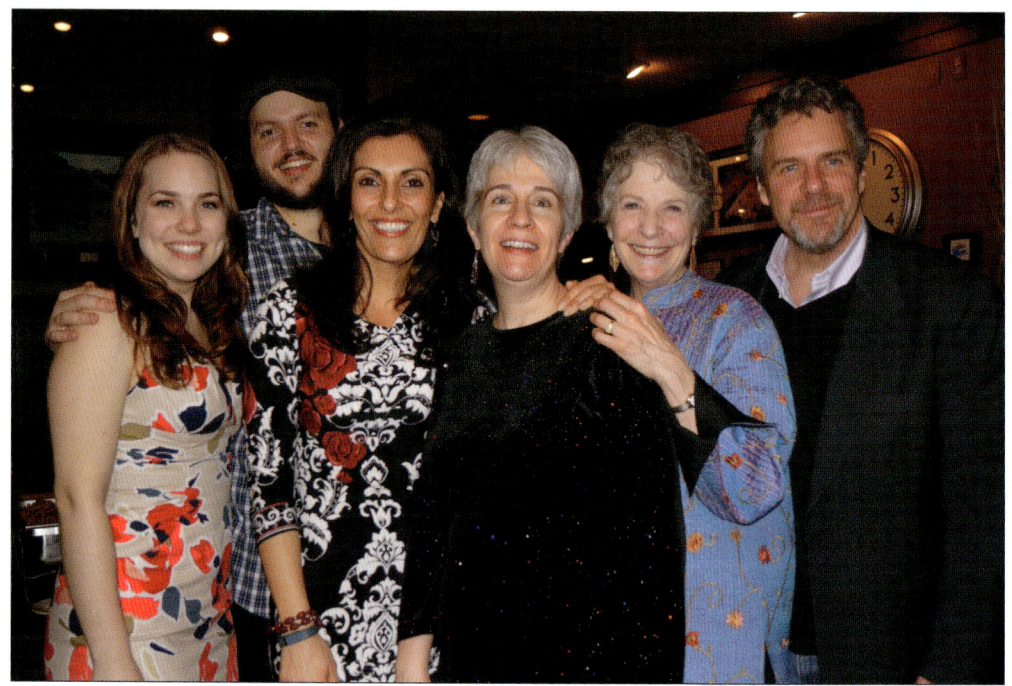

MBT celebrates *Falling*'s opening night in 2014 with a cast and staff party. Posing here are, from left to right, Lizzie Rainville, Daniel Everidge (reprising his Off-Broadway role), Sarab Kamoo, Deanna Jent (playwright), Carolyn Gillespie, and Chris Hietikko. (MBT.)

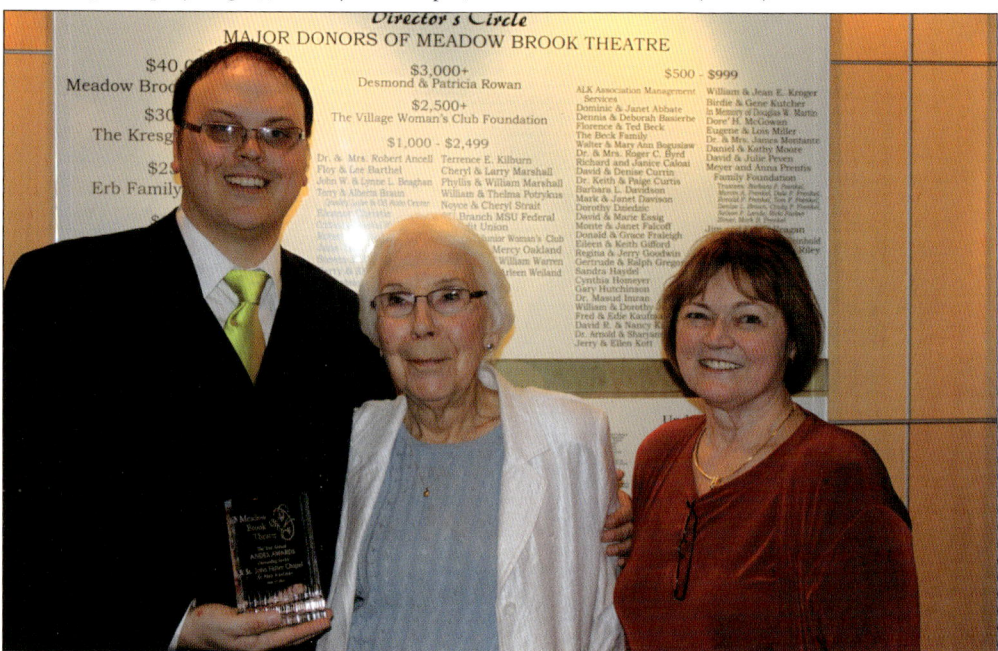

One of the oldest service traditions involved a Sunday post-performance potluck dinner for the actors and staff. This event started over 40 years ago at St. John Fisher Chapel. The person responsible was Sister Mary VanGilder (center), shown here receiving an Andes Service Award from Travis W. Walter and Cheryl L. Marshall. (MBT.)

Another longstanding group, the "Saturday Niters," was started by William and Phyllis Marshall in the early 1970s. Every third Saturday, the cast and crew are invited to a member's house for an afterglow party. Original members included professors Haskell, Simmons, and Boddy. Current "Saturday Niter" organizer Leslie Schneider (right) is shown with original organizer Phyllis Marshall (center) and her daughter Paula Marshall. (MBT.)

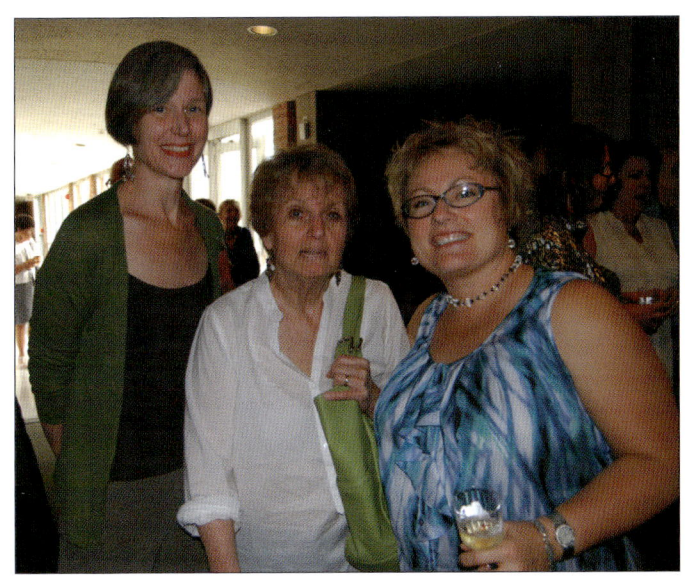

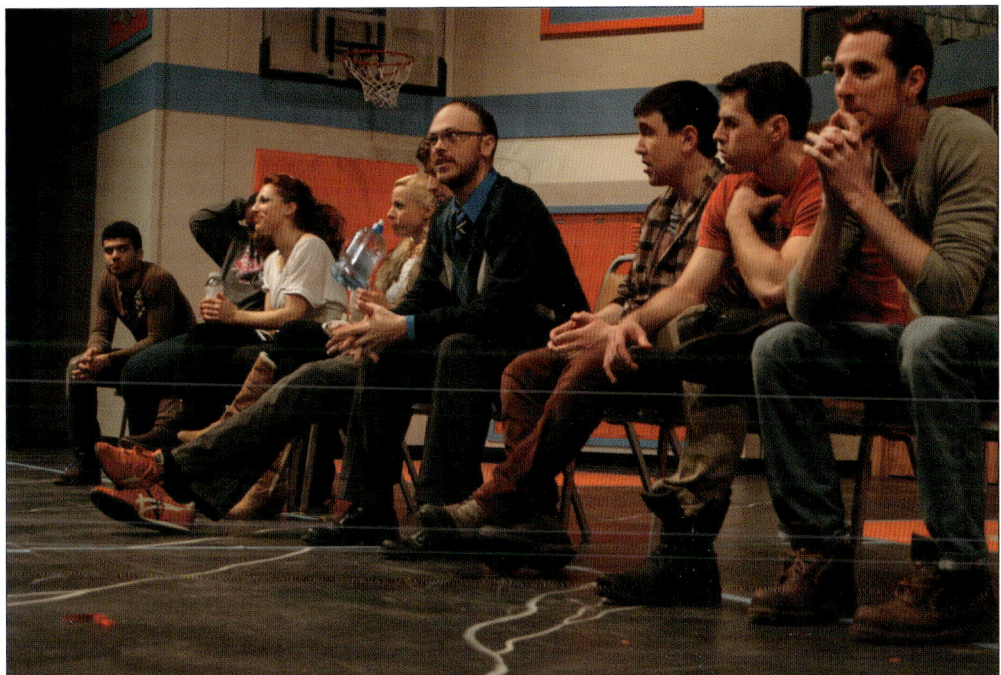

Post-show talkbacks are held during preview week and opening weekend to gauge audience reaction to the play. Artistic director Travis W. Walter (center) leads the discussion with cast members from *Lysistrata Jones*. Shown here are, from left to right, Michael De Souza, Tamara Anderson, Hannah Dubner, Kara Dombrowski, Greg Kenna, Walter, Ben Holtzman, Teddy Toye, and Tim Dolan. (MBT.)

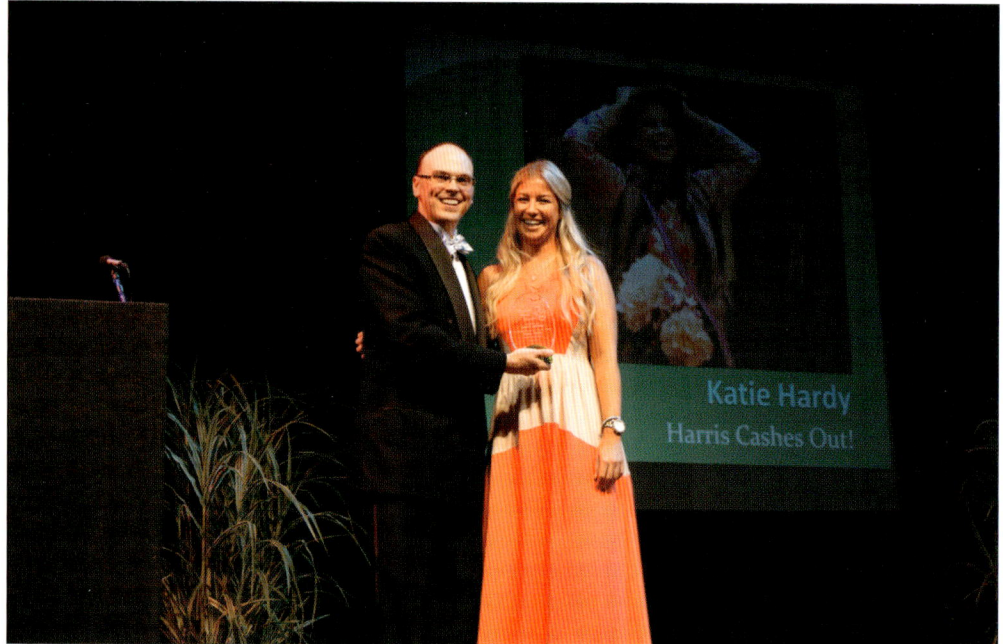

The Andes Awards is an annual event named after a longtime donor/supporter, who had a major impact on the success of the Theatre Ensemble. It is a night of celebration for all members of the Meadow Brook Theatre family. Travis W. Walter (left) congratulates Katie Hardy, named Favorite Actress in a Comedy for her performance in *Harris Cashes Out!* by Londos D'Arrigo (season 47). (MBT.)

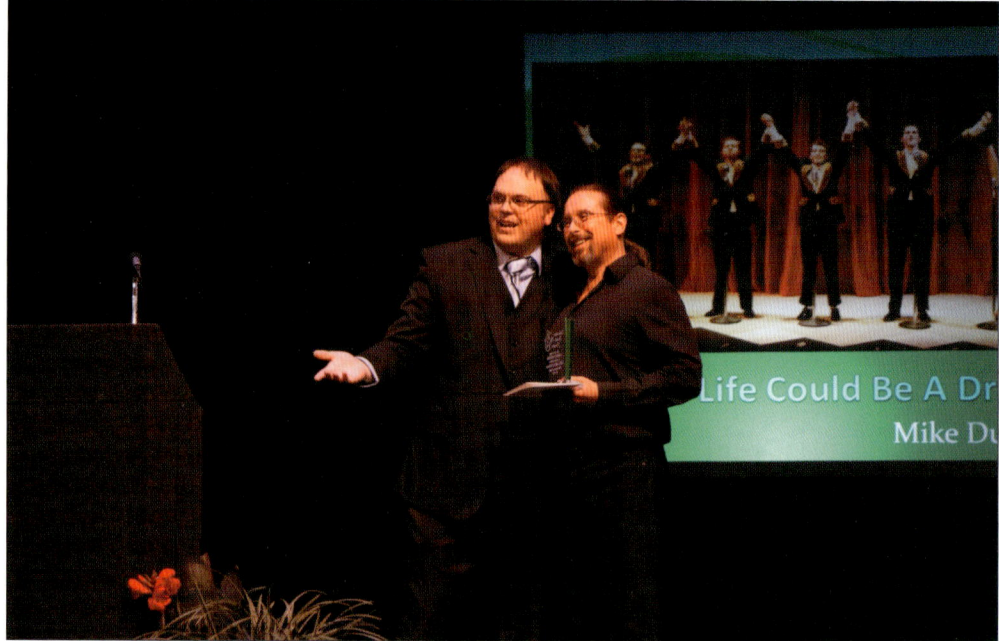

Artistic director Travis W. Walter (left) presents a 2013 Andes Award to Mike Duncan for his sound design for *Life Could Be a Dream* by Roger Bean. Duncan, resident audio engineer for 10 years and an accomplished musician, has composed scores for several productions. (MBT.)

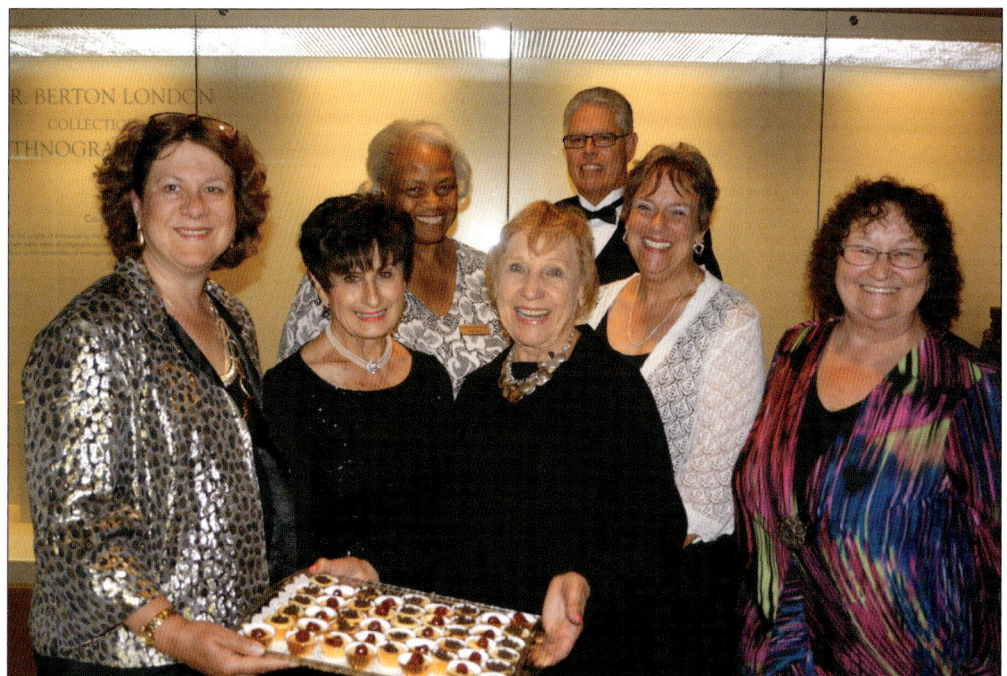

Each year, patrons at the Andes Awards are treated to an elegant appetizer buffet prepared by the guild. Pictured here from left to right are president Teresa Koempel, Corrine Alonzo, Gwen Ray, past president Flo Beck, Thom Foxlee, Speedy Bates, and actress/member Judy Dery. (MBT.)

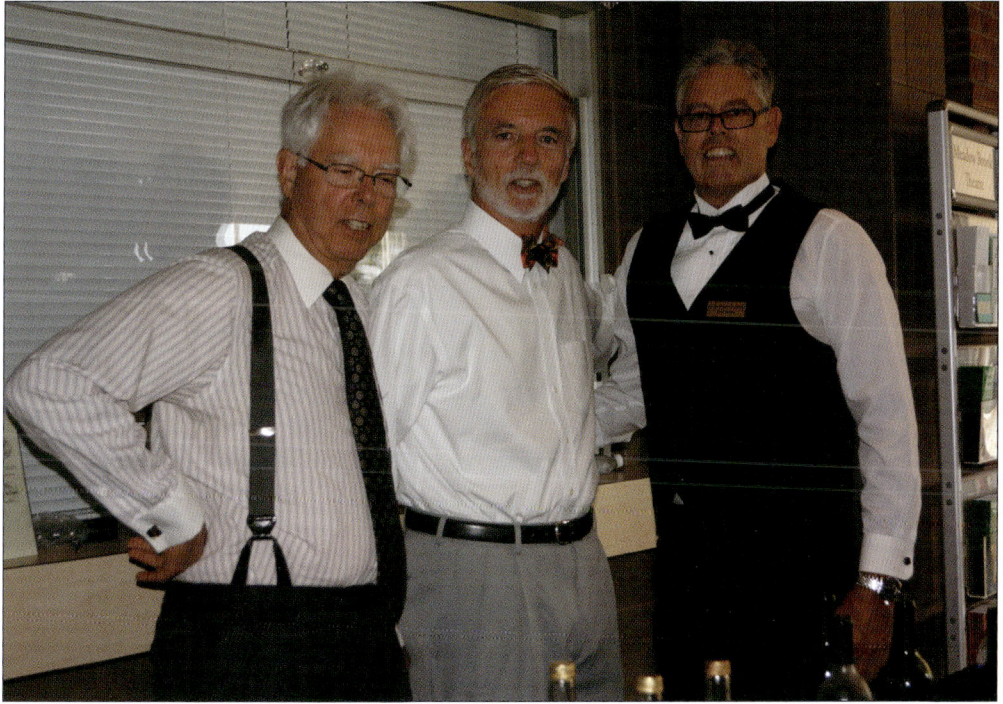

The bartenders for the 2013 Andes Awards ceremony are MBT board secretary Jeff Wurges (left), vice president John Savio (center), and board president Thom Foxlee. (MBT.)

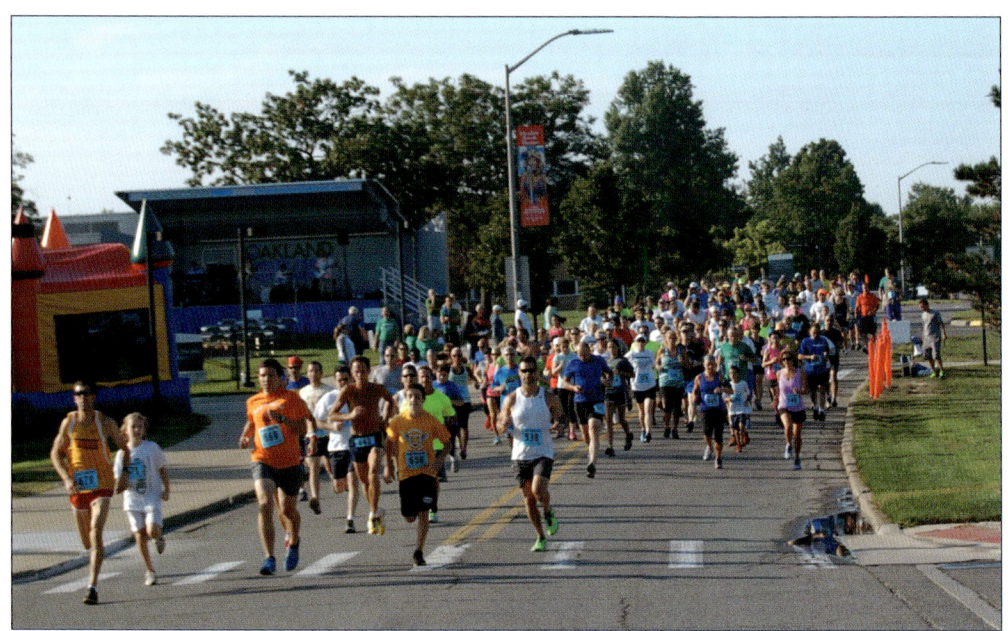

In 2010, Feet for Seats, a five-kilometer fun run, was created by Krista Reszewski to raise money for Meadow Brook Theatre. The original committee members included Jennifer Owens Vercruysse, Mary Caughlin, Maryann Foxlee, Liz Reckinger, Brian Kessler, Cheryl L. Marshall, and Travis W. Walter. (MBT.)

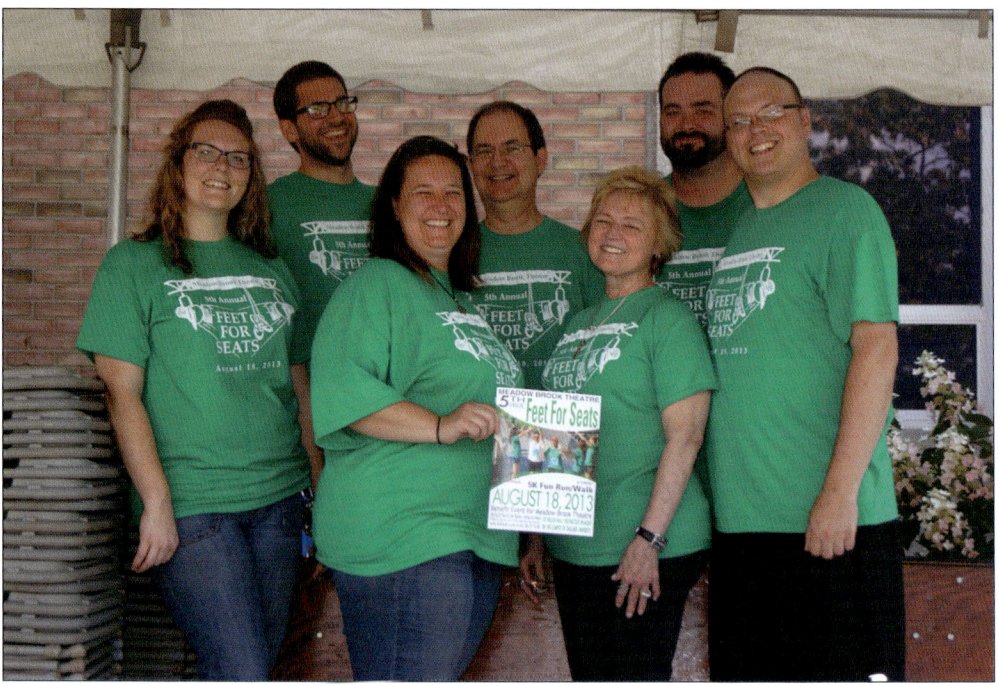

The fun run is operated by volunteers from MBT and offers family entertainment, including live music, food, and a bounce house for the children. The 2013 committee, shown here, includes, from left to right, (first row) Paige Vanzo, Liz Reckinger, Cheryl L Marshall, and Brian "BK" Kessler; (second row) Daniel Conway, Terry W. Carpenter, and Travis W. Walter. (MBT)

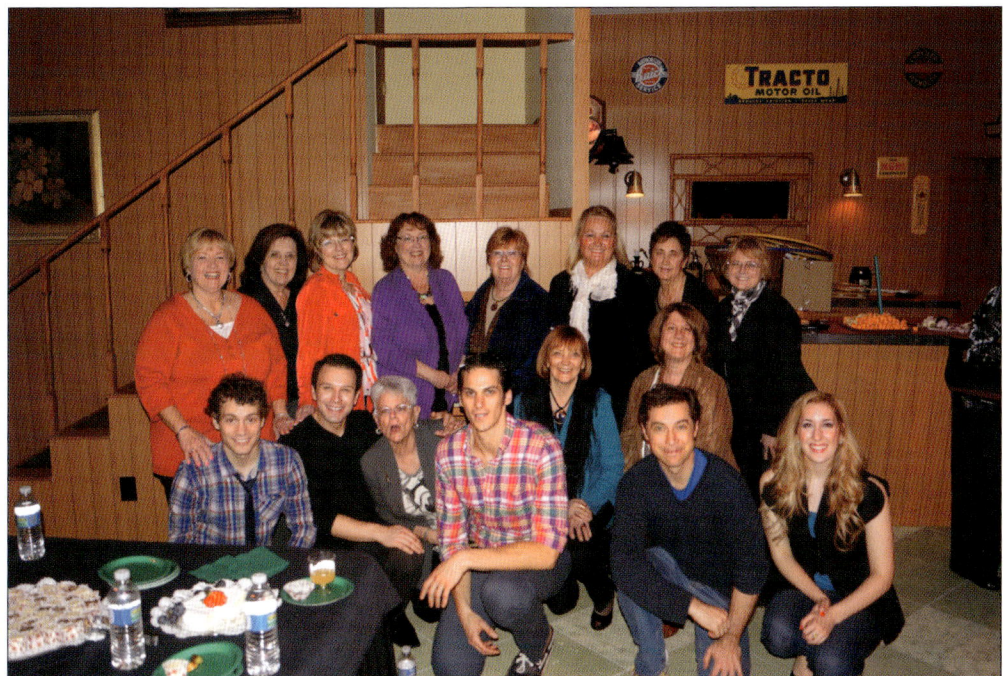

At the Director's Circle, major contributors and volunteers are invited to an afterglow with actors and staff, held on the stage. Here, the guild, MBT's largest contributor, is pictured with the cast of *Life Could Be a Dream*. (MBT.)

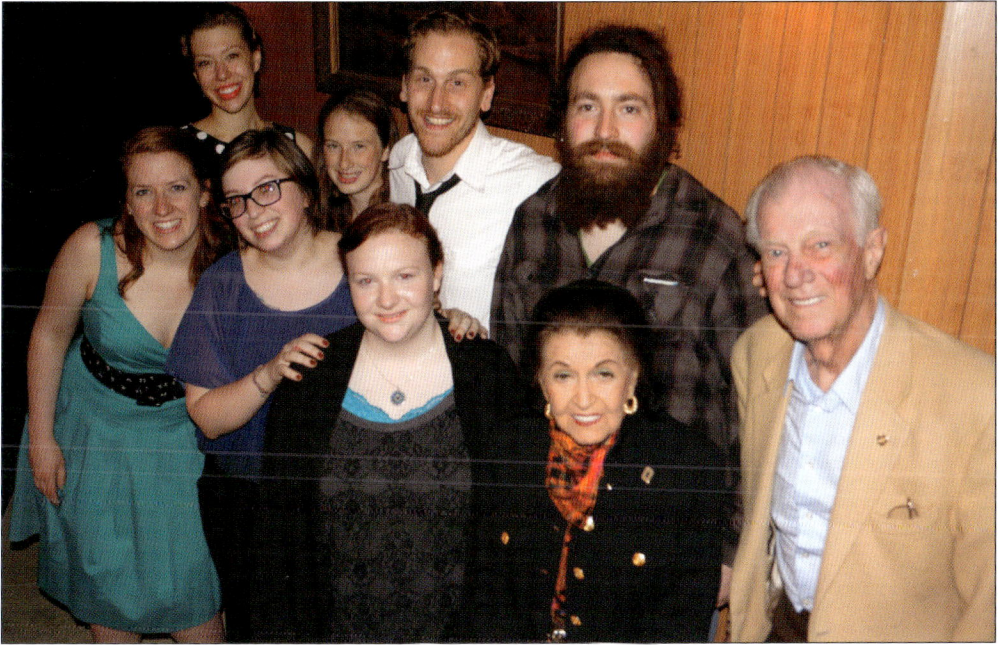

Intern sponsors Bob and Maggie Allesee (lower right) pose with the 47th season interns at the Director's Circle. They gather each year to thank sponsors and volunteers for their help and support, and to celebrate a successful season with the artistic and managing directors. Maggie is also a board member. (MBT.)

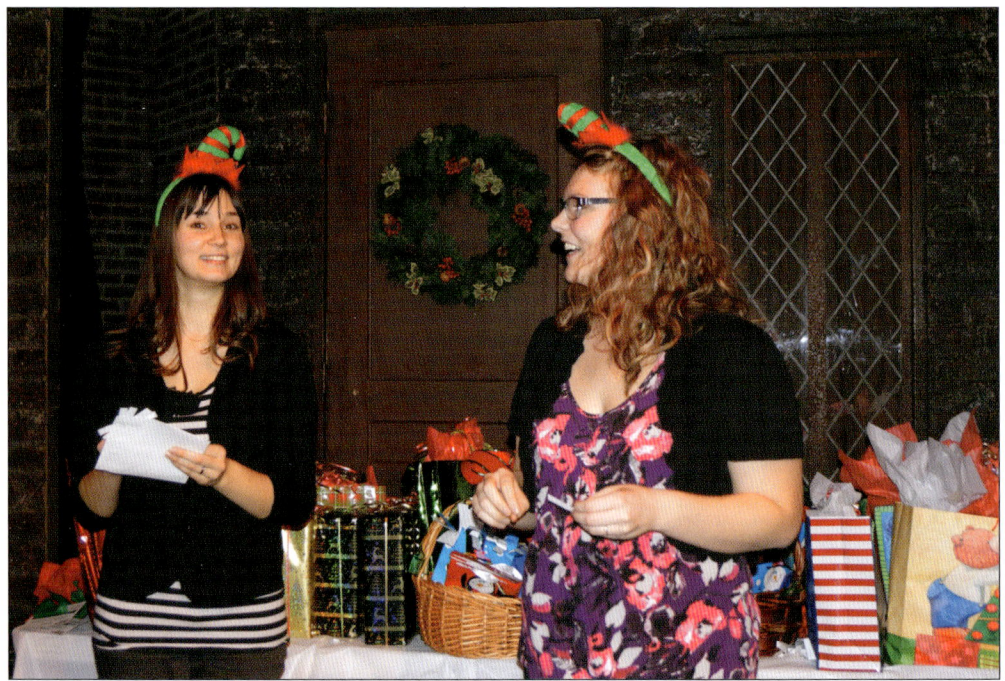

Group sales/administrative assistant Lee Ann Kostur (left) and marketing/communications coordinator Paige Vanzo are the elves at the annual staff Christmas party. They assist in all aspects of Meadow Brook Theatre business, guild events, and special projects. (MBT.)

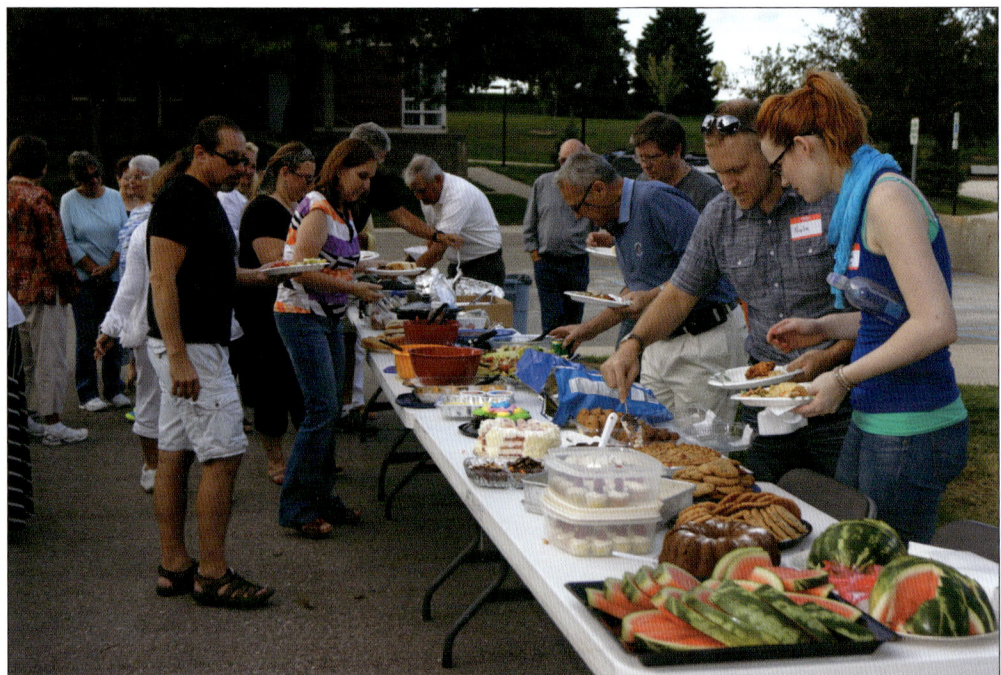

The Welcome Back Picnic hosted by MBT kicks off each season. It started as a thank-you gesture to the guild for all its hard work throughout the year. It is an opportunity to meet and mingle with the staff. (MBT.)

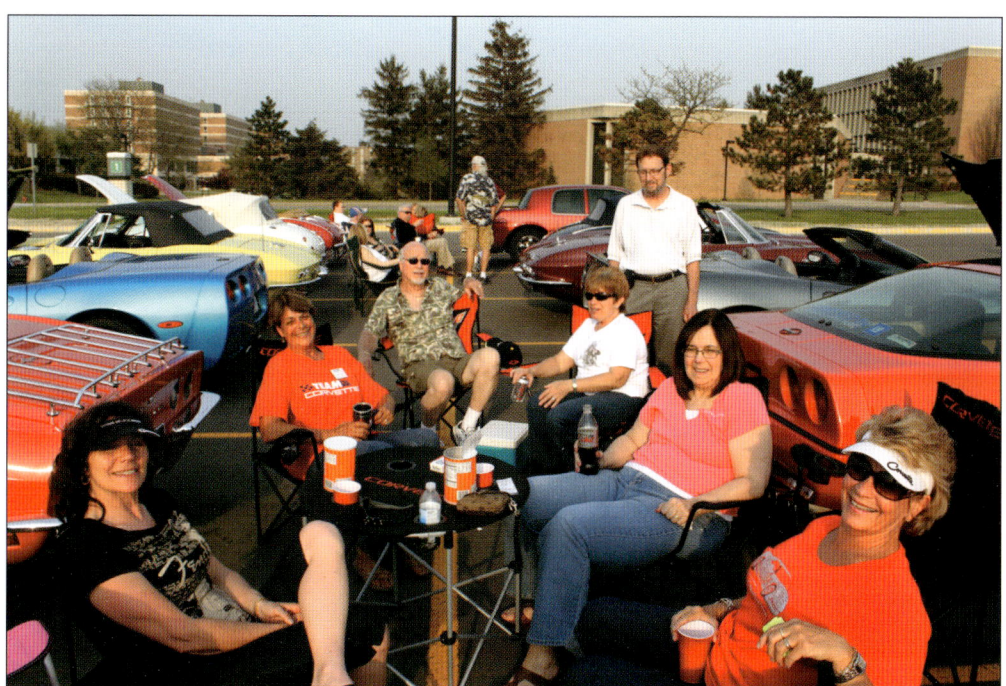

It has become a tradition to invite car clubs to the spring musical. The event has typically had an "oldies" theme. On Friday nights, club members gather in the parking lot, where playgoers can enjoy the cars before the show. (MBT.)

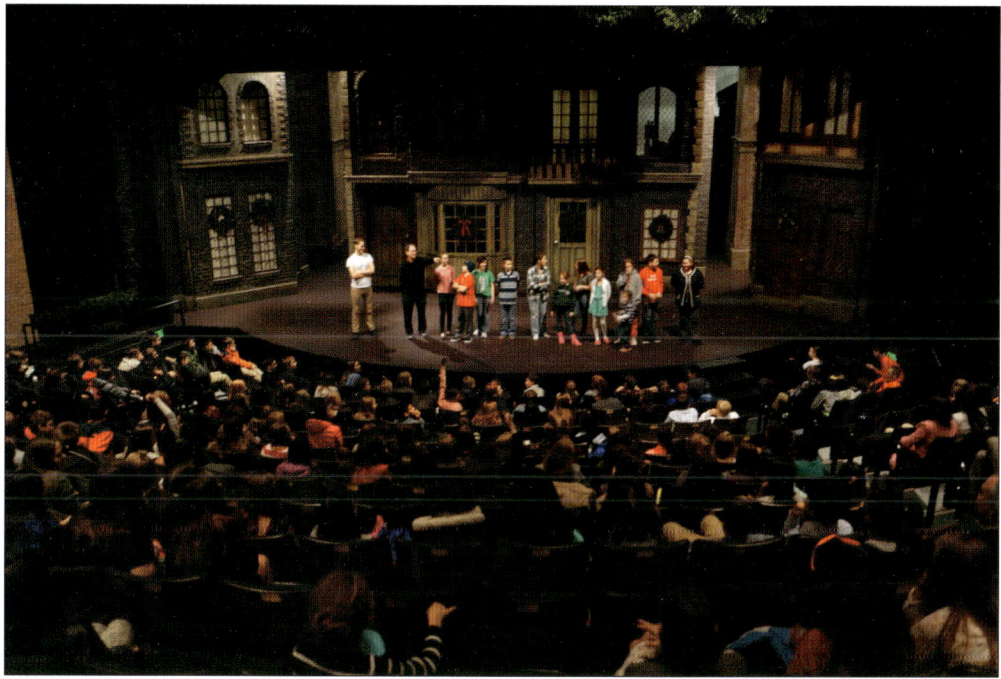

Meadow Brook Theatre schedules school matinees for age-appropriate plays. This matinee of *A Christmas Carol* included a talkback with some of the young actors and director Terry Carpenter. (MBT.)

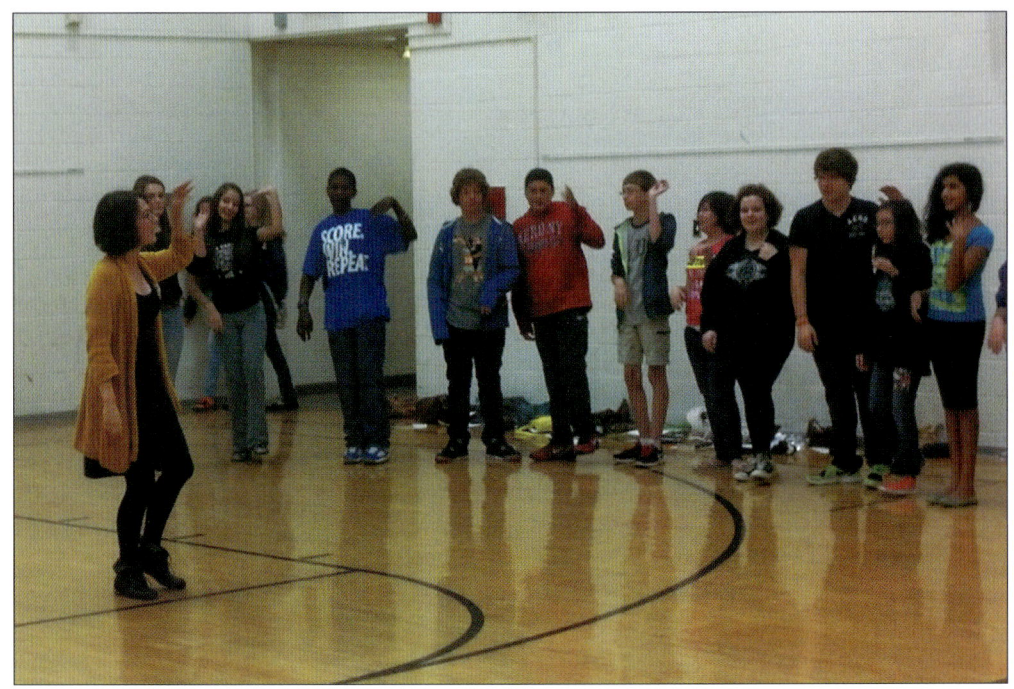

As part of MBT's Community Outreach Program, interns and staff conduct acting workshops at schools across Michigan to give students an opportunity to learn about theatre. Classes include acting, dance, stage makeup, script writing, and stage combat. (MBT.)

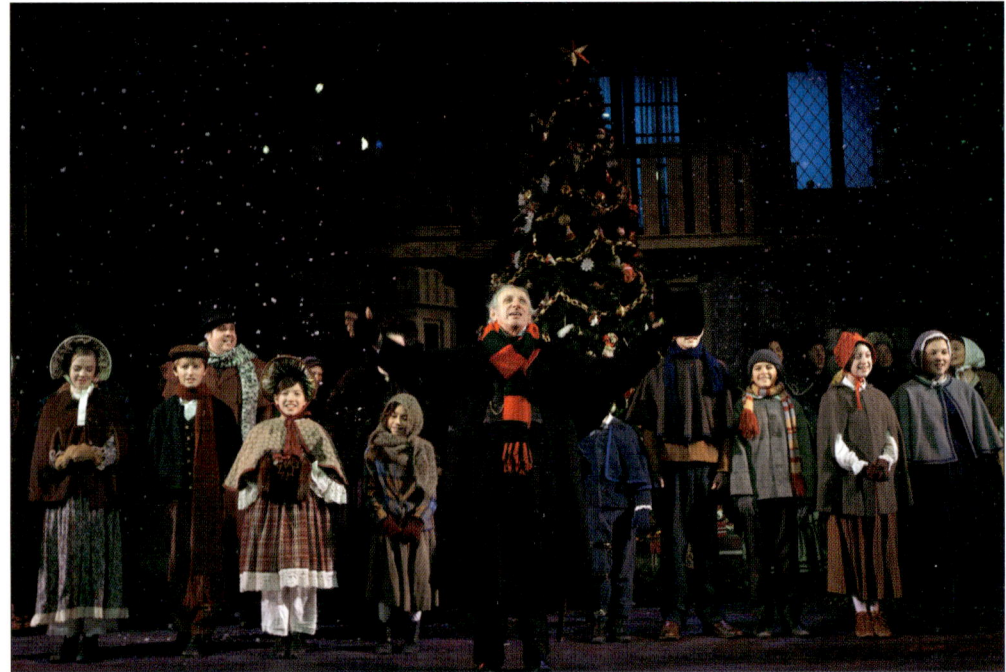

There are two complete casts of young actors for A Christmas Carol, so that school absences are minimized. Auditions for this show are highly competitive. Often, Peanut Gallery Players are included in the casts. (MBT.)

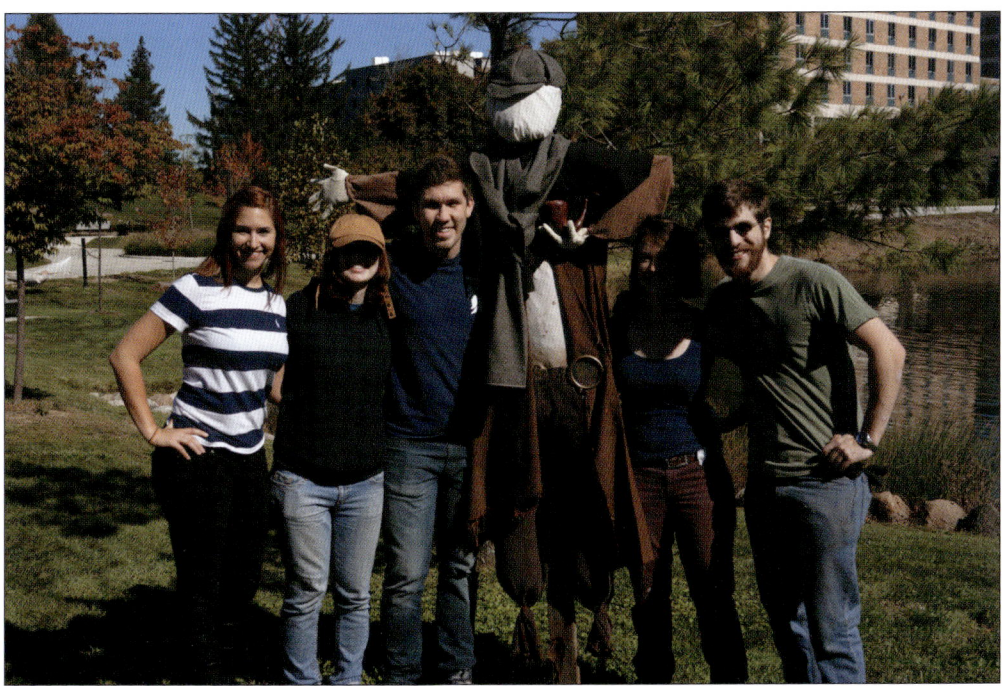

Rochester, Michigan, celebrates Halloween each year with an event displaying scarecrows throughout downtown. The Meadow Brook Theatre interns always sponsor and create a scarecrow. (MBT.)

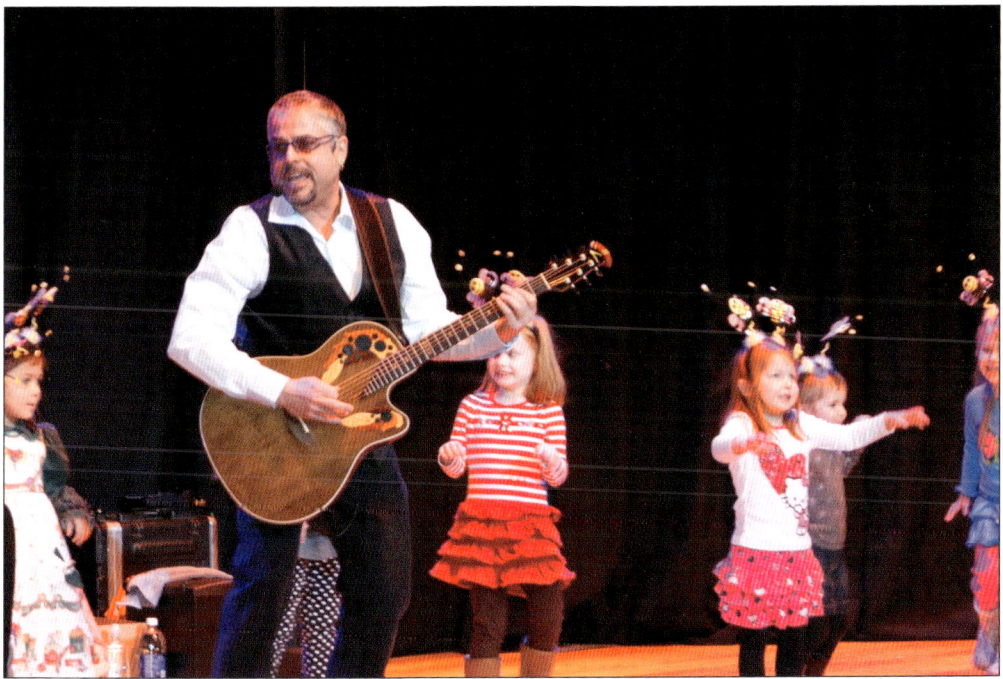

Each year, MBT's Children's Series provides local families the opportunity to share a live performance with their children. The show by Guy Louis (left) is made possible through a grant from the Michigan Humanities Council, which is awarded by the State of Michigan. (MBT.)

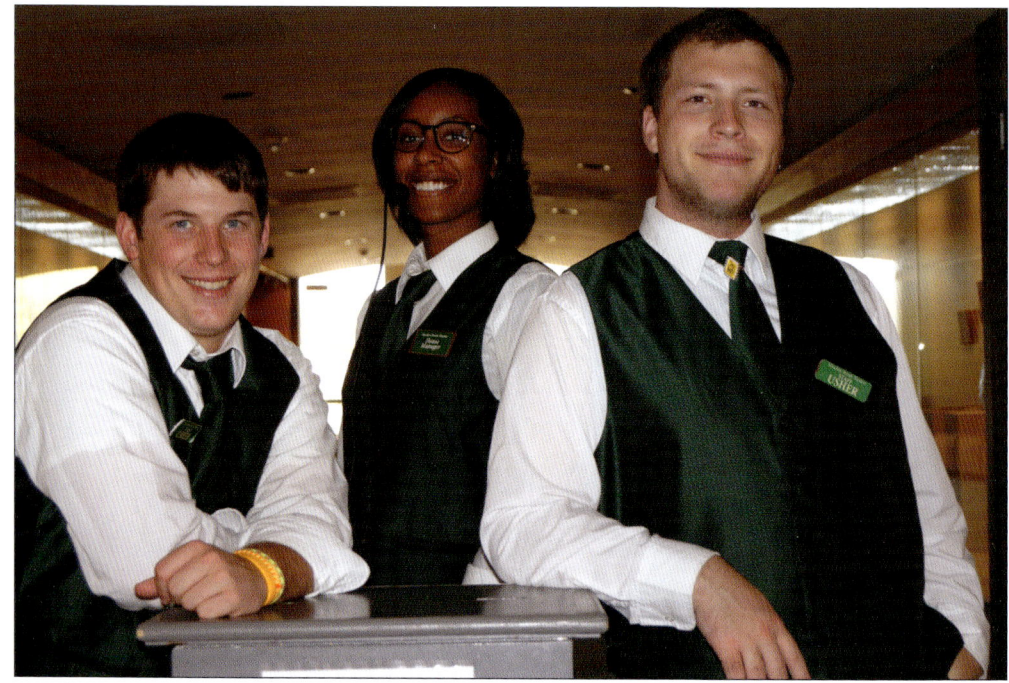

Meadow Brook Theatre started the 2009–2010 season with a new look for the ushers. Sporting the green vests and ties are ushers Matthew O'Brien (left), Nicole Davis (center), and Evan Heuker. The ushers set the tone for being courteous to the guests. (MBT.)

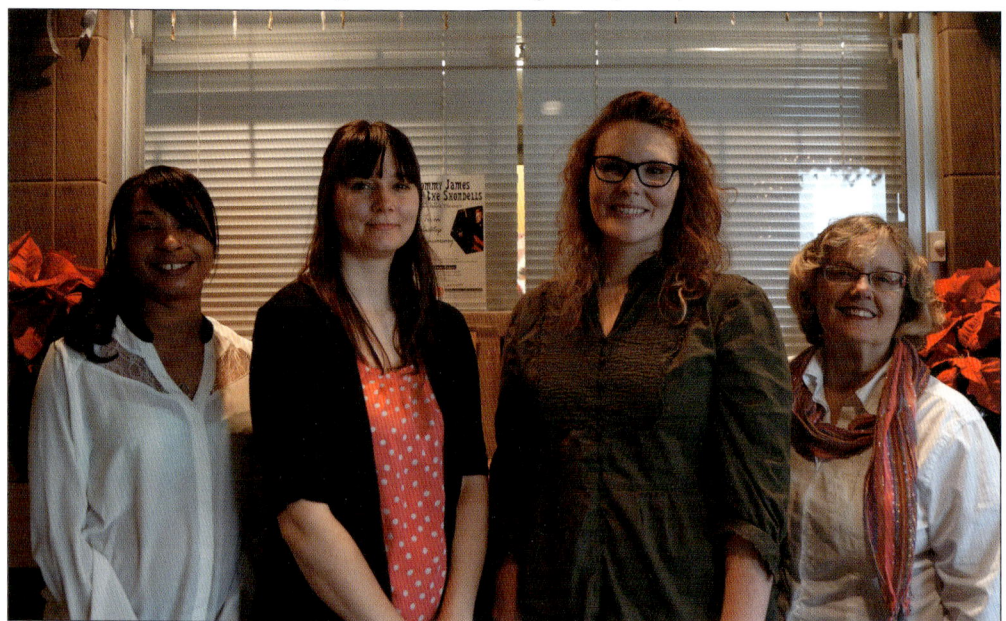

A key part of every theatre is the box-office staff. Shown here are, from left to right, box-office supervisor Sharon Harper, group sales/administrative assistant Lee Ann Kostur, marketing/communications coordinator Paige Vanzo, and box-office manager Barb Penchoff. Box-office associate Casey Hibbert is not shown. This group is the first line of contact and the public face of the theatre. (MBT.)

Six
Moving Forward

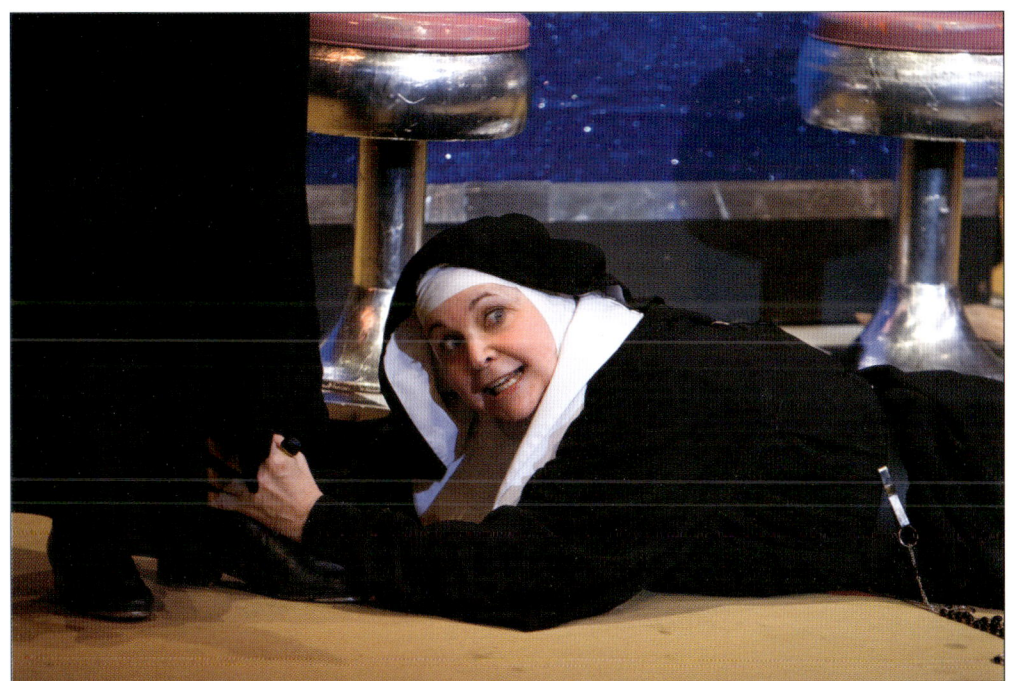

After a change in management of the theatre in 2007, the final show of the season was replaced with *Nunsense*, starring Cindy Williams. It was written and directed by Michigan native Dan Goggin. This production gave the theatre a much-needed boost in ticket sales and visibility. (MBT.)

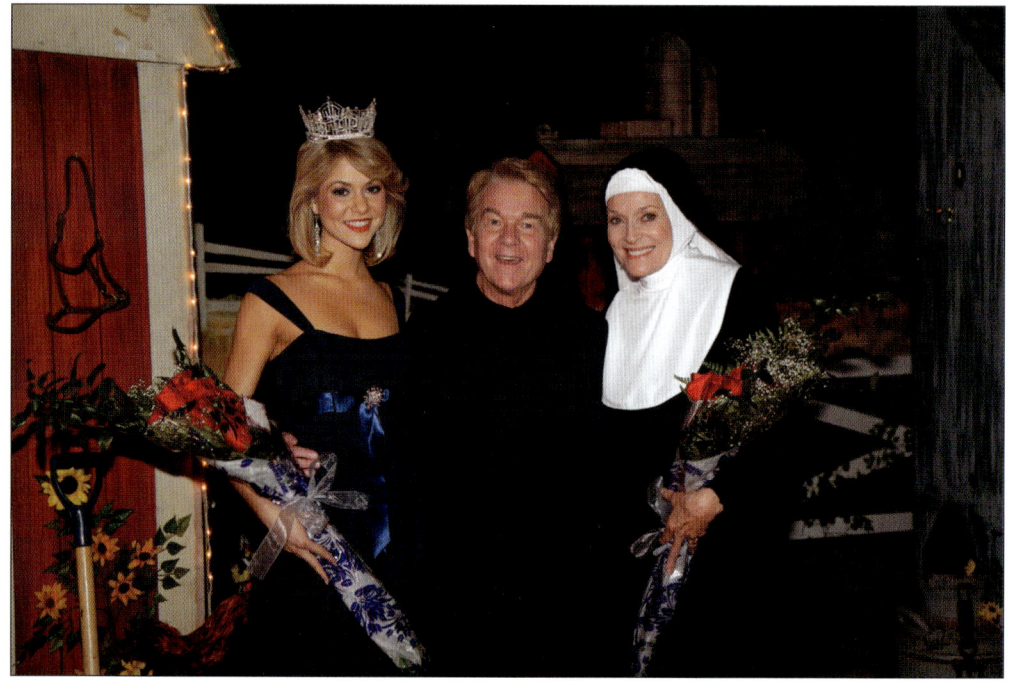

Following the success of *Nunsense*, Dan Goggin again helped the theatre by bringing in a bonus show at the end of the season in 2008, *Sister Amnesia's Country Western Nunsense Jamboree*. The show starred Lee Meriwether (Miss America 1955). At one performance, Kirsten Haglund (Miss America 2008) from Michigan joined Goggin (center) and Meriwether (right) on stage. (MBT.)

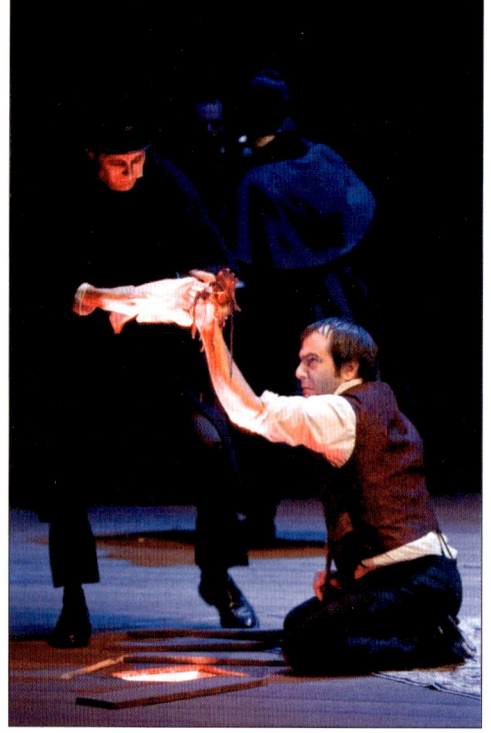

The 2008–2009 season saw a change in programming to feature Michigan premieres and the introduction of a Halloween and literary-themed show in the fall. Shown here in a scene from *Murder by Poe*, by Jeffrey Hatcher, are Dax Anderson and Chris Korte in a retelling of Edgar Allan Poe's "The Tell-Tale Heart." (MBT.)

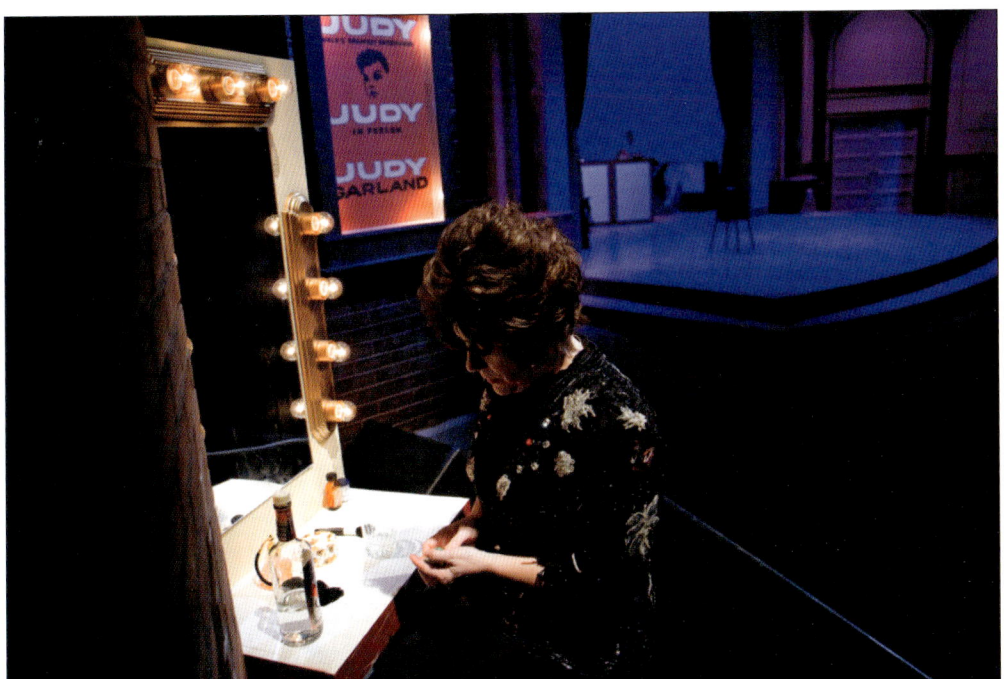

The Michigan premiere of *Beyond the Rainbow* by William Randall Beard opened in January 2009. Kimberly Vanbiesbrouck starred as Judy Garland at her 1961 Carnegie Hall performance. Directed by Travis W. Walter, this production won Best Actress in a Musical and Best Musical at the Wilde Awards, which acknowledges excellence in professional theatre throughout Michigan. (MBT.)

Cindy Williams returned to MBT in 2009 with her costar from *Laverne and Shirley*, Eddie Mekka, in the new comedy *Kong's Night Out*, written and directed by Jack Neary. This farce portrayed what could have happened in the hotel suite when Ann Darrow was taken by King Kong. The great ape's hand can be seen in this photograph. (MBT.)

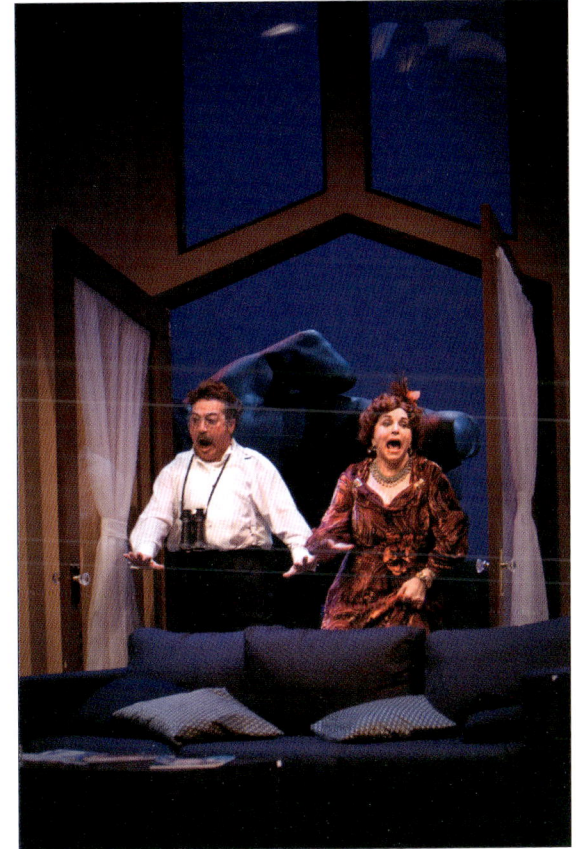

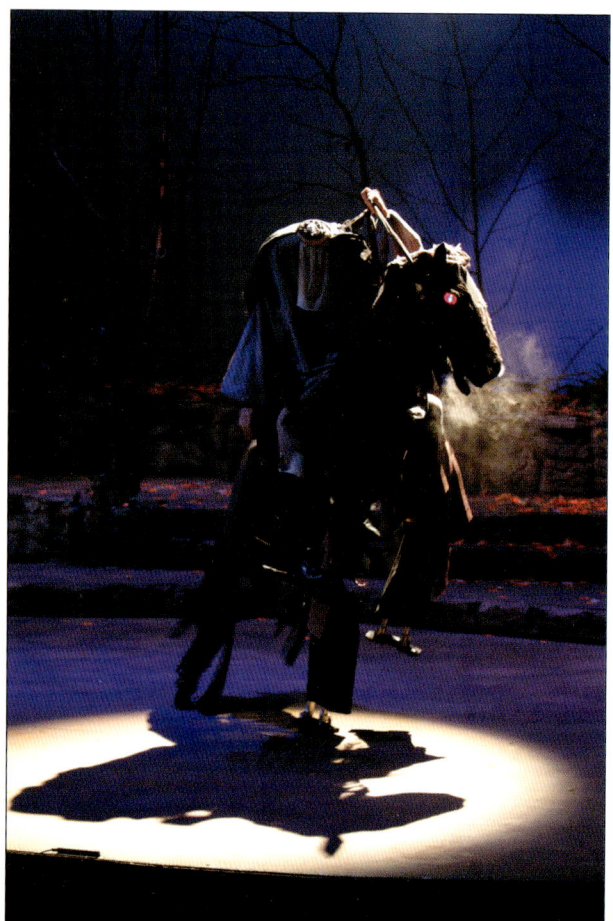

The 44th season at Meadow Brook Theatre opened with the world premiere of *The Legend of Sleepy Hollow*, by Washington Irving, adapted by Jefferson Garrett. Costume designer Liz Goodall created the headless horseman with glowing eyes and smoking nostrils. As seen here, the character is played by actor Rick Carver on stilts, menacing the locals. (MBT.)

Christopher Howe (left) and Steve Blackwood (of television's *Days of Our Lives*) starred in *Boeing-Boeing*, by Marc Camoletti, adapted by Beverley Cross in January 2010. This high-flying comedy about a man who is dating three different airline hostesses quickly became one of Meadow Brook Theatre's most popular shows. (MBT.)

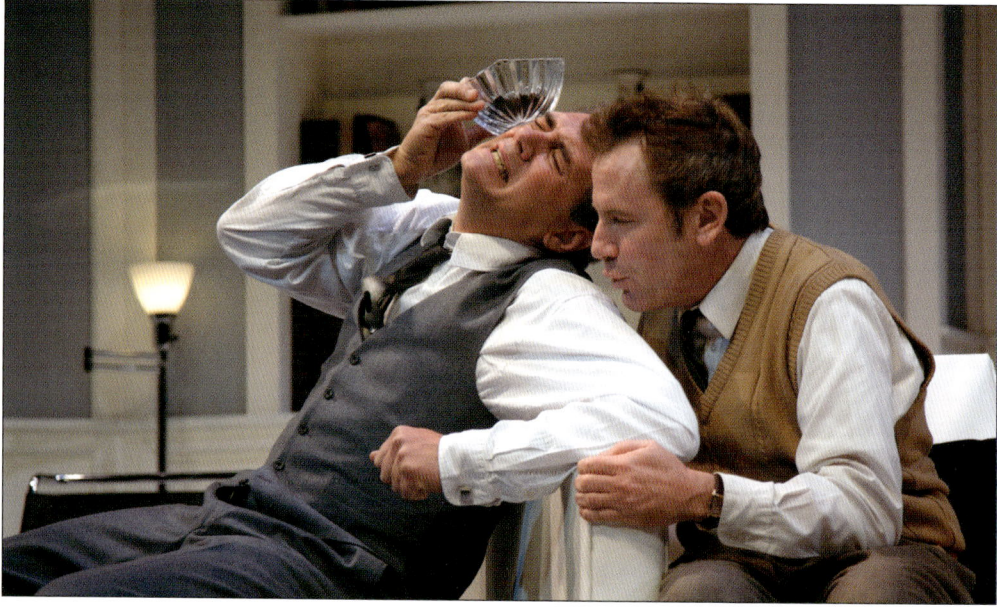

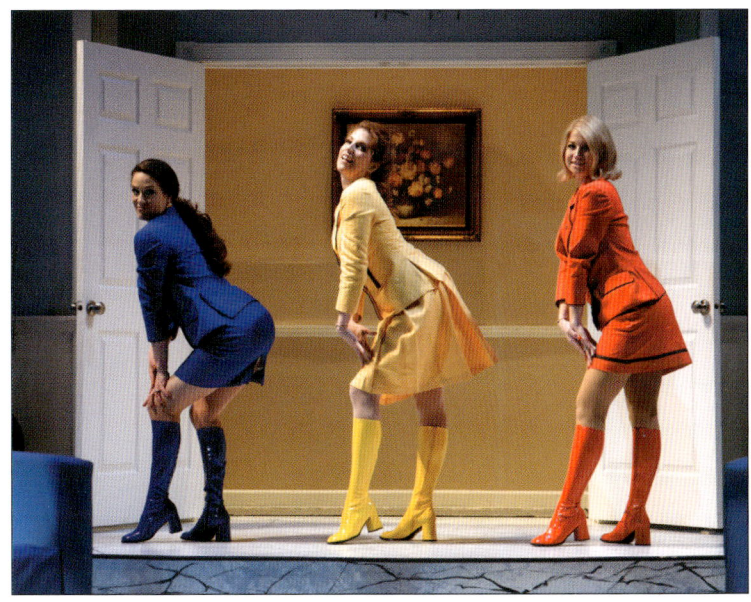

Boeing-Boeing, which won MBT a Wilde Award for Best Comedy, also featured a dancing curtain call choreographed by Stephanie Wahl, a former Rockette. This started the tradition of a dancing curtain call once a season at Meadow Brook Theatre. Shown here are, from left to right, Julianne Somers, Stephanie Wahl, and Katie Hardy. (MBT.)

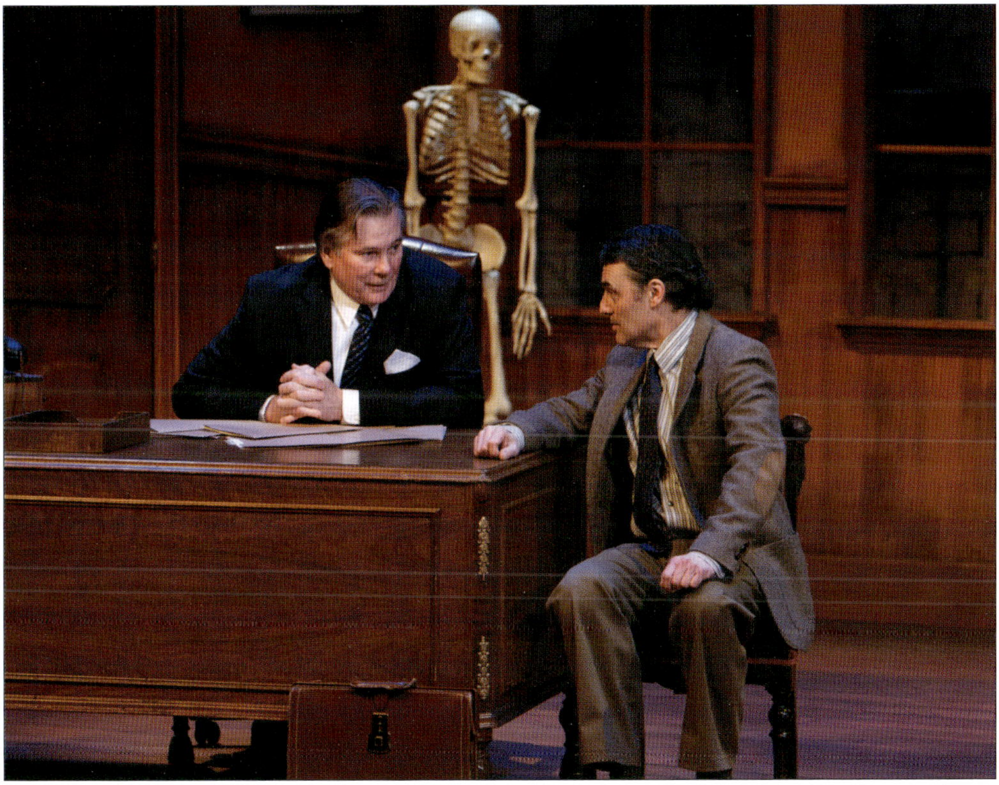

Associate director Terry W. Carpenter directed Anthony Horowitz's psychological thriller *Mindgame* in its Michigan premiere in February 2010. Mark Rademacher (left) and Loren Bass (right) starred with Inga Wilson. (MBT.)

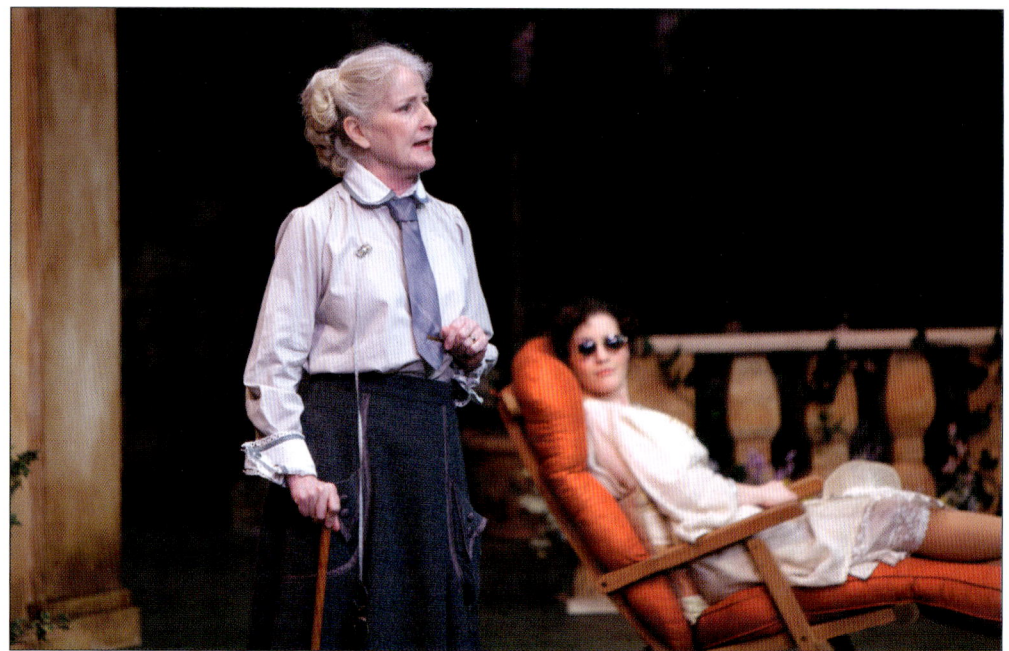

Pictured here in a scene from *Enchanted April* are Ruth Crawford (left) and Leslie Ann Handelman. This romantic comedy is set in London and Italy. Scenic designer Kristen Gribbin tackled the challenge of creating two different sets and won a Wilde Award for Best Set Design in 2010. (MBT.)

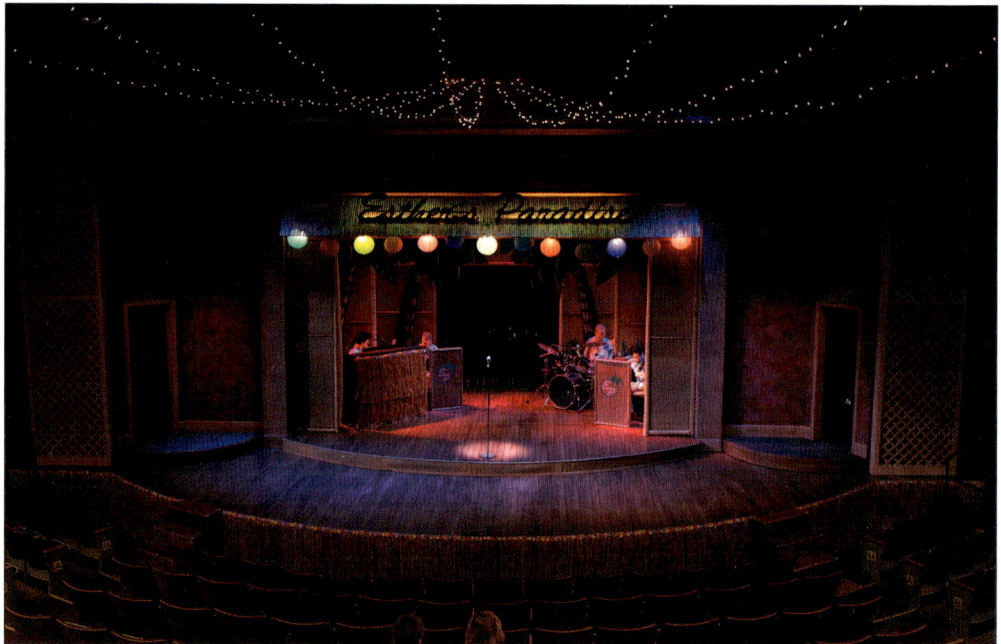

The Meadow Brook Theatre auditorium was transformed into Esther's Paradise Resort for *Breaking Up Is Hard to Do*, a show featuring the music of Neil Sedaka. The stage set was realized thanks to scenic designer Vince Mountain and lighting designer Reid G. Johnson. This 2010 musical comedy is still among the highest-grossing shows at MBT. (MBT.)

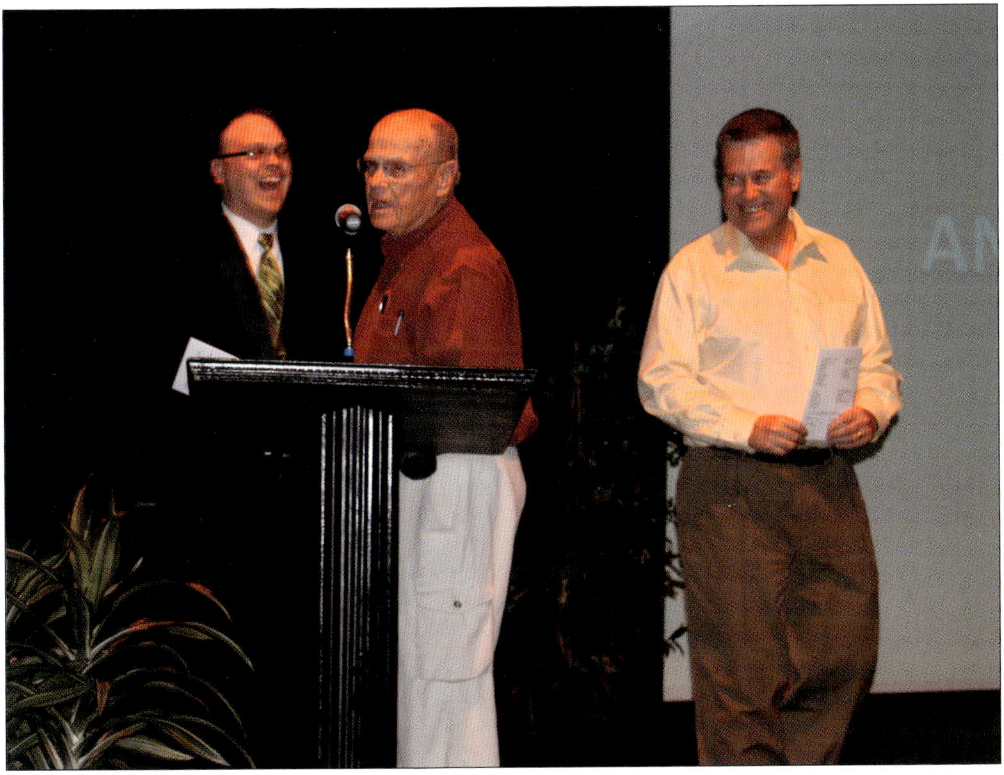

The end of the 2009–2010 season saw the creation of the Andes Awards (subscriber's choice awards), and also the naming of Travis W. Walter as artistic director. He had been unofficially doing the job since 2007. Pictured here at the awards are Travis W. Walter (left) and board members Bill Campbell (center) and Tim Caughlin. (MBT.)

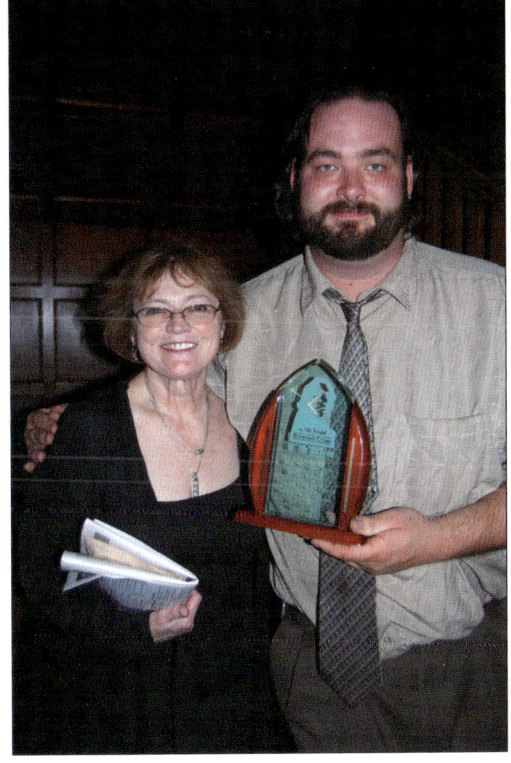

Technical director Brian Kessler (right) won a Wilde Award for the set design of *Dracula, A Rock Opera*. In addition to his great designs, he is responsible for creating special effects, including pyrotechnics and rain or snow on stage. Other set designers have commented that Kessler is always able to build sets to match their vision. (MBT.)

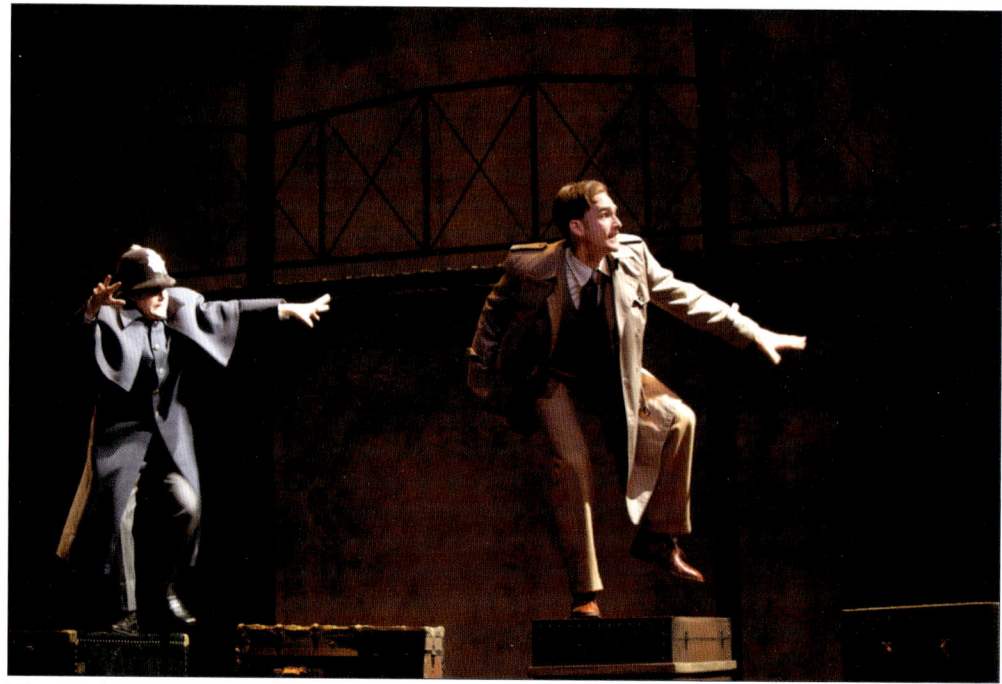

The Michigan premiere of *The 39 Steps*, adapted by Patrick Barlow from the film by Alfred Hitchcock, brought espionage, intrigue, and hilarity to the Meadow Brook Theatre stage. The show, which featured only four actors playing multiple roles, created exhilarating situations, including Rob Pantano (left) and Rusty Mewha jumping from train car to train car in this photograph. (MBT.)

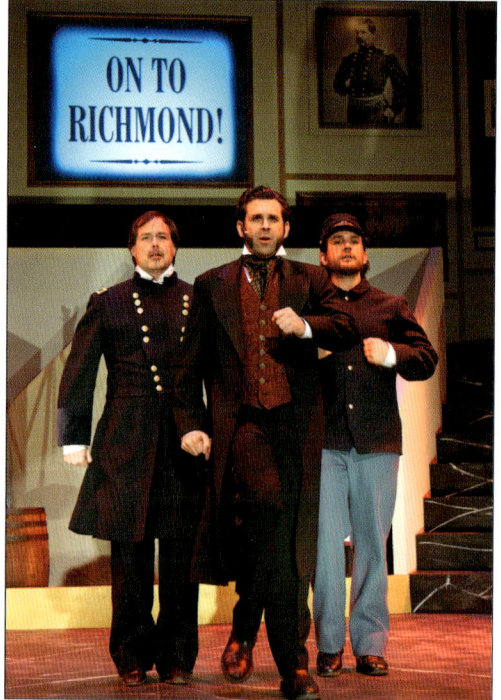

Meadow Brook Theatre honored the 150th anniversary of the Civil War with the show *Reunion: A Musical Epic in Miniature*, which looked at the conflict through the words and music of the people who lived and died for freedom. Tobin Hissong (left) has had a career spanning 20 years around metro Detroit. Eric Gutman (center) returned to Michigan after performing in *Jersey Boys*. Rob Arbaugh (right) has acted throughout the country and now teaches at Rochester College in Rochester, Michigan. (MBT.)

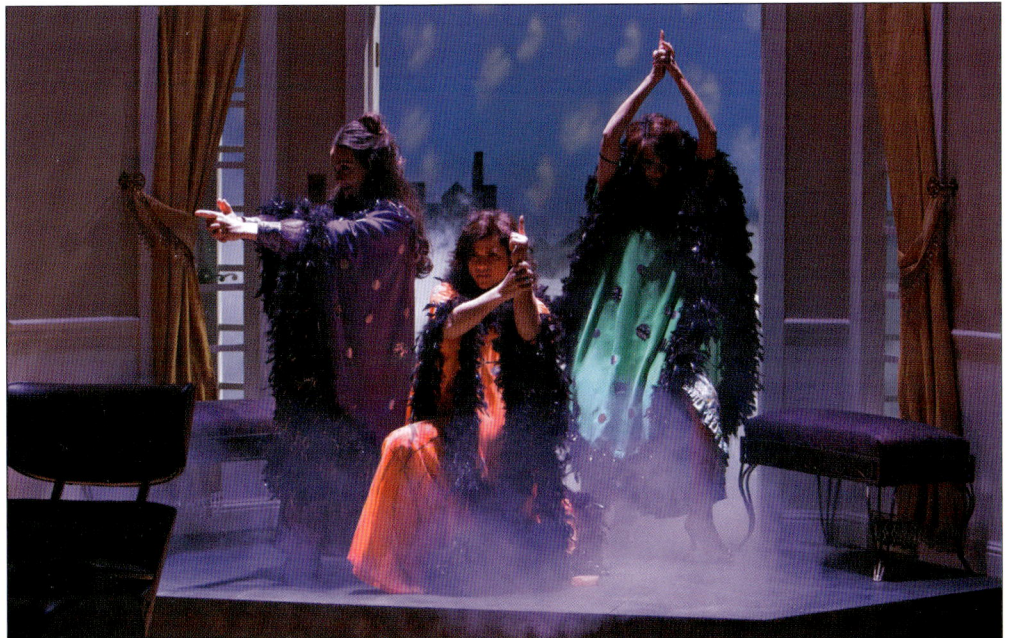

Meadow Brook Theatre produced the North American premiere of *Ding Dong*, by Marc Camoletti, adapted by Tudor Gates, in March 2011. This show continued the adventures of the characters from the hit *Boeing-Boeing* and featured another dancing curtain call, this time choreographed by Janet Caine (right), with Julianne Somers (left) and MaryJo Cuppone. (MBT.)

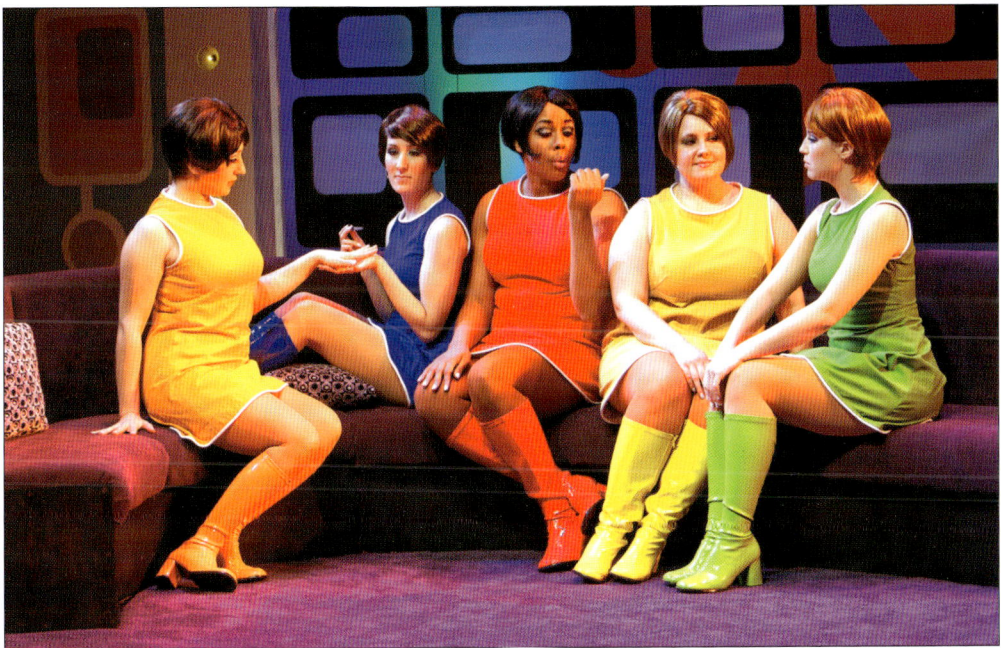

The finale of the 2010–2011 season was *SHOUT! The Mod Musical*, by Phillip George and David Lowenstein. This musical, which featured the music of the British invasion, showcased, from left to right, Liz Griffith, Allison Hunt, Charis Vaughn, Renee Turner, and Katie Hardy. These women made audiences stand up and dance. (MBT.)

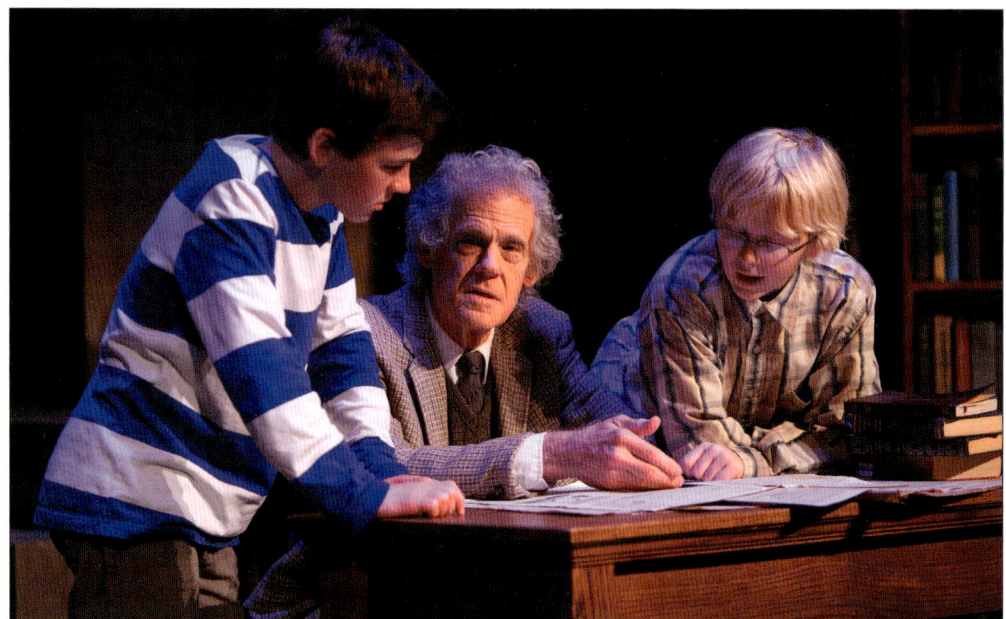

The 46th season opened with Ray Bradbury's classic *Something Wicked This Way Comes*. This well-attended season opener about coming of age starred local child actors Jacob Zelinski (left) and Ryan Lynch (right), seen here with Marty Smith. (MBT.)

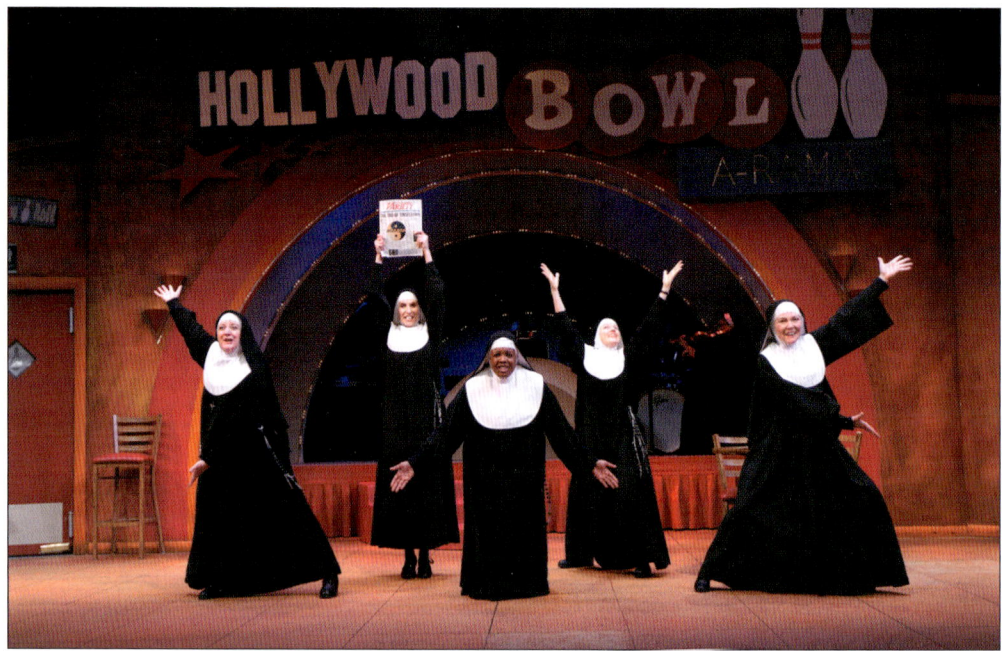

From left to right are Laurie Birmingham, Stephanie Wahl, Bambi Jones, Jeanne Tinker, and choreographer Teri Gibson in Dan Goggin's *Nunset Boulevard* from 2012. Goggin's *Nunsense* franchise is one of Off-Broadway's biggest commercial successes. The international phenomenon has been translated into 21 languages, with more than 5,000 productions worldwide. (MBT.)

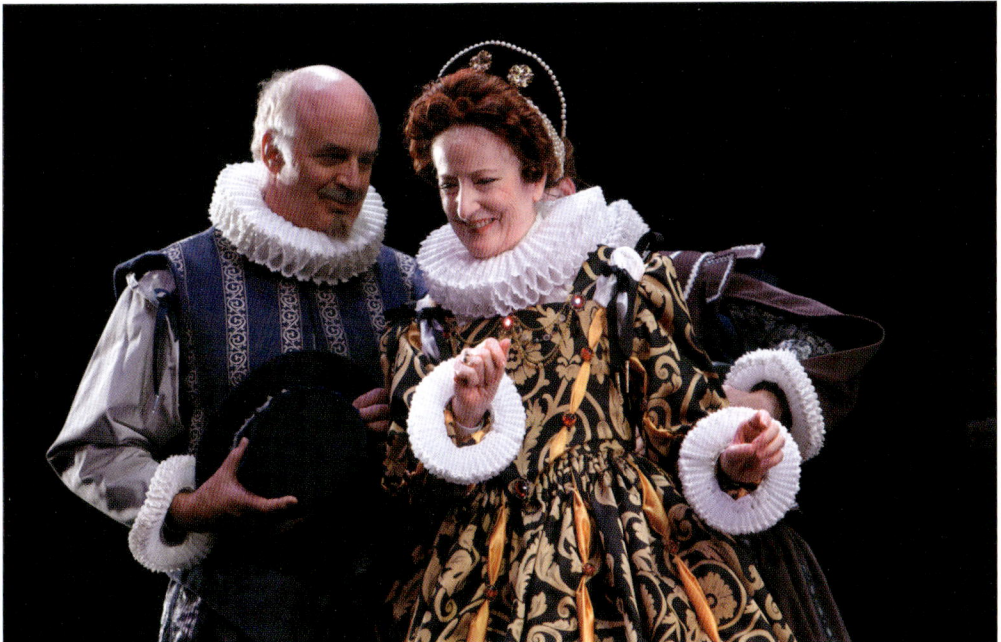

The Friedrich Schiller classic *Mary Stuart*, adapted by Peter Oswald, featured the rivalry between Queen Elizabeth I of England and Mary, Queen of Scots. Hugh Maguire (left) and Ruth Crawford were in the show, which featured Elizabethan costumes designed by Liz Goodall and constructed at Meadow Brook Theatre. With a cast of 14, this was a giant undertaking. (MBT.)

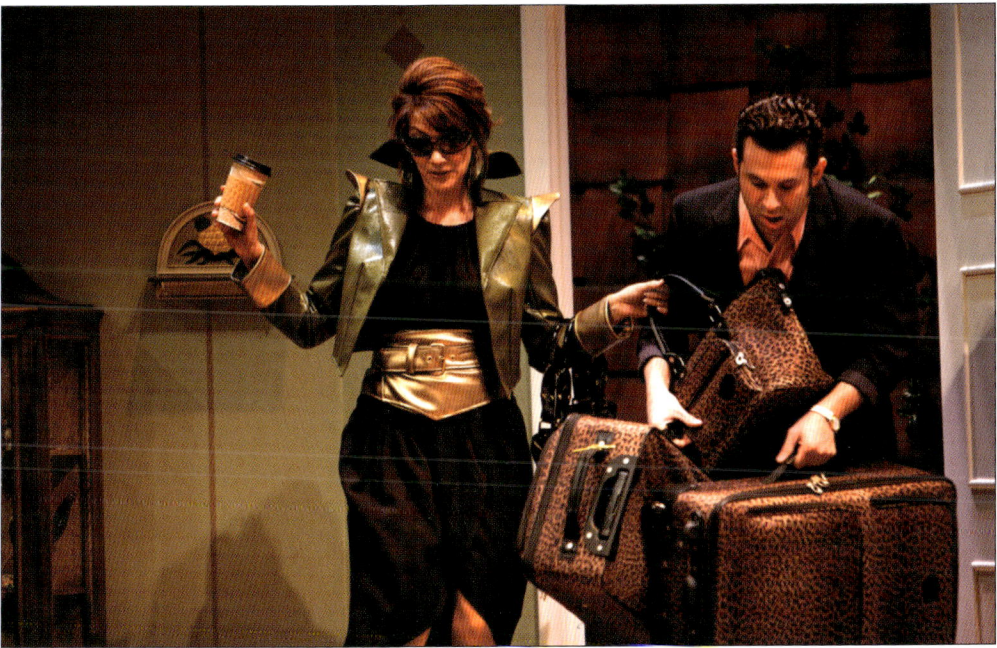

Meadow Brook Theatre audiences were delighted by Janet Caine and Eric Gutman in the Michigan premiere of the comedy *Spreading It Around*, by Londos D'Arrigo. Both have appeared in film, commercials, and in the *Forbidden Broadway* franchises at the Gem Theatre in Detroit and throughout the country. (MBT.)

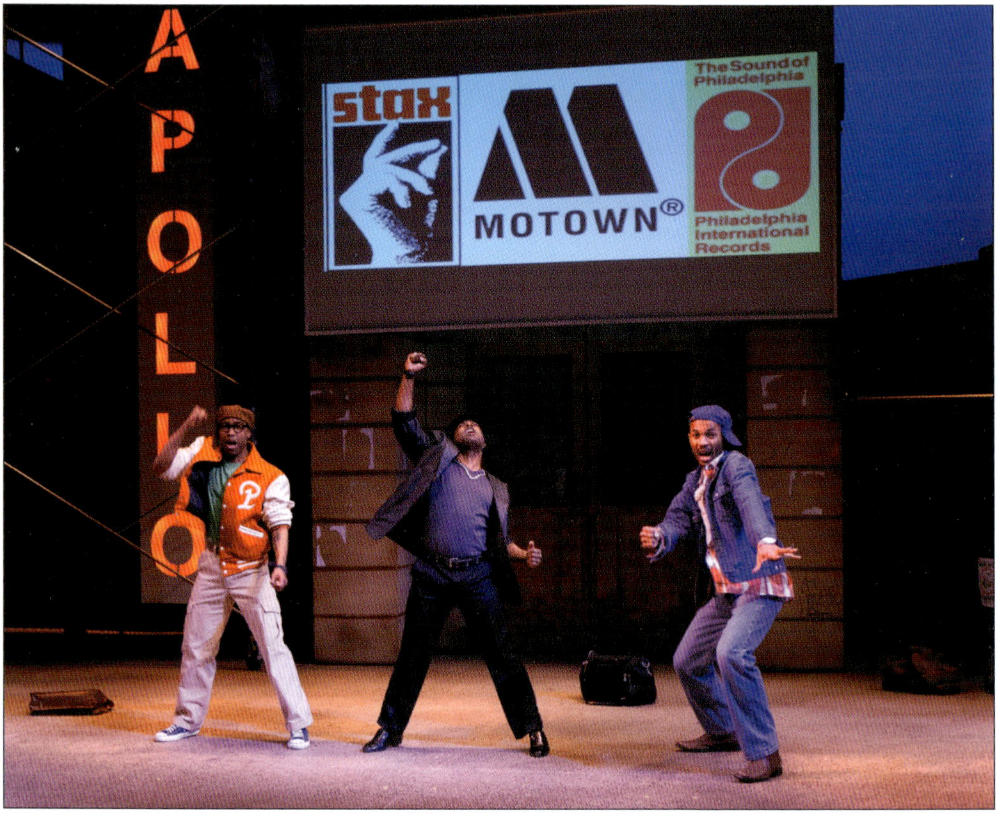

Tyrick Wiltez Jones (center) played Detroit in *From My Hometown*. He appeared in *Finian's Rainbow* at the St. James Theatre on Broadway and has been featured in numerous national tours. He is associate director for the Broadway Artists Alliance for New York City/Off-Broadway and is on the board of directors for Meadow Brook Theatre. Will Lee-Williams (left) and Alexander Elisa (right) also starred in this production. (MBT.)

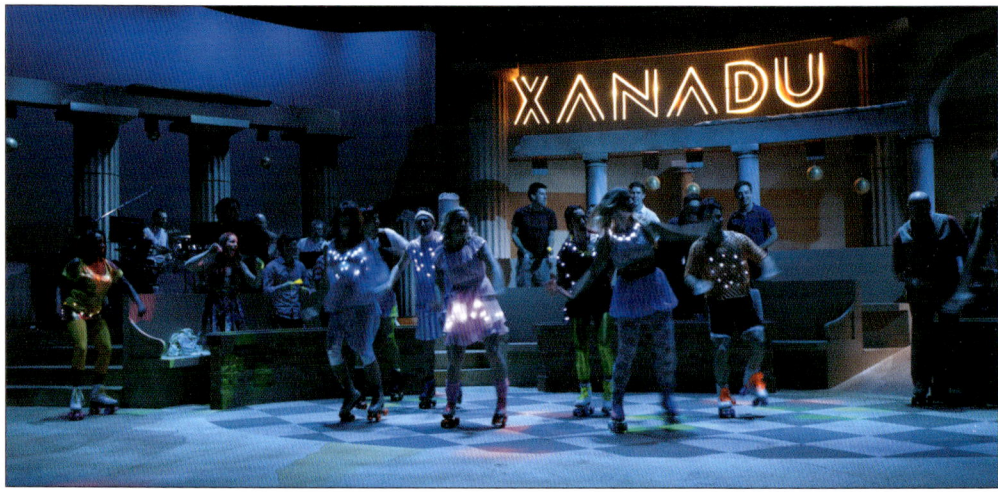

In 2011–2012, a sixth play, *Xanadu*, was added to the schedule. This play, made from a nostalgic movie, featured the musical talents of Allison Hunt and David Havasi. It included roller skating and dazzling lighted costumes designed by Liz Goodall. (MBT.)

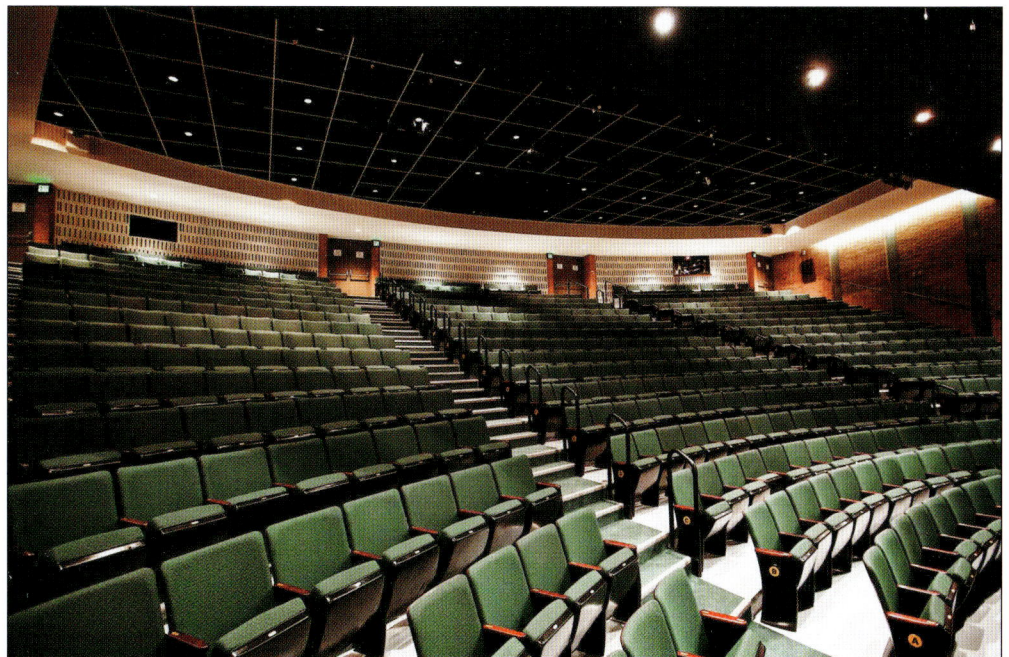

A much-needed makeover of the theatre was undertaken in 2011. The goal was to refurbish the seats, redo the floors, add accessible-friendly handrails in the aisles, and paint surfaces as necessary. The major fundraiser required for the project was fully supported by Oakland University, including matching funds donated for the seats. The goal was to be ready for the first show of the 46th season, Something Wicked This Way Comes. (MBT)

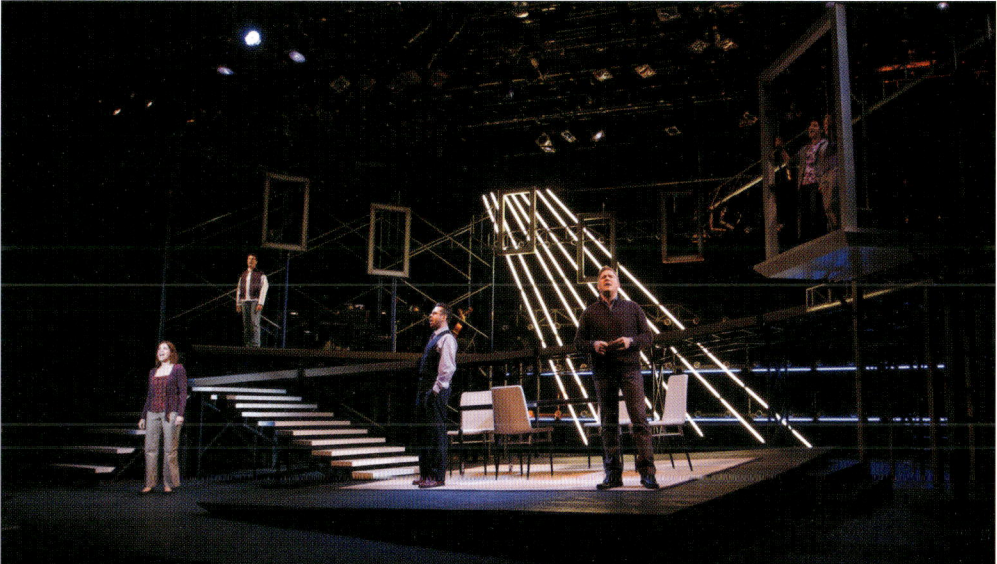

The Tony-winning musical and Michigan premiere Next to Normal was produced in February 2013. With a unique set by Jeremy Barnett and lighting by Reid G. Johnson, the audience was given a chance to see inside a family affected by bipolar disorder. Seen here on stage are, from left to right, Stephanie Wahl, Ryan Naimy, Eric Gutman, George Andrew Wolff, Jason Cabral, and Jessica Naimy. This production won the Wilde Award for Best Musical in Michigan. (MBT.)

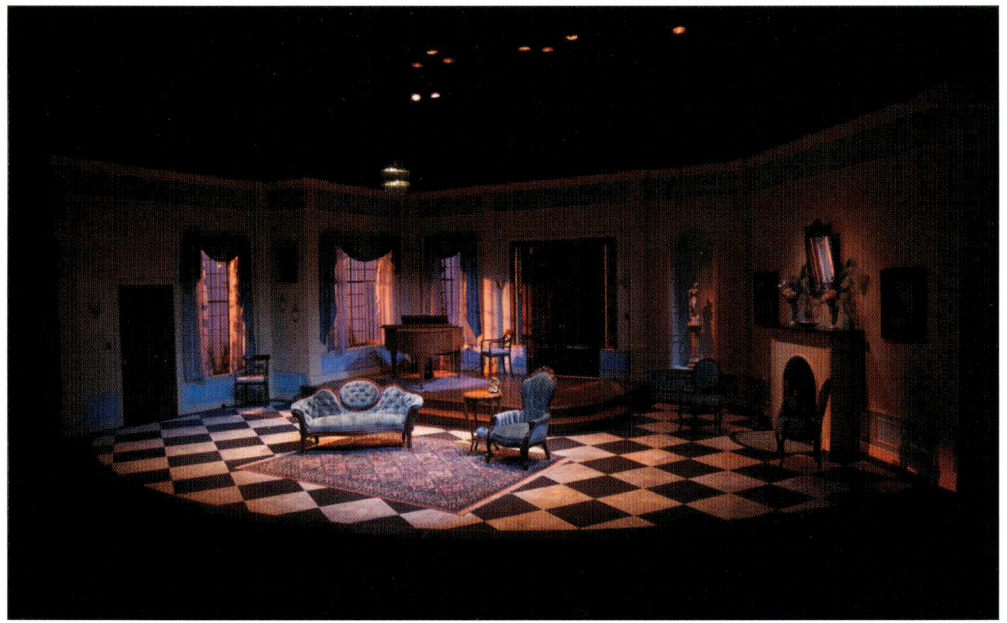

W. Somerset Maugham's classic story *The Constant Wife* was directed by Prof. Karen Sheridan of Oakland University's Department of Music, Theatre and Dance in March 2013. The set was designed by Jen Price Fick, an Oakland University alumnus, with lighting by Reid G. Johnson. (MBT.)

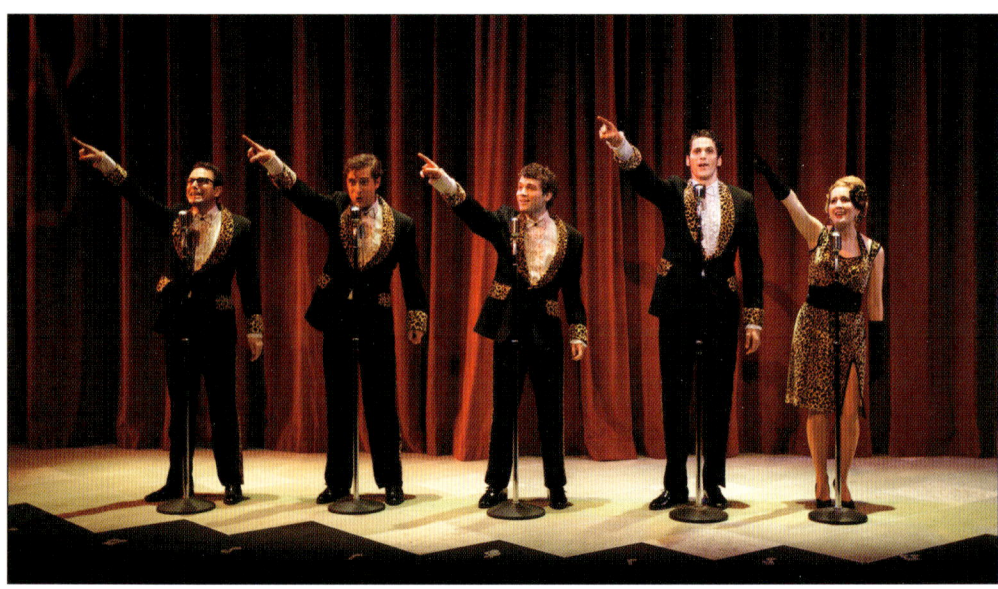

The Michigan premiere of *Life Could Be a Dream*, by Roger Bean, soared to great heights in April 2013, becoming the highest-grossing show since 2003. The stellar cast, shown here, are, from left to right, Mathew Schwartz, Joe Lehman, Lucas Wells, Sam Perwin, and Allison Hunt. (MBT.)

Paul Hopper, who starred in *70, Girls, 70*, first came to Meadow Brook Theatre in 1976. He has since appeared in 75 productions here and another 200 throughout the country. He received an Andes Award for Favorite Actor in a Musical, as Van Helsing in *Dracula, A Rock Opera*. (MBT.)

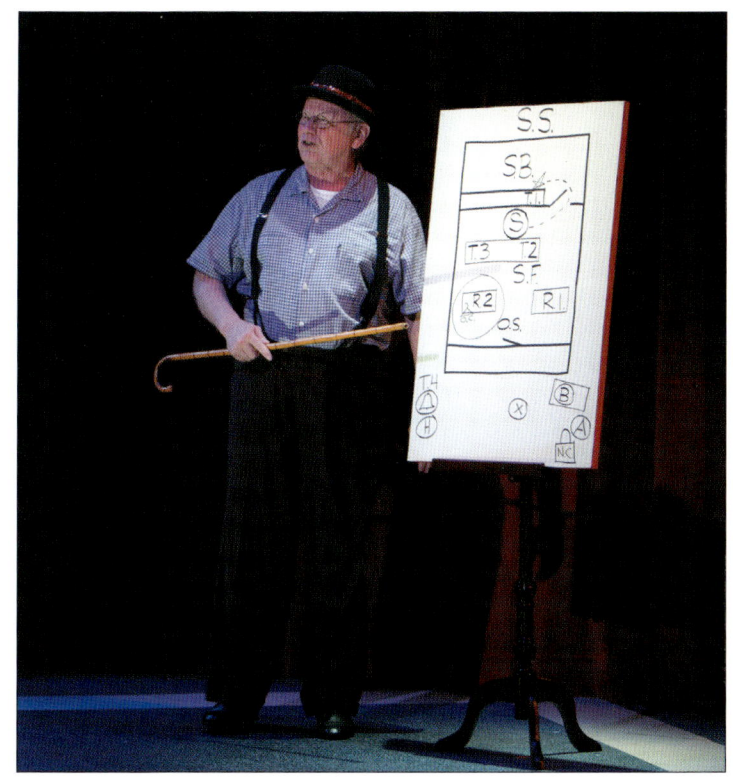

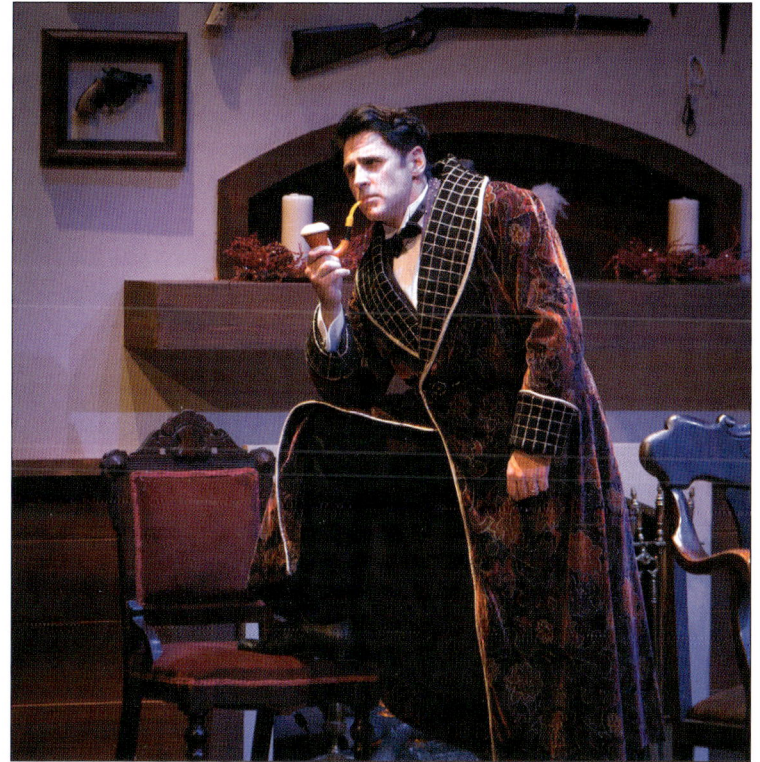

The 48th season started with the Michigan premiere of Ken Ludwig's *The Game's Afoot*. This Sherlock Holmes parody revolves around the actor William Gillette, who made Sherlock Holmes famous. He was played at Meadow Brook Theatre by Ron Williams. (MBT.)

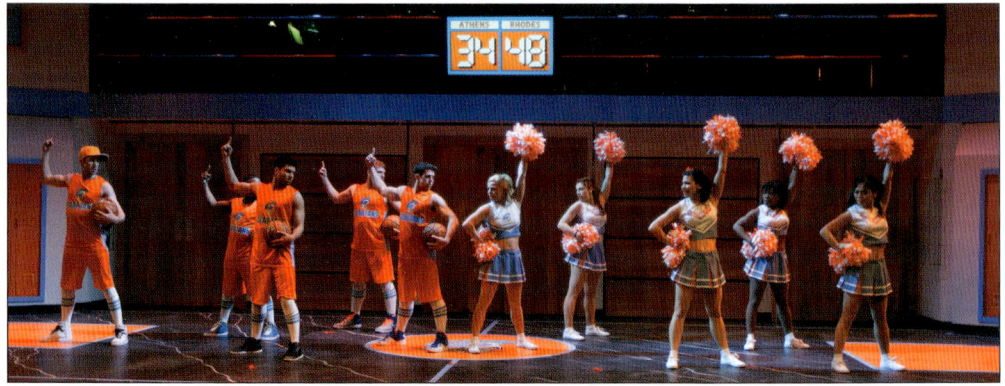

The Broadway musical *Lysistrata Jones*, with music and lyrics by Lewis Flinn and book by Douglas Carter Beane, was produced in February 2014. This updated version of the satire *Lysistrata*, written by Aristophanes in 411 BC, featured a large, diverse cast and an amazing band led by music director Greg Kenna. This production won a Wilde Award for Best Musical in Michigan. (MBT.)

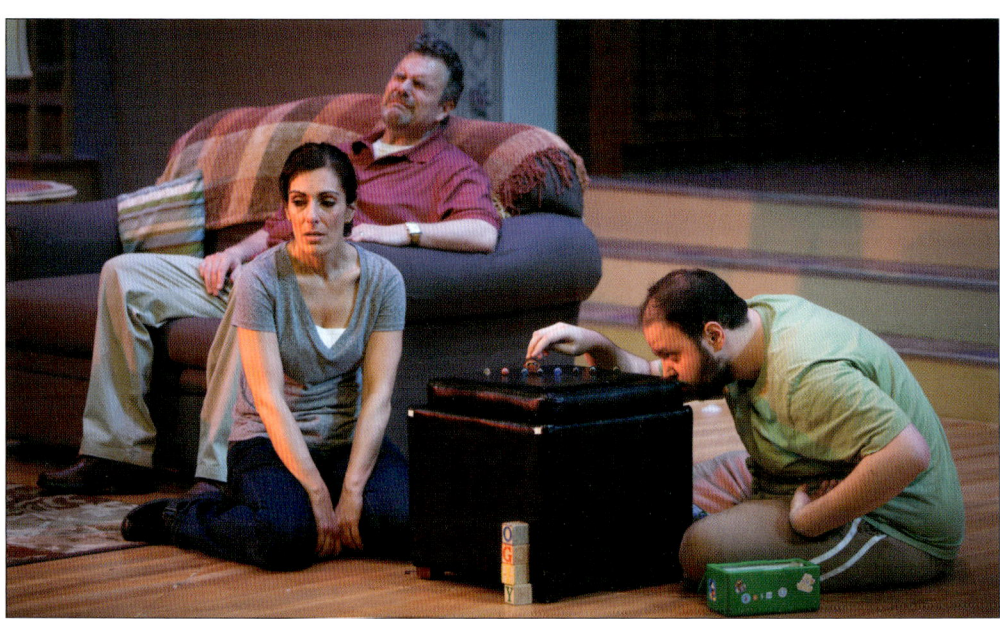

The moving drama *Falling*, by Deanna Jent, had its Michigan premiere at MBT in March 2014. This beautiful play starred Sarab Kamoo (left), Chris Hietikko (rear), and Daniel Everidge, who recreated his Drama Desk award-nominated role for the MBT audiences. The play, dealing with the issues of adult autism, is based on the playwright's life. (MBT.)

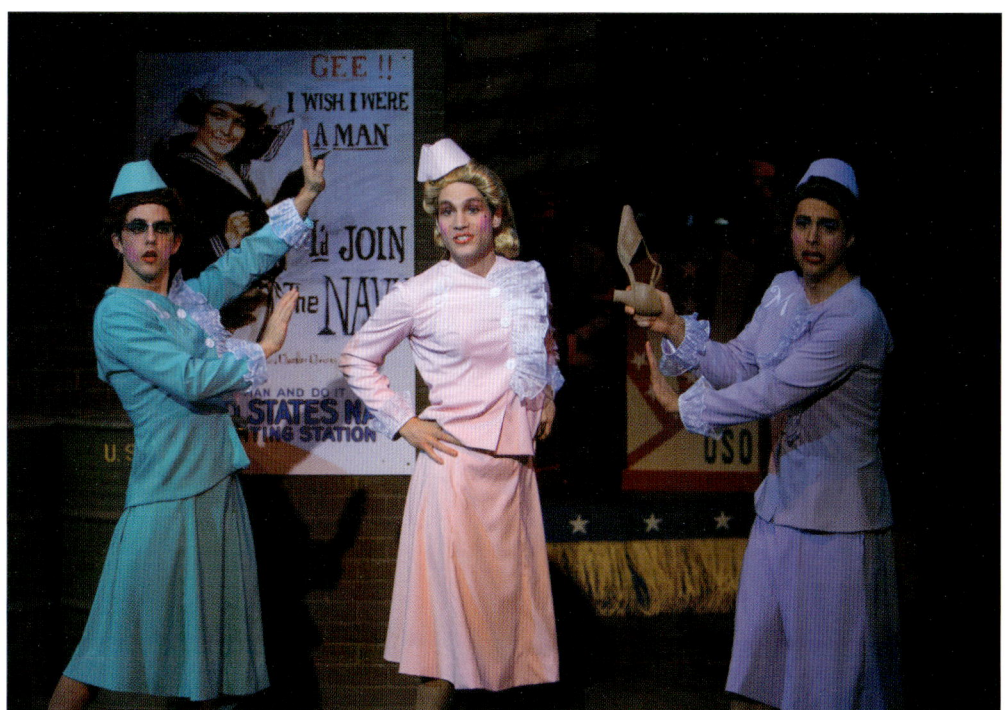

In the hilarious Michigan premiere of *The Andrews Brothers*, a trio of GIs decides to carry on with a USO show even though the Andrews Sisters have not shown up to perform. Seen here in costumes designed by Corey T. Globke are Ben Garrett (left), Lucas Wells (center), and Joe Lehman. (MBT.)

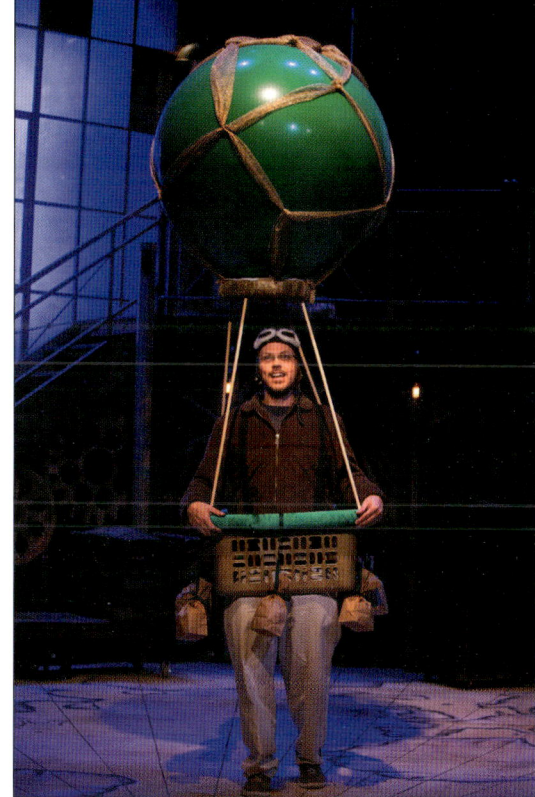

Travis W. Walter's curtain speeches have become an audience favorite. In *Around the World in 80 Days*, he appeared in an air balloon in order to not disappoint the audience who is expecting one based on the 1958 movie. (MBT.)

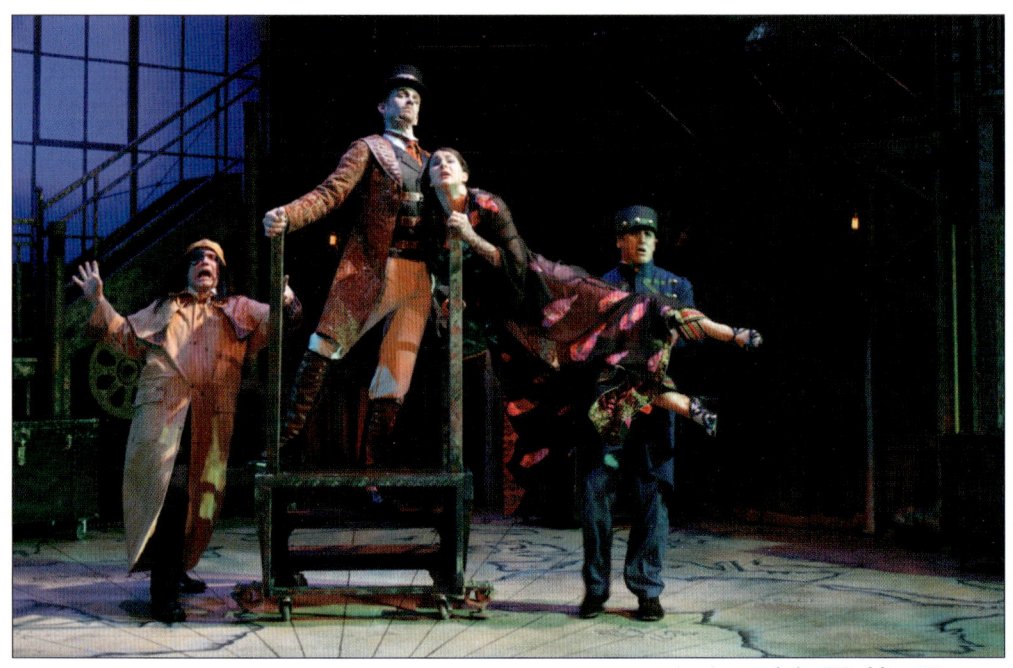

In *Around the World in 80 Days*, four actors play 39 characters. Here, the ship is hit by a typhoon. The costumes were designed by Liz Goodall. Pictured from left to right are Peter C. Prouty, Rusty Mewha, Kara Kimmer, and Ron Williams. (MBT.)

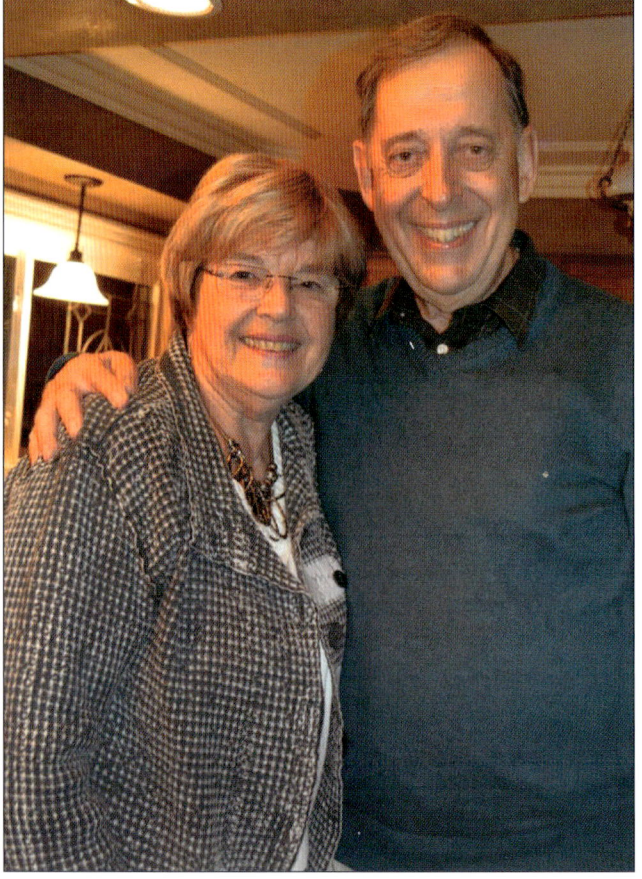

Dr. Richard and Edie Haskell were among the longest MBT season-ticket holders and original "Saturday Niters," who hosted dinner parties for actors and staff in their homes. Today, the legacy continues with the Bennets, Tans, Walchs, Vargases, Kollins, Foxlees, Guptas, and Dr. Hanna. (MBT.)

Tim Caughlin (right), former board treasurer, poses with Cheryl L. Marshall as he accepts his Andes Award in 2014 for Outstanding Service. He played a key role in establishing Meadow Brook Theatre as a 501(c)(3) nonprofit after the split with Oakland University in 2003. He and his wife, Mary, have generously donated over a decade of service and time to the board and guild, as well as being sponsors and rent angels. (MBT.)

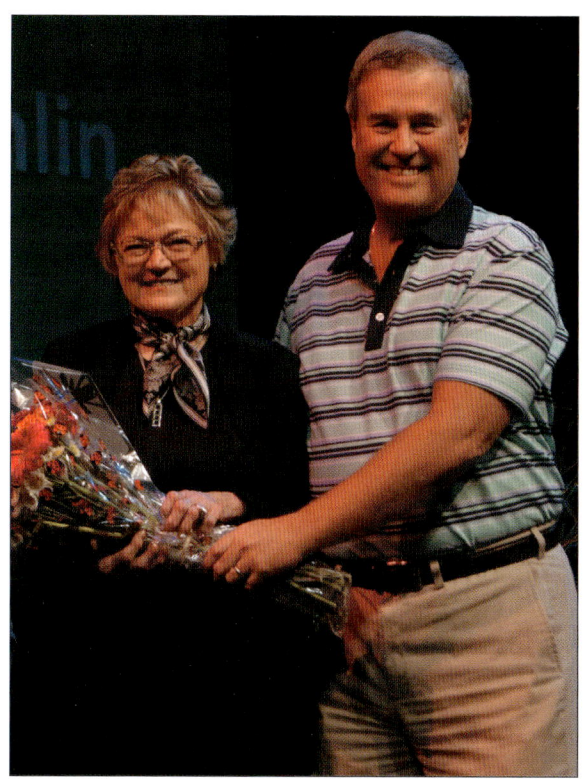

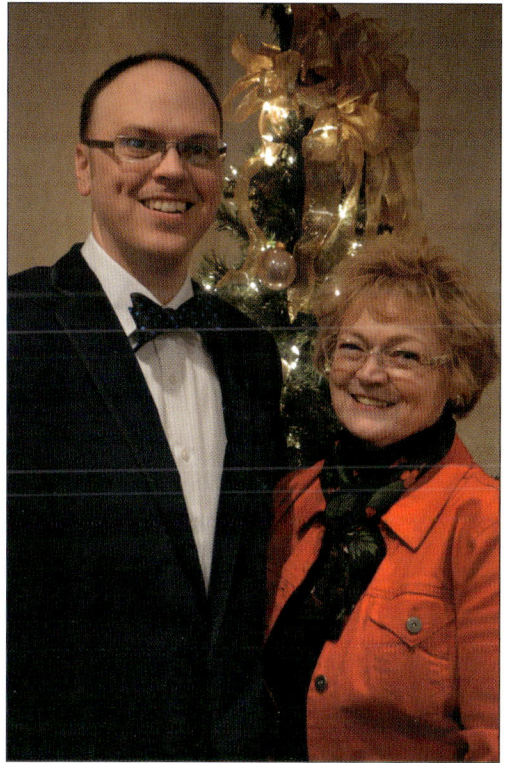

Managing director Cheryl L. Marshall and artistic director Travis W. Walter have been instrumental in moving Meadow Brook Theatre from OU stewardship to an independent nonprofit theatre. Their hard work, dedication, and passion set the standard for success. (MBT.)

Discover Thousands of Local History Books Featuring Millions of Vintage Images

Arcadia Publishing, the leading local history publisher in the United States, is committed to making history accessible and meaningful through publishing books that celebrate and preserve the heritage of America's people and places.

Find more books like this at
www.arcadiapublishing.com

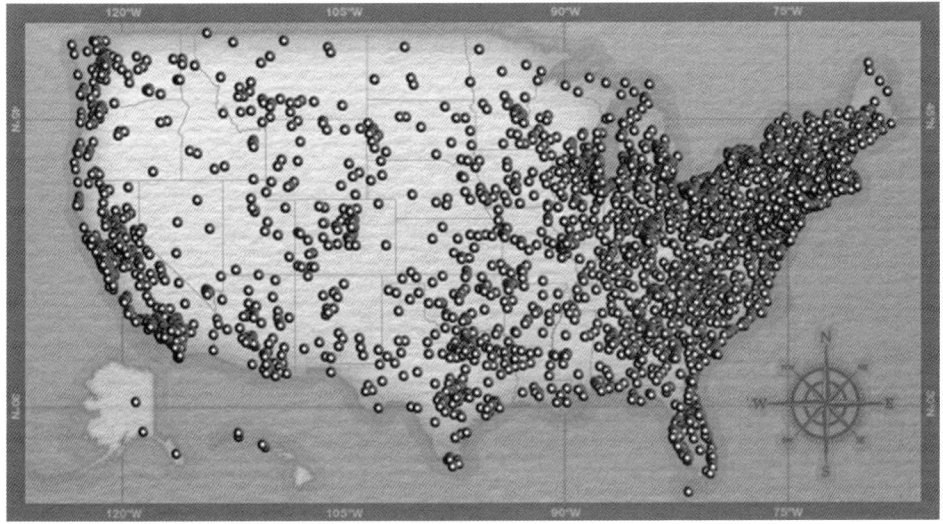

Search for your hometown history, your old stomping grounds, and even your favorite sports team.

Consistent with our mission to preserve history on a local level, this book was printed in South Carolina on American-made paper and manufactured entirely in the United States. Products carrying the accredited Forest Stewardship Council (FSC) label are printed on 100 percent FSC-certified paper.

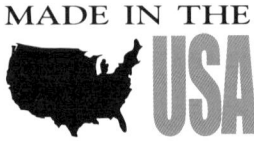